Copyright © 2021 Peter Vox

ISBN: 978-1-942500-74-2

All Rights Reserved

Boulevard Books

The New Face of Publishing

www.BoulevardBooks.org

The Psyche Ward Notes:

Surviving Anxiety & Depression

Peter Vox

Foreword

Did I know that things had become bad for Peter? Yes. *But this bad?* No, I didn't have a clue.

Over the past few weeks Peter has been forwarding copies of his journal transcriptions that were written while hospitalized in a neuropsychiatric center in New York City. These were the blueprints for what would become the book you're about to read. Within these myriad entries, Peter set out to describe his current life circumstances, and does so in considerable detail – sharing what he refers to as his ruminations. He is describing a variation of himself that seemed diametrically opposed to the version of Peter who I first met on a rainy Thursday afternoon during the summer of 1989. But things were different then.

For some perspective, please allow me to momentarily take you back to the magical time that was the late 1980s – the days of no internet, no social media, and no smartphones. Friendships were most often formed because of one's life circumstance, or the occasional chance encounter. I was about to embark upon my senior year of high school. My next-door neighbor and classmate, Scott Merlino, kept mentioning, "Hey, there's a guy who works out at my gym that you have to meet! He sings and loves your type of music." Scott wasn't a musician, so I approached his referral with a degree of skepticism. However, and not wanting to sound rude, I would say, "Oh Yeah? I'll look forward to meeting him one day."

A couple of weeks later, while returning home from summer school, I was surprised to see Scott sitting on our front porch. He was accompanied by an unfamiliar guy sporting a mullet. It was Peter Vox.

Over the years I have often thought about how grateful I am that Scott took the initiative to make this introduction happen. It was one of those seemingly random introductions that would end up changing the course of my life for the better. If one is willing to surrender to the infinite wisdom of the cosmos, the alignment of circumstances that led up to that fateful afternoon are not a matter of mere coincidence.

In many ways, the version of Peter who you'll be learning about during the ensuing chapters isn't quite the same as what I'm describing here. The Peter who I met and would become close friends with during the early 1990s was very social, outgoing, industrious, and most notably, *hilarious*. Peter was blessed with an abundance of comedic wit.

Of course, Peter *is still all these things*. But time has a way of etching away at smooth surfaces. The gravity of chaos is heavy. This realization also highlights that you never truly know the extent of someone's mental strife. Exterior presentations can be misleading. When I first met Peter, he looked the part of a rock star. Because of this superficial observation, I just assumed everything was okay.

In truth, the pain, tumult, and internal anxiety Peter had been coping with since at least 1984 wasn't overt or readily observable when I first met him. I mean we had discussed things and shared some of our personal stories. But the notion that the 1990 version of Peter would eventually become suicidal or institutionalized would have seemed unfathomable. In those days, Peter was the life of a party. People were naturally drawn towards his presence – this is something I witnessed many times. His good looks and charm gave no indication of what simmered beneath the surface.

It's a world of contradiction, where two opposing realities can both be true. I have since become aware of his struggles with anxiety, and now understand that it had probably existed from the very beginning. And despite it, Peter managed to perform on stage before large crowds while exuding an aura of total confidence and ease.

It has been said that music has an ability to tame a troubled soul. Perhaps this is the explanation. When Peter and I first met, we shifted our lens towards recording and performing music together. That was our bond and focus.

I would be remiss if not to mention Peter's greatest attribute; it's his generous and kind spirit. Peter is a team player and the type of friend you're grateful to have in your corner.

I could provide many examples but for now will share this one. I lived in a small town in Upstate New York. During my senior year of high school, Peter drove me to my music school auditions in New York City when no one else would or could. It was a three-and-a-half hour drive each way. He didn't volunteer for this because it was easy or convenient, but rather because he believed in me. I'll never forget that act of kindness and gesture of true friendship.

Another extension of his generosity is demonstrated by virtue of what he is willing to share with readers within this book. He has adopted a no-holds-barred approach to writing, and I'm guessing that some of what gets revealed in the following pages wasn't easy to share. It's very up close and personal.

I sense that Peter's willingness to share his story in an open-book capacity is part of a healing process. This public acknowledgment represents definitive steps towards his liberation from the incarceration of trauma. Although some of the details are not always pleasant, in the end, this is a story about survival and creating a pathway towards personal salvation. This book provides anecdotes of hope for anyone who is confronting similar adversity.

Darren Wilsey
June 12, 2021

***DISCLAIMER*:** I am not a licensed medical doctor, psychiatrist, psychologist, social worker or any other mental health professional. Therefore, any mental health theories, information or descriptions of myself/other persons discussed are based on personal research and are strictly my own opinions. In addition, people's names have been changed to protect their identity.

Introduction:

The following is a journal that was written while I was committed to a total of 5 psychiatric hospitals that are located on Long Island, Queens and The Bronx, New York. In total, my hospitalizations added up to 14 months. The longest stint in these hospitals lasted 11 months and 1 day from Aug 21, 2019 - July 22, 2020.

The mental illnesses I have include major depression, severe anxiety disorder and PTSD. All of those disorders are mostly caused by my experiencing non-stop existential crisis/sadness; that's where you are constantly aware during every second of every day that you are going to die someday and you are left living in a frozen state of fear. These are unwanted obsessive-compulsive thoughts. It also distracts you from day-to-day life and can contribute to relationships ending with friends and family. The reasons for these illnesses are both genetic and environmental and are covered as the journal goes on.

An awful habit that I have is ruminating about the past, the present and the future. Ruminating is when you constantly think of negative events in your life, and you are having difficulty getting over them and moving on.

While this journal contains sections of ruminating, I kept them word for word and in order so that the reader can get a glimpse into that type of thought process. Because ruminating can get tedious, I will give a Rumination Warning to the readers just in case you're not up for it. In addition to writing down my own personal thoughts and experiences, I took the time to write about the other patients, their illnesses, their life stories and what life is like when you are living in a psychiatric hospital.

While being born with mental illness, I was also lucky enough to be born with a creative side; I sing, play drums, draw and I was blessed with a quick wit and sense of humor which thankfully made it to these pages. Humor is a great coping mechanism. Thank you for being interested in my journey.

Chapter 1: The 11 Month Hospitalization Begins

Aug 28, 2019

I was admitted to Jacobi Hospital in The Bronx on Aug 21, 2019, for taking 15 Ativan after finding out my pension and finances were not what I thought they would be upon retirement. This was my 3rd stay at Jacobi since May of 2019. This combined with divorce, having to sell a nice house in the suburbs, bankruptcy, being put on food stamps, going on social security disability, the loss of my father, car accident, back surgery and being falsely accused of assaulting my students and my being pushed out of a 19-year teaching career caused the camel's back to break. Basically, it was a culmination of 10 years of constant major life changing events and fighting mental illness at the same time.

Below is the first entry into a journal on Aug 28, 2019, 4pm Jacobi Hospital

Description of my anxiety attacks: The catalyst will be usually something that gets me to start obsessing over death; like a news story about someone who has a terminal illness . Physical symptoms start with either a stomach cramp or a cold wave of adrenaline that feels like a cold needle that got injected into my sternum. My head, face, toes, hands, and fingertips all go numb. After that happens, I get dizzy and get the sensation that I'm in a cold dark tunnel, where every sound is amplified and it echoes throughout my head.

The worst part of my anxiety attacks is that they make me vomit. The vomiting usually happens in the mornings, so its more like the dry heaves because my stomach is empty. I wind up coughing up stomach bile instead of food. It also happens to be extremely painful. This phenomenon is called retching. It makes you feel like you're being beaten up by a ghost.

Every 15 minutes or so today, I get the tinge of fear when I start thinking about the reality of my situation: I need a job, I need money, my pension is not what I thought it would be.

I get tremendous amounts of fear that I won't survive, or I ask myself, "How will I survive?" I then start to obsess over death: How will I die? When? What happens after? What was I before I was born? What does forever mean? What existed before the universe and The Big Bang (not the TV show)? All these questions that have no answers then cause tremendous fear which quickly turns into feelings of sheer terror and hysterics. It leaves me feeling that life has no meaning.

Every anxiety attack feels like it's the first time I've ever had one. Even though I have had hundreds of panic attacks, each one feels like the worst one I ever had. I also experience heart palpitations which can make some people with anxiety think that they are having a heart attack.

Right now, I'm looking forward to medication time so I can get some sleep.

Aug 29, 2019, Jacobi Hospital, Bronx, NY

Every morning I wake up at around 4 a.m. and immediately have the fear of death and the onus of knowing that I have to fight it all day until I go to sleep at night. This has been happening every day since 1978. An anxiety attack can happen at any time during the day without warning. As a kid, I could be playing ball with my friends and then I would start thinking about that one day I will die. My adrenaline would start pumping as I couldn't stop the fear of death from happening and all the physical symptoms I mentioned above would start taking over. I would either leave my friend's house or I rode it out until they stopped. This also led to me feeling socially awkward and insecure at a very young age.

After a 4 a.m. anxiety attack subsides, I am somehow able to fall back to sleep for a couple of more hours.

Today I feel like giving up, it feels like there's no other way and I'm frightened at the same time. I'm having heart palpitations, dry mouth, fearing I could die at any second and overwhelming feelings of helplessness and hopelessness. I have three sons to live for and this illness is winning?

That is unacceptable. Why am I afraid of getting a new job or being strong enough to survive? Giving up is the easy way out, however it will hurt all the people that I love, so I have no choice but to fight like I have been doing my whole life. Maybe I'm in the hospital because I need to pause and reset my life. I guess after fighting since I'm 9, I'm burnt out and I need more intense help. I'm looking forward to shock therapy, especially the anesthesia, so that I get a break from reality if only for 30 seconds. (Shock treatment did happen when I transferred to Elmhurst Hospital in Nov 2019). I am hoping that electroshock treatment helps to make me strong enough to survive, go to work, be a good father, and maybe someday I'll fall in love again. I also hope to regain my interests in all the things I enjoy; music, art and fitness. Right now, I don't see a future. I know this thought pattern will eventually change because it always does when I go through rough periods. However, this is THE mother of rough periods and the emotional pain won't stop no matter how much I want it to. When I had my sons, I wanted to make sure that I hid my anxiety and depression from them so that it would not affect them and look where I am now.

It's 2:15 p.m. and an anxiety attack hits me like I've never had one before in my entire life. I retired too early based on anger and fear. I fear looking for a new job because it's going to be difficult if I must talk about being hospitalized. I'm tired of staying here too. I have a very cold feeling in my chest as my heart pounds and my face gets cold and numb. When I walk laps around the unit, which is called 7A, I ruminate and worry the same as I do when I lay in bed or when I sit watching TV.

Another cycle of anxiety hits again and the subject matter is about my divorce; my children spending more time with another man then with me, the fact that I must sue the Department of Education to clear my record and the worry about how I'm going to survive financially when I get out of the hospital.

August 30, 2019, Jacobi Hospital, Bronx, NY

It's morning time and the anxiety hit like a sledgehammer on my back. Today I'm getting out of bed on time so that the nurses can take my daily vitals; that would include my blood pressure and my pulse. After my vitals are taken, I go to the day room and wait for the announcement for breakfast. As I sit waiting for breakfast, I navigate an anxiety attack from being very bad to being tolerable. I concentrate on the other patients, talk to people and try to keep busy. When breakfast and all meals arrive on the meal carts, patients must stand in the hallway and wait until their names are called so that they can take their trays into the day room to eat. As I sit in the day room looking at my breakfast this one morning, I realize that I must eat in order to feel better just a little bit. I wind up eating some pancakes, which are good. It turns out that I was surprisingly hungry, and I asked for seconds and thirds, since they were available. If there's one thing that hospitals make the best in terms of food, it's their pancakes and waffles.

There are activity groups here, but I don't really think they help. For example, the fitness group is made up of extremely light stretching and doing arm circles. To me as a fitness buff and physical education teacher, I do not get anything from exercise like this. It's almost as if the instructors don't try. They are so mellow like how therapists are parodied on TV shows. They talk with this quiet mellow voice as if everything's going to be okay just because they're talking that way.

When your brain is so consumed with worries that are quite frankly, not real; doing arm circles, coloring like a five-year-old, playing ping-pong and having a dance class where you barely dance is of no help.

There's not enough real group therapy and individual therapy. People who are truly insane may not get the full benefits of psychotherapy because their illness is something that is permanent and unfortunately there's a limit of how much they can improve. However, maybe pushing the limit by just a wee bit could help them. They truly live in a different world. I have now seen it up close and personal.

People like me who have anxiety and depression are not insane and are aware of reality. With intense therapy, someone with cognitive awareness can benefit and improve. There's no cure for anxiety and depression; only strategies or medications; which I strongly advise that you research what you are taking should you decide to go on meds.

It's very tempting to lay in bed all day, however, I ruminate when I'm in bed about everything that revolves around what happened in my life and the unwanted death obsession.

Instead of laying in bed I decide to sit in the day room and watch Kelly Ripa and Ryan Seacrest blow bubbles.. I'm living the dream!

Watching TV has become especially painful because I know all the people on television shows are successful and wealthy. It's all I can think about and then I ruminate about my crazy ass. I worry about the day-to-day grind about working. It's not that I don't want to work. The issue is that; all day at a job I'm under constant self-imposed paranoia that I'm doing a bad job, or I did something wrong. It's mentally and physically exhausting. Every time a supervisor wants to talk to me, I panic. I then worry I will get fired, end up homeless and broke. Conceivably, I can waste about an hour of my day worrying about getting fired from a job that doesn't even exist.

One of the nurses said this to me: "Don't try to figure out what you can't control while you're still in the hospital like what job you're going to have.

Don't fantasize about being fired from a theoretical job that you don't even know what it is yet. The first thing you have to do is take care of you and be around for your children. One thing at a time. And you need to take it slow when you get out. If you try to push too hard and too fast, you will wind up back here". The one thing you learn about staying in the hospital for a long time is that the nurses know more than everybody else, including the doctors.

Aug 30, 2019, Jacobi Hospital, Bronx, NY

I'm sitting on my bed in my room, looking out the window while it starts to get dark out as I get ready for sleep. I took my medications for the night and when they take effect it's very sudden; you lay in bed awake and then the next thing you know it's 4 in the morning. I'm feeling especially homesick; I miss my kids, and I'm feeling scared of what my life has turned into, hence, more rumination for you to read about and for me to whine and complain. But I'm too tired to write more because even my complaining repeatedly gets tiring. Sometimes I think I'm just a big baby.

Chapter 2: Barry and the Others

One thing I wanted to accomplish and was interested in while writing this journal was discussing the patients that I met and gotten to know very well during this surreal experience. I attribute this to having an inquisitive mind and want to know how certain clocks tick. When I introduced a patient in my handwritten journal, I wrote their name with a semi colon next to it, like below:

Barry:

Barry is 61 years old, my roommate, an accomplished musician and loves to give the nurses a hard time. If I would have to describe what Barry looks like it would be Sherman Helmsley from The Jeffersons, who played George. The difference between them is that Barry has gray hair.

 Barry likes to help clean the tables in the TV room and is OCD about his hygiene. That's a blessing given some of the smells here that punch me in the nose without warning. Unfortunately, Barry lost his wife five years ago to Lou Gehrig's disease. He took care of her for her entire sickness. We talk about her a lot and shed many tears about her and the wonderful memories that he had about her.

Barry also has another side; he likes to deal weed, smoke weed, he's very hyperactive and he likes to be the center of attention like a typical Leo. In addition, he thrives in and gets off on chaotic situations. Barry also likes to flirt with every woman on the floor whether it's a patient or a nurse. Barry also loves to tell stories about how he likes to be out all-night smoking and dealing weed. He said to me once, "I love being out all night, carrying guns and being around niggas on the street".

Plus, he is on the phone constantly with family members either laughing maniacally or cursing out those who owe him money. The medical staff has him on many drugs to calm him down so he can sleep. He fights the drugs and stays up all night pacing our room and the hallway. While he does this, he becomes loud on purpose as he tries to keep everyone awake. I had to eventually switch rooms because he had me up every night.

There is also a generous side to Barry: He's always ordering food and soda for everyone from his family members that come to visit him almost every night. I got to meet his son and daughters and I thought they were very nice and none of them had mental illness. I couldn't understand how Barry was their father because he was so mentally ill. But then I asked myself; How could I be my sons' father when I'm so mentally ill or the son of my father?

Barry was brought to Jacobi Hospital, Ward 7A after some gang members at a basketball game thought he was a police informant. They made Barry strip down to his underwear to check that he wasn't wearing a wire. When the gang members realized he wasn't a cop they took all his clothes, sneakers and weed. They left them in his underwear. He was then brought by ambulance to Jacobi Hospital for his 10th or 12th stay.

When Barry speaks, he drools, which is a side effect of the numerous medications that he is on. Lots of the patients here drool due to medication side effects.

Barry usually starts a conversation talking about his fast lifestyle and then eventually will start crying at the same time about something depressing. Barry's major run-ins on 7A were with a woman in her 20s named Shalika:

Shalika in my opinion is,

bipolar, schizophrenic and she believes that she is Beyoncé. However, her appearance looks nothing like Beyoncé. Unfortunately, Shalika is overweight, missing teeth, drools from her meds, and walks with a water jug that is just tilted enough that she spills water on the floor constantly. In addition, Shalika has a bladder problem and wears diapers, or is supposed to wear diapers. There are times where she will be standing in the hallway and just start peeing in her pants. She's not even aware of it.

Barry and Shalika are constantly fighting and their arguments center around the use of the radio or the TV in the day room. On a day-to-day basis, Barry would instigate Shalika to lose her temper. His goal was that she would get a shot of Thorazine that would knock her out for 8 hours. His theory was that it was better to have her sleeping all day then to be a pain in the ass to everyone. Although mean, I could see his point.

In addition to being hyperactive, talking all the time and causing trouble, Barry loves to dance. In fact, he's one of the better dancers I've seen in my life.

Barry loves to dance in the day room. When he dances, he doesn't seem to have a care in the world. He enjoys his stay here saying, "It's cheaper than living home. I get three meals a day, I love giving everybody a rough time and they'll never kill my spirit".

While at this latest stay at Jacobi Hospital, Barry befriended a 21 your old kid named German. German sliced his arms open with a 6-inch knife in front of a police officer as a distraction so that the officer wouldn't arrest his sister for dealing weed. Instead of being arrested, Herman was brought to Jacobi Hospital 7A. Herman's forearms had several deep cuts that were held together by thick black stitching. In addition, the cuts had yet to start scabbing up and they were somewhat bloody. Given this, German refused to wear bandages. In my opinion, the cuts looked like a suicide attempt.

Barry was quick to adopt German as his "son" and promised him a job dealing weed when he gets out of the hospital. German also lost his mother about a year ago. If you mention his mother, even in a caring way, he will either get violent or have an emotional breakdown and start mutilating himself with anything he could find. One night, German got so upset that a female patient asked what happened to his mother from an empathetic stance, he had a seizure. In addition, at a group meeting, German started chewing on his stitches. That was the most emotional pain I've ever witnessed from a person.

When I watched German chew on the stitches they eventually started to bleed. Blood dripped down his arms, on the table and on to the floor. Yup, this is happening.

Tobin:

Tobin is a 50-year-old male who was born in Russia and raised in Israel. He also served four years in the Israeli army and fought against the Palestinians. When Tobin was brought to Jacobi Hospital, he was unconscious due to alcohol poisoning. The alcohol poisoning was so bad that there was blood in his lungs that had to be drained. He went on a huge drinking binge for weeks because his wife and the mother of his two kids wanted a divorce. His resume is impressive; after serving in the Israeli Army, he owned an IT company, and now owns a liquor store and rental properties. One would think that life was going pretty good for Tobin and his family. He came to the USA with nothing and built a great life.

According to Tobin, his wife no longer wants to be with him, giving no concrete reason other than she doesn't love him anymore. He started drinking a lot. He never cheated, never abused her mentally or physically and is very family oriented

Tobin is also very strong-willed and doesn't understand my illness. He thinks that I can just turn off the negative thoughts that have plagued me for most of my life. I try to explain that it's mostly a chemical imbalance. He tries to be uplifting, positive and always gives support whenever we are talking socially, playing ping pong or in group therapy.

 We've had many talks about staying strong and moving on from divorce. Tobin eventually must go through his divorce, and I can see the pain on his face. It reminds me of how I feel about my own divorce.

During his stay at the hospital, Tobin became a pretty good artist. Tobin's artwork consisted mostly of superhero drawings like Batman and

Superman. He also worked on a pretty good pencil drawing of President Obama.

After Tobin was discharged from the hospital, he would call us to check in and let us know what he was up to. Tobin said he had first come home, the house was empty, no electricity, phone or food. His Rabbi helped him get started along with Adult Protective Services who got his electricity turned on. He sounded happy on the phone although he hasn't seen his wife and his kids and doesn't know where they are. The last time I spoke to him on the phone he talked about becoming a singer and that he wants to record songs with me. It's very far-fetched considering he does not have a good voice and I don't have the heart to tell him that. I suggested he get his business and rental properties back in order and unfortunately face a terrible divorce in which his wife will try to take everything.

Shirley:

I met Shirley at Jacobi Hospital and we were both eventually transferred to Bronx Psychiatric Center around the same time in February of 2020.

Shirley is about 65 years old she is African American, overweight, missing many teeth, drools from medication, and it's constantly talking nonstop about her life and how she will sue these hospitals. Shirley pushes a chair while walking because the hospital won't let her have a walker. When Shirley speaks, she can pinpoint everything from the day, date and year of different events in her life. In my opinion, she has a photographic autobiographical memory in which she remembers every second of every day of her life. The actress Mary Lou Henner from the 80's TV show Taxi has that ability as well. There are many interviews of her on YouTube about it that you can check out.

In my opinion, Shirley is bi-polar and gets angry very easily at the nurses and calls them bitches and hoes. She always yells," Y'all are fat, and you need some dicks in your lives!" Shirley gets mad at things like not getting a tea bag with lunch, always getting a cheeseburger, and not being able to watch the shows that she wants to watch on TV. When
Shirley is out of control; she gets an injection of Thorazine which knocks her out for the entire day. Sometimes I wish I can get a shot of Thorazine,

and I could be knocked out for a day. Maybe we all do.

An interesting story about Shirley was an incident when she entered a younger male patient's room and tried to have sex with him; first, she exposed her breasts in a gesture of seduction. The male patient screamed, and the nurses quickly took Shirley back to her room.

Try to keep in mind that the behavior I'm describing of these patients are not things that happen occasionally; they happen daily, by the hour and sometimes by the minute. When one incident ends, another one begins. It's non-stop 24/7.

Zane:

Zane is African American, in his mid-20s and wears horned Rim glasses like Steve Urkel from Family Matters. Zane has obsessive compulsive disorder tendencies and rituals: he must touch the floor in a certain pattern while he leaves his room, when he sits down for a meal and even during a basketball game. He bends down and makes shapes on the floor with his right hand after outlining his feet and tapping his feet as well.

If I met Zane on the street, I would never guess that he has a mental illness. He speaks extremely eloquent, dresses nice, has impeccable hygiene and seems to have cognitive awareness when I speak with him. But, during meals, he puts food on his soup bowl cover and leaves it on the floor for invisible friends to eat.

Chapter 3: Aug 30, 2019, Jacobi 7A

There was an incident today between two women: Shalika and Carmen. Shalika spit on Carmen based on lies that Barry supposedly told to both women about each other. Barry loves chaos! This happened right when Barry was being discharged. Carmen is 57, homeless and can barely walk. I'm guessing she is heavily medicated. This is not the first incident for Carmen. She had many arguments with Shalika based on turns with the radio and just talking trash to each other. All the incidents end with Shalika getting the needle and being knocked out for the rest of the day. Shalika likes to threaten everyone by saying she'll call her mother, brothers or sisters to come here and beat everybody up.

Kalida:

Kalida is about 35 years old, African American, extremely thin and has one daughter. She told me she is a meth addict with anger/violent issues. She is also very loud. When she wasn't yelling at someone, she would yell to herself.

Whenever Kalida is on the phone, she's yelling at the person on the line saying, "You better bring me my fucking stuff first thing in the morning!" Some patients think she's smuggling drugs. I believe she is getting soda, iced tea and chocolate. She has offered me chocolate. I decline because I don't want to owe anyone anything, especially someone who gets violent.

Just about all of Kalida's arguments end with her taking a swing at someone. Too many incidents eventually led to her being transferred off the ward.

Benny:

Benny is in his mid-twenties is from Latino descent and in my opinion, has schizophrenia and many other illnesses which I don't know how to describe. Let's just say in layman's terms; he's pretty fucked up!

He shaves his head bald and has many scars on his forehead. In addition, he has a cleft palate scar under his nose. Benny is also missing teeth. When he watches television with us, he reacts to the shows and becomes paranoid about the characters either coming to get him, us or any other scenarios that make him part of the show.

 I spent part of the morning writing down everything that Benny said word for word. Most of it is confusing and doesn't make much sense.

According to Benny, while talking about different movies like The Matrix and John Wick; other actors besides Keanu Reeves are interjected into Benny's mind. According to Benny," Keanu Reeves is being charged with rape. Everyone who worked on the Transformers movies are being charged with copyright infringement and will be sentenced to death. Brandon Lee was killed because of copyright infringement. Real life predators are also coming after Danny Glover and Mel Gibson." Benny is combining lots of different movies here.

According to Benny, every actor in Hollywood is being charged with rape, murder or copyright infringement. "The way the police get these actors is to watch the movies and pull them from out of the screen", Benny says.

Benny also claims to have worked for Sony, PlayStation, programmed streetlights, satellites and programmed the Transformers; like Artemis Prime and the Decepticons. He spends most of his day walking laps in the hallway of the unit, which is a rectangle. 15 laps equal a mile.

Benny laughs a lot to himself in a high-pitched, whining voice. When he walks the hall, he will also enter the TV room, stop at the TV, look at it for a moment and then leave to continue his "laughing laps". Benny always has the same facial expression; his lips are puckered like he's about to whistle but he never does. Benny also always wears a long white t shirt, basketball shorts with black long johns, and Crocs on his feet. His favorite channel is the Disney Channel and he likes the shows that are meant for teenage girls. In group therapy today Benny said he is waiting for Section 8 housing.

The only thing you can do when someone is obviously very ill is to be friendly, smile and try to contribute to the conversation.

I feel for Benny because he truly does not know what the real world is: his head is filled with voices and visions that trick him into believing they are real. That's got to be painful and confusing.

Chapter 4: Aug 31st, 2019, Jacobi Hospital 7A

A woman named Colima started screaming and cursing today about getting the wrong breakfast again. She wanted an omelet. Instead, she got two hard boiled eggs and a few slices of American cheese. When she saw her breakfast, she lost her mind and started screaming, "The same fucking mistakes every day! What's the point of telling the dietitian what I want if I don't fucking get it? I swear I'm going to go crazy on everyone". At that point, she kept screaming, slamming her tray and throwing food all over the place. She finally had to be calmed down and given a Thorazine needle. How come I never get the needle!? Usually when I talk to Colima, she is calm and friendly. It was off putting to see her angry side come out like that. It was literally like Dr. Jekyll and Mr. Hyde.

Christopher:

Christopher is African American, 25 years old and in my opinion, is highly schizophrenic. During his first night here, he tried fighting with just about everyone. He yelled at a patient calling him a "Motherfucking Latino". After that, he pushed and choked another patient named Maria.

During Christopher's second night here, I was walking laps around the unit and saw Christopher standing naked in his doorway. He just showered and forgot to get clean pajamas. When I first saw him, he was in a trance and staring into space. I said, "Chris, you know you're naked, right?"

Christopher asked me to help him get clean clothes. So, I called the nurse and she got him clean pajamas. I couldn't help but see the humor and oddness of the situation.

On 7A, a good laugh is hard to come by. At least I'm getting along with everyone and am making friends. Sometimes the most mentally ill people have true wisdom to share. It's as if for just a moment, they have total clarity, share something deep and then revert back to their usual selves.

Rosa:

The story of Rosa is quite a sad one. Rosa is about 23 years old, extremely overweight and has incontinence problems. As a small child, Rosa fell out of a 2nd story window, landed on her head and suffered brain damage as a result. She lives here at Jacobi Hospital and has been here for over two years. The family is unable to care for her because she is violent. Rosa likes to call every new male patient on the floor her boyfriend. She called me her novio when she first met me. When she said that, I smiled and said thank you. On the inside, my heart immediately broke for her.

When Rosa doesn't get what she wants she lays on the floor with her two stuffed animals and can be heard wailing from her room. Sometimes she runs around screaming while her nurse gives chase. She spends about 90% of her time in her room, sedated. One afternoon she attacked a nurse, who collided with me while trying to get away from Rosa. Rosa has a meltdown at least three to four times a day and at a certain point you go from being shocked to being numb to it.

Kasey:

Kasey is a Jamaican from Kingstown. In my opinion, he is schizophrenic. Kasey sleeps all day but when he is awake, he sits in the day room and repeats what he hears and sees on TV. He constantly says that he lives in a small community and pays his rent. He says that every time he's at the medication line. At night, Kasey walks with my old roommate Barry in the hall. Kasey and Barry like to talk loudly while they walk in order to drive the nurse's crazy. Kasey talks about political conspiracies that make zero sense. For example, New York's weather is controlled by the government. I wrote down some of his rants in a later entry.

Dijon:

Dijon looks like Lurch from The Addams Family. He's about six foot four, very thin and missing most of his teeth. He is always wearing a University of Wisconsin t-shirt, blue sweatpants and brown slippers. He can also barely speak. He sleeps all day while he farts and shits the bed. Dijon needs to be woken for every meal and for every medication dosage. The room we shared got so bad with the odor that I could not stay there anymore. When he is awake, he walks laps around the unit. His walking routine includes doing a lap, walking into the day room, staring out the window for a moment, he then farts and walks out. The night that I got clearance to move out of the room from Dijon, the nurses finally got him to shower. However, he put back on his feces covered clothes. So again, the nurses made him shower and got him clean pajamas. In my opinion, Dijon is extremely schizophrenic and talks very softly in a language in which I cannot decipher.

Chapter 5: The Origins of My Mental Illness

Where does my mental illness come from? Well, like I've stated before, I believe it's a combination of my past environment and genetics.

The first memory I have of my life was being brought to the cemetery at around age 2 for the unveiling of my uncle Wayne's gravestone. I remember hearing people cry as I was looking up at some clouds and the blue sky. My memory of it is only a few moments of the event, but it is crystal clear in my mind. I can see it still and feel it.

My anxiety and depression started to become apparent at about age 5. I remember having what I know now were panic attacks about going to school and leaving the house for nursery school up until 7th grade.

By age 9, I had my first existential crisis about death and mortality: it was the summer of 1978, we were on vacation in Vermont. I was fishing in a stream with my family. I remember using a yellow fishing rod. Suddenly, I started to think about that one day I will die. I remember my entire body going numb and cold. I then started to cry and screamed to my parents, "I'm afraid of dying!". That day opened the door in my mind to being involuntary obsessed with and scared of death. The existential crisis/sadness became permanent.

I believe this was partly brought on because of the untimely deaths of family members and friends of my parents. In addition, mental illness runs in my family especially with my father, who was also instrumental in fueling my disorder.

So, who died an untimely death in my circle of family and friends?

My maternal Uncle Wayne died in Nov of 1969, from a brain aneurysm. He was about 41 years old. 9 years later in Jan of 1978, Wayne's son Paul died of a heart attack at age 33, leaving a wife and infant daughter. The autopsy showed that he had the heart of an 80-year-old man. These deaths made my Aunt Sheena a widow and losing her son within 10 years. It left my cousins losing a dad and brother. It left my grandmother (an undiagnosed schizophrenic too) and grandfather losing their son and Grandson within 10 years and so on and so forth.

On my father's side of the family, my uncle Joe, who was my dad's brother had a wife named Beth, who died of cancer at age 42, leaving a young son behind; this was just three or four years after my uncle Wayne died.

A few years after my Aunt Beth died, Joe married a woman named Shannon. She had a son named Terry who was my age at the time; 8 years old. It was the first time I had a cousin that was my age, and I was excited to meet him. Unfortunately, I only got to meet Terry once at Thanksgiving dinner with my family at my childhood home. I remember playing with him in our basement and he got his butt stuck in the laundry hamper. I remember all the laughing and thinking that I had a great new cousin. A few months after I met Terry, he was killed by a drunk driver while riding his bicycle in Harlem in front of my uncle's apartment building.

Around the same time that my cousin Paul died, a newlywed couple had moved into the house next store. Teddy and Shelly were their names. Teddy was a great guy. He was nice, funny and I spent a good amount of time with him. My bedroom window faced their driveway, so I would always yell out my window to him. If Teddy was outside at night, I would joke and yell in a funny voice, "Hey! I'm trying to sleep up here!" He would always play along and make jokes. It was like having an uncle living next store.

 Not long after Shelly gave birth to their daughter, Teddy was diagnosed with a brain tumor. I watched this man deteriorate before my eyes. He went from having a thick head of hair, thick beard and good physique; to looking like a concentration camp victim. The last time I saw Teddy, he was being brought out on a stretcher to an ambulance. He had suffered the seizure that eventually killed him. Another person close to me gone. More people left widowed. More children left without their fathers.

 More deaths: both of my paternal grandparents died before I was 6, so I have memories of their deaths. Furthermore, during the 1970's, I had a lot of great aunts and uncles who were in nursing homes to where I was brought not only to see them, but I had to see all the dying elderly spread about the nursing home hallways. If you mix that with all that had happened to the people I was close to, I began to obsess about death even more. By age 10, I was constantly questioning the meaning of life and the existential questions that have no answers. Not knowing the answers gave me anxiety and the overwhelming feeling that life was meaningless. Mind you, this was all happening during my formative years. Every time the phone rang in my house, I feared it was someone calling to tell us someone died.

My mother blames herself for bringing me to cemeteries and nursing homes at such a young age. She says she looks back and it was a stupid thing to do. When she told me that, I told her in a nice way that it wasn't the smartest thing to do. I'll be honest by saying that I am extremely resentful that I was taken to those places. I remember how it scared the shit out of me.

Like I stated earlier, this would be one part of how my environment shaped my views on life and how it triggered my mental illness to reveal itself. My brother has gone through the same losses, lived in the same house with me and our parents and he only gets panicky occasionally. He went to therapy a handful of times and has never had extended episodes of anxiety or depression. This makes me believe that genetics plays a huge role in mental illness. As a result, if your environment is unhealthy, it will feed the illness.

By the time I was 14, I felt I was suffering and I asked to go to therapy in February of 1984. The final catalyst that led to this was: I was obsessing over the cold war between the USA and USSR. I would watch the news every day to see if anything was happening. If I heard the local fire department's sirens, I would think it was a missile warning and would have to put on the TV or radio to make sure we weren't getting attacked. There was also a made for TV movie called, "The Day After", which depicted what a nuclear holocaust would be like. I believe that Jason Robards was in the movie.

I tried to avoid watching the movie until it was shown in my English class. This made me worse. On the Monday following February break in 1984, I had a huge anxiety attack while walking to my friend Andy's house to pick him up so we could walk to school together. I never made it to his house. During the anxiety attack, I started to vomit and lost control of my bowels (I shit in my pants). I immediately ran home after and that was when I told my mother that I needed to see a psychiatrist.

By age 24, in 1993, I started taking medication, Xanax. Coming up in the next chapters are more in-depth explanations about my family, my divorce and what going through life like this has been like.

Chapter 6: My Father

My father's name was Irwin, and he was born in June of 1931 and died in April of 2019 from a series of heart attacks in one day. The first heart attack he suffered was while he was playing poker at an illegal card room in Queens. After that heart attack, he had 2 or 3 more at the hospital and was in a vegetative state with barely a pulse. We followed his Do Not Resuscitate orders and took him off life support and kept him on a high morphine drip until he passed away. My mother, brother and I were not there when he passed away. We had all gone home to shower and change our clothes and then go back to the hospital to wait for it to happen. I have mixed feelings about it, but not because of my fear of death. It was more that I knew he was going to die because the doctor told us he had no brain function; that's when he died to me. My mother and brother were hoping there was a chance he would wake up even knowing what the doctor said. With all the death that happened around me, I've never actually seen a person die in real life. There's a certain irony there.

Back to my dad. Dad sold advertising for a fashion trade newspaper. The cool thing about his job was that the company would give him NY Rangers and Knicks tickets if their clients didn't want to go to a game. Because of that, I saw Michael Jordan's rookie debut at MSG against the Knicks. The game is on You Tube.

My father was born and raised in Brooklyn, New York by 2 Russian immigrants. My grandfather, Harry, was about 6 ft 5 and weighed approximately 250lbs of solid muscle (Think Rob Gronkowski). Harry fought in World War 1 and was in the cavalry. In Harry's early twenties, he competed in a handful of bodybuilding shows, winning most of them. My grandfather was a gentle giant; very loving, always giving hugs and kisses and words of praise for my brother and me. Unfortunately, my grandfather died when I was approximately 5 years old. The memories I do have of him are wonderful. Before my grandfather died, he suffered a stroke that left him looking unrecognizable; emaciated, face deformed, and he couldn't talk or walk. When I went to visit him at the nursing home with my mother, I couldn't accept the fact that this is what my gigantic, strong, and wonderful grandfather had become. I remember feeling hurt, mad and scared all at the same time. I had two awesome grandfathers. More on my maternal grandfather later on.

My grandfather Harry was a car salesman and also drove a cab. He was married to my grandmother Ethel. According to my father, my grandmother was a grandiose narcissist. In addition, she was also a very talented opera singer who turned down a job with the Metropolitan Opera in New York City in order to get married and raise children. This decision was something that my grandmother always regretted. With that being the case, she took out all her anger and resentment on my father, my uncle and especially my grandfather. My grandmother also neglected my father and uncle and quite frequently left them unbathed for days and weeks at a time.

According to my father, his mother would call him a "bitch" as her main word of verbal abuse. Can you believe people were using the term "bitch" in the 1930's and 1940's? Their family dynamic and energy centered around what my grandmother wanted and what type of mood she was in. Between her neglect, abuse and genetics; my father grew up to be a very mentally ill man.

My father's anxiety disorder displayed itself in the form of him being a hypochondriac, being afraid of everything, lazy and not motivated. In addition, he rarely bathed, he used to have my mother cut his toenails for him and wash his hair in the kitchen sink. This is a grown man living in an upscale neighborhood. In addition, my parents had the bathrooms renovated and he still didn't shower. He also would sometimes sleep in bed with his sneakers on under his blanket.

Every night until I moved out in my twenties, my father would examine himself in his bathroom mirror and look for things to be wrong on his body. For example, he would be looking for tumors, cysts or other uncommon growths on his body. He would do this self-examination just at about the time my brother and I were going to sleep for the night.

Every single night, my father would stand at the top of the stairs and yell down to my mother to come upstairs and examine his body. My father would yell with a neurotic shrill that immediately does damage to you when you hear it. All I would hear was fear every night in his voice.

So, after bellowing to my mother a few times in a tone like he was being skinned alive, my mother would scream in her neurotic tone that she was on her way. There was zero consideration from my parents about the fact that they are both screaming at each other in fear while their kids can hear them. I knew it was madness. As a kid, it scared me. When I got older, it pissed me off because my father had been in therapy most of his life and didn't use much of what he learned. In addition, my mother was his enabler and they had more of a mother to son relationship than an equal partnership in the marriage.

Anyway, my mother would then stomp up the stairs, make her way through their bedroom and into their bathroom to examine my father for what he perceived to be cancer. I would hear exactly what they would say because they were so loud. Even just normal conversations were loud. My father would ask my mother what a particular pimple or scratch looked like. My mother would say she didn't know. My father would get angry if my mother said that she didn't know what it was. I would always hear my mother tell him "It's nothing, it's a pimple" or "It's a scratch". My father wanted my mother to be his nurse and mommy. I think my mother knew well enough not to say that it looks like a bump, because that would set my father off for another few hours. Imagine trying to go to sleep every night and your father, who is supposed to be the example of bravery and masculinity in your life is in his bathroom basically freaking out that he has imaginary cancer. Never at one time did my father ever lower his voice, try to curb his behavior or even take any time to do some self-reflection on how his nightly mental breakdowns could be affecting his sons. Many times, I was awoken from sleep by my father screaming for my mother to come upstairs. It was like being woken up by an air raid siren. After a while being jolted out of sleep like that starts to erode your nerves and mental health.

While at the same time being a hypochondriac, my father was also hyper-vigilant on ingredients in foods, electronic devices and even toothpaste that could pose a threat of cancer.

Every day of my childhood, we were yelled at as to why we couldn't eat or have certain things because they cause cancer. Now, telling a five-year-old that he can't have something to eat because it can give him cancer which WILL kill him is not something that I would put in a book on great parenting.

One of my father's irrational fears was the use of the artificial color called Red Dye #5, which was a possible carcinogenic if you ate excessive amounts of it. Red M&M's were infamous for being made with Red Dye #5. When my father heard Red Dye #5 was a possible carcinogenic, he went on a personal crusade to find out everything that contained Red Dye #5 and banned it from our house and forbid us to eat food that contained it. He would always speak in this fearful shrill, "It causes cancer, and I don't want you to eat it!"

Soon after red M&M's were banned in our house, all red candy followed suit and were removed from our house. Luckily, my favorite candy flavor was grape, and there was no Red Dye #5 in grape lollipops and candy.

Another one of my father's fears was saccharin, the sugar substitute. In the 1970s some scientific reports came out that said that high doses of saccharin given to laboratory rats caused them to develop cancer. After hearing that news, our family was not allowed to have anything that contained saccharin. Here was the problem with that; there is saccharin in all major brands of toothpaste. My father, with his new fear of saccharin, made my mother take all the toothpaste out of the house and buy toothpaste from the health food store. My dad would always make my mom do his neurotic work which made her look like the bad guy until we got old enough to understand what was really going on. The natural toothpaste tasted and looked like window caulking and didn't get foamy like regular toothpaste does. Brushing my teeth became yet another thing to remind me of cancer. I would brush and think, "I have to use this horrible white clay to brush my teeth because my dad is scared." Children emulate their parents' behavior. If you act scared all the time, you're going to raise scared kids. It's simple. If you have kids, do them a favor and don't let them see your behaviors that will fuck them up in the future.

Other things that my dad cut off were foods like salami, ham, any delicious cold cuts, bacon and hot dogs were off-limits too because they contained sodium nitrate, which also causes cancer. Even before we found out about those food additives, we weren't even eating those foods in small quantities let alone enough to cause cancer.

 Other things that were prohibited were certain electronic gadgets and appliances that my father read that emitted radiation, which caused cancer. Color televisions, microwave ovens and cordless phones. Once again, don't forget that my father is telling his son during his formative years that basically everything causes cancer. How do you grow up in a world with those messages constantly being tattooed into your memory and not be affected by it?

For a man who spent his entire life trying to escape cancer by eating mostly healthy and exercised a lot, my father wound up getting prostate cancer in his 70's (he never got checked starting at age 50 because he was afraid to go to the doctor) and had some precancerous melanomas removed from his face in his 50's. As a kid, my dad spent a lot of time in the sun, never used suntan lotion and would burn every summer. Luckily, the prostate cancer was cured as well as his skin. There are certain things in life that are unavoidable and it's important to put those things in perspective and live your life. We are all going to have illness in our lives. Something has to kill us, right?

Because of the skin cancer scare which was in 1986, my father would avoid going outside at all costs. If he did have to go outside, he would wear a wide brimmed hat and white work gloves on his hands that looked like Mickey Mouse's gloves. He would wear long sleeves and pants even in the summer. He would also put way too much sunblock on his face, and it would clump up, making it look disgusting. This behavior became an issue in that my father missed out on events in mine and my brother's lives; my brother's college graduation and all my years of playing lacrosse in junior high school, high school and college. He came to one game: I was a freshman in college, and we were playing the US Merchant Marine Academy in Great Neck, NY. My family lived in Nassau County, NY, close to Great Neck. So, my parents came to the game. Mind you, I was a freshman and a goalie, which means I get maybe 5 minutes of playing time in the 4th quarter if we are either up or down by a lot of goals. I got 5 minutes playing time and let up one goal.

 As I grew up our relationship was strained at times because he refused to curb his behavior for his own dignity and ours as well. Over time, I was fine not having or counting on my father to be there for certain things: most of it was due to his addiction to gambling. He was a poker player and there's a long history there which I will touch on down the road. My dad would miss many family events or just blow off seeing everyone because he wanted to gamble.

After my lumbar fusion surgery in April of 2018, the day I was released, I was going to send an Uber to get my parents, pick me up at the hospital and take us back to my apartment. At my apartment there was a brand-new recliner chair for my dad, as a surprise, because he complained he had nothing comfortable to sit on at my place. The nurses informed me to start making the phone calls to my parents and Uber because I'd be leaving in 60 minutes. I called my parents, who lived in Queens, NY since 2000. My mother answered the phone and said that they couldn't come because my father slipped off a curb getting into an Uber. This was a lie because my father was 86 at the time, only had a flip phone, never used Uber and didn't know how. While I understand that my parents were in their 80's I set them up with a big SUV to pick them up and they would have been comfortable and wouldn't have to worry. The plan was to go to my apartment, order in some food and surprise my dad with the chair. None of this happened. Like I said, my dad never fell. He had my mom lie for him. He went to play poker instead. I had to tell the nurses that I didn't have anyone to meet me at the hospital or meet me at home. I'm divorced and live alone. The nurses told me that if I felt that I can make it home in the Uber alone and get into my apartment, then they can send me home. I told them I could do it. During my surgery, I had 3 of my lumbar vertebrae fused together with two titanium rods, 6 titanium screws and 3 artificial discs grown from human bone cells. In addition, I had 33 staples that kept the incision closed.

I called the Uber, the nurses helped me into the SUV and the driver dropped me off on my corner with my duffle bag and walker. I live in a basement apartment as any appropriate divorced father would, and I had to let my walker and bag just flop down the stairs to the entrance to my apartment. I climbed down the stairs slowly, got inside, looked up to the ceiling to curse my father and then smoked a big fat joint that I had waiting for me.

My parents did eventually visit a couple of days later. My dad only visited once. So, the chair I thought would maybe motivate him to come here with my mother more to see my kids never worked. My dad sat on the chair once; from April 2018 until he died in May of 2019, my dad came to my apartment with my mom only once during that 11 month period. Luckily, my wonderful youngest son quickly claimed the chair as his own. I love seeing him all bundled up in a blanket and having a good time at my place. Meanwhile, although neurotic as well, my mom was a spry 84-year-old and was still driving and working at the time and would drive to my house and even to my brother's house in Connecticut. There was no reason for my dad to let my mother drive to these places alone other than he was gambling.

Every time my dad would skip out on family to go play poker; he would have my mom relay the message. My mom would always add, "You know he loves you; this is what he likes to do". I would say, "This is bullshit". My brother wasn't as kind as I was particularly because he knew how much money my dad was losing as he got older. I had no clue how much. If I had to guess, I would say over 300k. My parents made a good profit after selling their home in Nassau County, NY and buying a condo in Bayside, Queens. My father lost that money and other savings, forcing my parents to sell their condo and move into a studio in the same building. Even after we thought it was settled that there would be no more poker after they moved to the studio, he lost 40k more. My father died leaving my mother 1/4 of what she should have had if he didn't gamble. In addition, my brother and I were left nothing. Not to sound ungrateful, but when my father was alive, he would brag and say that there's money for us. He would say not to worry, and that even though it's not a million dollars it will be a nice addition to our own savings. So, when you find out you got nothing? It leaves you feeling a bit jilted; not because you didn't get the money, but because my dad let his gambling affect his honesty towards us. At one point I was being told by my parents that there was no poker playing going on. My brother knew and did not know that I was unaware. When he told me the gambling was still going on, I officially gave up on my dad. I was done.

As I stated earlier, my father refused to curb his behavior even though he knew he would be causing unnecessary and uncomfortable scenarios which put me, my mother, and my brother in awkward and infuriating social positions.

Examples: my father wanted to me to tell my friend/bandmate, Shane, to not walk around barefoot in our house because my father had a fear of getting AIDS. Shane was living in Manhattan and had a gay roommate. This was the mid 1990's and my father thought all gay men had AIDS. He never did any research or reading up on AIDS, only the hysteria he saw on the news. Shane's

roommate did not have AIDS and neither did Shane. However, once my father found out that Shane's roommate was gay, he immediately assumed that Shane had AIDS. I told my father that I refuse to do this since he had no clue of how AIDS was transmitted. In addition, I told my father that I did not want to be embarrassed this way and make my friend feel uncomfortable in our house. He then began to yell with that cowardly shrill to his voice where it sounded like he was going to start crying if he didn't get his way. When our argument got to that point, I stormed out of the room and the house.

Another example of an embarrassing situation occurred when I was dating a girl named Kim from 1993 to 1996.

One night, my father was in his bathroom doing his nightly examination of his body and he noticed a bloody glob of mucus in his toilet. He then called me into his bathroom to ask me if I spit in his toilet and left this bloody mucus. I told him no and walked out. He then called me back into the bathroom and asked me to ask Kim if she went into his bathroom and

spit a bloody mucus into his toilet. I immediately got enraged because I didn't want to be put through this shit again now with my girlfriend. I remember telling Kim what happened and leaving to go to her parent's house. Being that her parents were of a younger generation, we spent more time at Kim's house than my parents' house. In fact, little did I know that Kim's dad was smoking weed every night in the basement of their house while he played video games and practiced archery. Now that's a dad I want to hang out with! It's too bad that weed would cause me to panic back then. I definitely missed out on some fun with Kim's dad.

These stories about my father are just but a few of dozens and dozens of events like this that happened over my entire life. Dealing with that behavior becomes intolerable. In addition, when I had my own children and saw my father's behavior around them, I would immediately speak up and tell him to knock it off or else he's not going to see my kids anymore. My father also has a habit of asking people the same questions repeatedly while knowing the answer beforehand. My friends nicknamed him "The Quizmaster".

My father also enjoyed mispronouncing words on purpose to get a rise out of somebody. For example, he would do this to my children while talking about their games and toys. He would say PokeMAN

instead of Pokémon. He knew the correct pronunciation but thought it was funny to get a rise out of my sons. They felt he was diminishing what they enjoyed.

My sons grew to not like him at all. One day my father asked me if my sons liked him and I told him, "No, because you ask them the same questions over and over, you mispronounce the names of their games on purpose to bust their chops. You also constantly bring up who recently died in the news and other morbid subjects. It annoys them and it annoys me. So, no, they don't like you". Soon after my twins were born, my resentment towards my father started to grow because I began to find out from him how much he didn't do and how lazy he was when my brother and I were kids. He would tell me that he NEVER changed diapers, fed us, cooked, did laundry, yard work, shoveling snow, fixed anything etc. My mother did everything. What made it even more irritating was that he would say this in a bragging tone as my ex-wife and I were on zero sleep because our first babies were twins. We were overwhelmed, scared, tired; and there's my dad making it worse with stupid comments.

After he passed away, I didn't grieve or even cry. I mostly just thought about it a lot. A part of me feels free. That might be a mean thing to say, but it's one of the feelings I have about it, and it's worth analyzing. Technically, my dad was a nice man with a good heart. He provided me with a nice home with my own room in a beautiful town with the best schools this country could offer. I went on many vacations, professional sporting events, sleepaway camp, a teen tour, tennis camp and lacrosse camp. He also paid for me to go to college, gave me money to get a CD that I recorded mastered, helped pay for my wedding and gave my ex-wife and I about $70,000 total as gifts and loans for our house down-payment and renovations. It was great to have all those things, but they came with the price of being around my dad and not knowing what irrational thoughts and behaviors were around the corner based on his mental health or whether he was winning or losing at poker. If he was losing, he would look suicidal. In addition, being given those things were also held over my head for guilt trips especially if we had a disagreement.

I would rather have grown up with less and my dad not mentally ill. Not a different dad, the same person. It's an easy decision. I may have been the youngest in my family, but my dad was the baby.

My Mother:

My mother grew up near my father in the Brownsville section of Brooklyn. She lived with her parents and my uncle in an apartment that was located above a pool hall, which was where she met my father.

My mother is too nice and too accommodating to a fault: it leads her to asking you what you need in an obsessive way; listing too many things to choose from and then repeating it 4 or 5 times.

Like my father, she asks the same questions over and over while fully knowing the answer. I believe they both felt that it was some sort of game to them and they got joy out of the frustration that it caused. In addition, if you complained back to them, they would ask why we were yelling at them, which they already knew because they were told dozens of times to stop. My dad never stopped before he died and my mother still hasn't stopped.

After my being hospitalized and finding out that her brother was schizophrenic and my grandmother went undiagnosed, in my opinion, my mother's behaviors started to make more sense. She was neurotic as well but was made worse by my father. I also feel that my mother has an undiagnosed mental illness.

My mother was the enabler to my father: instead of trying to help him push through his emotional problems, she let them continue and gave my father the unhealthy space to act as he pleased, thus making his illness worse.

My mother doted on my father by doing everything he asked. It was very similar to the relationship that Archie and Edith Bunker had on "All in the Family".

My father also put my mother in those awkward situations where she had to look like the bad guy if something was going on that was setting off my father. For many years, I thought these crazy beliefs and idiosyncrasies were from my mom. When I got to be about 6 years old, I quickly realized it was really my dad.

My mother would also act like my father's secretary: if he wanted to talk to my brother or myself on the phone, he would first have my mom call us. My mother would then announce on the phone that my dad wanted to talk to me. I would always ask, "If he wants to talk, all he has to do is pick up the dam phone and call! All of these unnecessary steps for a simple phone call are ridiculous! Does he not know how to use a phone, or does he not know the same phone number I've had for 21 years?"; which very well may be true considering he would still get lost driving around our hometown, even though he lived there for almost 30 years. I chalk it up to him not paying attention and relying on others to pay attention for him.

Needless to say, my mother did everything to keep the household running with zero physical help from my father; yet, he had no problems jogging 5 miles a day or staying up for 27 hours straight playing poker. 27 hours was his longest stint sitting at a card table. I'm sure he took piss breaks.

Another aspect about my mother that might be cruel to say is that I feel she lacks common intelligence and common sense: she always had a tough time grasping simple ideas and concepts. She would nod along like she understood. However, when she would bring up such concepts again, they were completely different than what was discussed.

In addition, my mother is unable to answer a simple closed ended question: Instead of answering "yes" or "no", she would go off on a tangent about the question and then never actually answer the question. You are then stuck asking the same question over and over which may take you 5 minutes to get an answer to a simple question like, "Are you hungry?" By the way, this is not due to her age, these behaviors have been going on since I'm a child.

I feel that she got so used to taking care of my dad's unhealthy dependent needs, that she truly forgot about her own needs and wants. You can then add two sons who fought all the time to the mix and understand why she lost herself.

Like I said before, these constant behaviors erode one's sanity and confirms my belief that a person can be made schizophrenic as well as being born with it. When a person is fed so many mixed signals and conflicting messages, the brain crashes like a hard drive, which

causes a change in the brain's chemistry in a form of brain damage. It's similar to what I read about Post Traumatic Stress Disorder (PTSD).

I do love my mother for the basic fact that she is a wonderful woman. However, there are times where I can't take the behaviors.

Chapter 7: My Maternal Grandfather, My Hero: Lewey

The only relative that was my saving grace from my neurotic immediate family was my maternal grandfather, Lewey. My grandfather was born in Brooklyn and was from Russian descent. He

was Jewish along with everyone else that lived in Brownsville, Brooklyn in the 1920's and 1930's.

As a kid, my grandfather took up boxing along with all my great uncles on both sides of my family. My great uncle, Nat Pincus was a professional fighter and fought at the original Madison Square Garden. His boxing record and career summary is on Google.

My grandfather grew up with a bunch of friends that would be later known as "Murder Inc." or The "Jewish Mafia".

My grandfather's best friend growing up was the leader of Murder Inc., Meyer Lansky. They met when Meyer immigrated to Brooklyn from Russia as a child.

I don't know the extent of my grandfather's involvement in Murder Incorporated except that they were his friends and he hung out with them. My grandfather sometimes carried a gun when he had to and smoked Camel cigarettes with no filter.

My grandfather was the strong and soft-spoken type. He didn't waste time with words. He didn't start fights, he finished them. A popular story about my grandfather was that he had knocked out the toughest hitman in Murder Inc. named Abe Reles. Apparently, there was a beef between them, and they were to meet to settle it. My grandfather brought his gun because he heard that Abe was bringing his. It was decided they would fist fight. The fight was one punch; my grandfather hit Abe once, knocking him out on the hood of a car.

In the mid 1970's, we were visiting my grandparents after they moved to Florida. The phone rang and my grandmother answered and said, "Lewey, it's for you", My grandfather said, "Who is it?", my grandmother answered,

"Meyer", my grandfather said, "Tell him that he knows that we can't talk on the phone". My father then asked, "Meyer who?", my grandfather answered, "Lansky. The feds still watch him and bug his phones". At this point, Meyer Lansky was an old man, but I'm sure still had some old friends around too.

As an occupation, my grandfather was a commercial painter and a well-respected union official. Even though his group of friends were criminals, my grandfather was a stand-up guy and never got involved in union shenanigans that were popular back in those times. My grandfather didn't want to risk going to jail and knew when to stay away from his friends. Nobody tried to force him to do anything because they knew he would say no. In addition, he wasn't afraid to knock someone out who tried to intimidate him into breaking the law.

Lewey eventually married my grandmother and had two children, my uncle Wayne and then my mother a few years later. As I mentioned earlier, Wayne would eventually die in Nov of 1969, and his son Paul would die in Jan of 1978. One tragedy after another.

My grandparents still lived in Brooklyn after I was born, and we used to see them all the time.

I loved hanging out with my grandfather. He was funny, wise, tough, patient and very loving. If I didn't know any better, I would say he had Buddhist tendencies. Being that my grandfather was also a calm person, it was unusual to be around because I was used to the chaos of my family. His calm, cool and collective demeanor drew me to him even more. I would hang on every word he said. I think he saw I was a tortured soul and would often remind me to slow down, take a breath and be patient.

When I was about 5 or 6, my grandparents moved to Florida to help with my uncle's widow and my first cousins. I would forget that he was their grandpa too. Nobody wanted to share him. At the time, I didn't understand, and I was crushed when they moved. I went from seeing him every couple of weeks to now only the summer when they would stay with us for a month. During their visits, I would spend most of my time with my grandfather sitting on lawn chairs in our driveway. If it was raining, we would sit in the garage with the door open so that we could watch the rain. We spent countless hours playing checkers, cards and Monopoly. Somehow, he knew how to roll the dice so he would land on the "Go To Jail" space on purpose. He would do it over and over and I would laugh so hard because I thought he was having bad luck and he would react to it saying, "Oh boy! Not again!" My grandfather was also a self-taught piano player.

In the middle of June 1980, I was in the 6th grade, and I had to write a 20-page written report about the history of Great Britain. I was sitting outside with my grandfather as I was writing the final draft. I was complaining and he talked me through it. The best part was that I had signed a book out from the school library about Great Britain and cut out photos of Stonehenge and London and glued them to my report. My grandfather asked, "What are you doing to that book? Is that a library book?", I said, "I'm cutting out pictures for my report", he then asked while he started laughing, "Are you going to return the book to the library?", I said, "Yup, I'll slide it in the return slot. They'll never check the pages". He continued to laugh and said I had ingenuity.

Whenever my grandparents came to visit, my father's peculiar behaviors seemed to go down a few notches. I believe that he was so distracted by them that he didn't think to check up on what I was eating, what I was brushing my teeth with or if I was sitting too close to the TV wearing a Geiger counter on my head. There was one instance where my father was so distracted by his thoughts while watching TV, I ate a dog biscuit in front of him to see if he would notice. He didn't. I must have been about 8 or 9. I remember sitting on the kitchen floor eating it.

Anyway, during my grandparents' visits, all my father's food restrictions were lifted for them because he couldn't control what my grandparents chose to eat. It was great! I felt like a prisoner getting smuggled contraband; Virginia ham, bologna, hot dogs, iced coffee, red M&Ms and even real toothpaste! I was in heaven!

My grandparents knew my father's hang ups about food, so they would sneak it to me without him noticing. We had drop off points located around the house. My grandfather would signal me to the kitchen and whisper, "There's a ham and Swiss on Wonder Bread with mayo in the bottom draw of your dresser. We never had this conversation. Capiche?". I'm obviously exaggerating about the drop off locations but they would sneak me food especially if we were sitting outside because my dad rarely came outside.

I also spent a lot of time with my grandfather learning how to box; he was a former Golden Gloves Champion in Brooklyn for his weight class. We had a heavy bag at our house, and he would show me how to jab, hook, cross and throw combinations. When my other great uncles who fought visited, I would goof around with them too at the heavy bag. Eventually as I got older and more into fitness, training like a boxer became my favorite thing to do. It is a fun way to exercise, you get in shape really fast and it keeps anxiety at low levels. I recommend it highly.

 I was 23 when my love for it really kicked in and it became a very consistent hobby. I would train on the heavy bag for least 2 hours a day and I got so good at the speed bag, I could hit it with my eyes closed(I attribute that to my drumming). One time my neighbor, who was a Golden Gloves fighter was watching me train in my backyard. I had an extra heavy bag outside hanging from a tree. I was 27, 6 feet and 225 lbs of solid muscle and I hit hard. My neighbor suggested I fight in Golden Gloves. I told him I felt I was too old and just did it for the exercise and the fun. Three years later, when I started teaching, the school social worker was a boxing trainer and heard I had been training consistently for almost 10 years. I was 31 at the time and Matt, the social worker, had me do some mitt work and some heavy bag work. After 30 minutes, he told me he wanted me to enter the Golden Gloves and fight professionally for 5 years after that. I told him I was too old. Matt told me the cut-off age to enter Golden Gloves was 35. His thoughts were that I could make a few thousand dollars and get out quick. I told him he was crazy. He would keep telling me I was good enough to be a professional if he and his friends trained me. Matt worked with a former professional fighter who gave me the compliment that I had a jab like Lennox Lewis. I didn't believe that was possible and he was blowing smoke up my ass. Still, it was a nice way to try to motivate me. I was only training because it felt great. I didn't believe I was any good at it.

My Golden Gloves experience was short lived for I am near sighted and wear glasses or contact lenses. When it came to sparring with no contact lenses, I couldn't see the punches coming at me and would end up a bloody mess. We all quickly realized that my eyesight would prevent me from competing. The last day I sparred, I got my nose broken and ruptured a vein in my lower right lip, which you can see just under the surface of my lip.

I never stopped training however, because it's so much fun. I would have liked to have one fight for the experience of it.

But I digress. One of the last great stories that my grandfather told me was during my last visit with him in Florida in the Spring of 1983: Lewey, who was in his 70's was at the dog track with his friend when two guys in their twenties tried to shake them down for money. I asked my grandfather what happened next. He put up 2 fingers. I asked, "What does that mean?". He said, "Two shots. I hit one guy, knocked him flat and then I hit the other guy and knocked him flat". That story cemented my grandfather as my ultimate hero. He was tough, calm, confident and had a charm that everyone wanted to be around. It's hurts in a way to say that he was everything my dad wasn't.

I remember during the 1983 visit to Florida; my grandfather was having a tough time walking and needed to hold my arm as we walked down the street. I remember my heart breaking because he was getting older and with death always on my mind, I knew I was going to lose him one day. I was mad too. I was mad that he was old. To me, it wasn't fair; my Superman was mortal.

My grandparents last visited New York in the Spring of 1984. It had been a rough winter for my grandfather with his mobility, he had some eye problems and had just gotten over pneumonia. However, it never stopped his positive attitude and all I wanted was to spend as much time with him as I could.

The last time I saw my grandfather alive was in the spring of 1984 when we dropped him and my grandmother off at the airport. I didn't know it would be the last time I saw him in person. I remember saying goodbye, but mostly remember waving to him from the car window and then watched him enter the airport. I wish I could have told him how much he meant to me.

I was in touch with him for the rest of the spring and into the summer. During the summer of 1984, I went on a teen tour which is a traveling camp on a bus for Jewish kids from Long Island and

Westchester. When we arrived in San Francisco and got settled where we were staying, I was told to call home as soon as possible. I started to cry because I had a feeling, I lost Lewey. I called my mom and she told me that he died in his sleep. The person that I loved the most in the world was gone. I don't ever remember telling him that I loved him, but he had to have known I was crazy about him as I never left his side. As I write this, I cry just like the day I found out he died, and it's been over 35 years. I think of him every day and even have a tattoo of the design of a tie clip he gave me. It's on my arm so that he is always with me.

My grandfather represented the man that I wanted to be and that since we were blood, I always felt it was possible. Sometimes when things get too wild in my thoughts, I focus on him, and I can feel his spirit guiding me to relax. I still miss him terribly.

Chapter 8: Retired So Young?

On dating sites, I mention that I'm a retired teacher. The other day, a woman responded to my message starting with, "Wow, you retired so young". I then thought about that I eventually have to explain what happened to my career and my subsequent 11 month stay in Psychiatric Hospitals if I meet someone and we get close. When and how does one bring that up? I would assume it's best that I do inform before anything sexual happens. Can you imagine if I had sex with a woman and then after saying, "Oh, by the way, I was committed for almost a year for almost killing myself, I got falsely accused of pushing my students, I have anxiety and depression, I take meds, I lost my shirt in my divorce and I'm starting over and looking for a new career, maybe a home inspector. It's good money and you set your own hours."

It's not something that fuels my self-esteem as I move forward building relationships with new people. Below are the events that led to my retiring from work and when I started being admitted to a total of 5 psychiatric hospitals. These are actually excerpts from a letter that I sent to an attorney who was considering my case and wanted to know what happened:

I was a Physical Education Teacher at a middle school for NYC Schools for almost 19 years. On December 11, 2018, two 8th grade girls walked out of the gym without permission or the hall pass. I called to them loudly, "Girls, where are you going?". I got no answer. I went to the gym door and yelled down the hallway, "Girls, where are you going without the pass?", once again, no answer. So, I trotted down the hallway to catch up to them and saw they were wearing ear buds and didn't hear me. So, I tapped one girl on the shoulder lightly, and took out her ear bud. And then I asked with an annoyed tone, "Where are you going?". The girl responded, "I don't feel good, I'm going to the nurse". I then said, "So, go to the nurse". I then told the 2nd girl to go back to the gym, she said no. I then yelled to try to be a little intimidating, "Get back to the gym now!", she said no and threatened to tell the assistant principal on me. I then said, "Ok", and I walked back to the gym alone. The first girl never went to the nurse. Standing in the hallway next to me was the dean from the school we share the building with and a security guard. They were there because the other school was traveling to their 2nd period class. So, there must have been 200 kids walking the hallway.

After I got back to the gym, my assistant principal showed up and asked if I laid my hands on the girls. I said no, and he left. Apparently, the girls wrote statements that I physically abused them by swinging them by their coats into the walls. In addition, a 3rd girl who was never in the hallway with us wrote a statement that I pushed her into the lockers: there are no lockers in the school. She made it up and the administration still accepted her statement. By the time I was at lunch duty, the police had been called by one of the mothers of the students and wanted to talk to me. As I was on my way to talk to the police, I was walking with my assistant principal who was telling me to try not to freak out. We were met in the hallway by the principal who came out of her office and said, "Never mind". So, I never spoke to the police, was never arrested, never got sued and no parents ever came to the school to confront me or have a meeting with the principal and the girls never went to the nurse or a doctor for "injuries". According to the principal, the mother calls the police all the time (I have her on recording saying that during my first disciplinary hearing). She also said she couldn't stick up for me and had to do what the Department of Education wants her to do. That's recorded too. A few weeks later I got called in to the principal's office for that very meeting.

There were many things about this investigation that were shady. We had video cameras in that hallway, and the videos show nothing. According to the assistant principal, the angle of the camera doesn't pick up where we were standing. That area would be the entrances to the boys' and girls' bathrooms near the cafeteria. Those bathrooms are the busiest for kids to go when they cut class. Sometimes they drink and smoke. But more dangerous is the chance for fights. If I were assaulting my students; the dean, the security guard and the 200 kids walking that hallway would have reacted in some way. There would have been a melee of kids reacting on at least one camera. Furthermore, when students are in the hallway, most of them have their phones out. So, not one video? Not even a video of me yelling to the girls to get back to class?

When the investigators started interviewing people, they interviewed the dean who said he saw nothing, they never interviewed the security guard, and they lost the statement about the third girl being pushed into the lockers that never existed. My first disciplinary hearing was with my principal. Before the meeting, the letter that claims she agrees with the Department of Education was already completed and given to me halfway through the meeting. So, it didn't matter what I said, The DOE wanted me out and put in the rubber room. I asked her if she thought I assaulted the girls. She wouldn't answer the question. Later that day at a staff lunch in the library, the principal asked if she could talk to me in private. We went into a little computer room. She had crocodile tears in her eyes, and she said, "Mr. Vox, I just want you to know that I am very uncomfortable with this, and I am sorry for what you are going through". I just nodded OK and walked out of the room. After that, I was sent to the rubber room, which is another name for being put on paid administrative duty. You sit in the cafeteria all day at the district office.

Occasionally, you help make photocopies. A few weeks later, my 2nd disciplinary hearing came up.

At that hearing, the girl's statement about being thrown against the lockers was still missing. I recorded the meeting. The 2 reps from the Dept of Education were particularly nasty and asked questions to lead me on to make it seem like I was incompetent. I fired back at them and told them to stop trying to be a Monday morning quarterback and second guessing my decisions. I told them that they were incompetent if they were going to try to use hindsight against me, especially when they know that all their reports are false. When this meeting had come around, I was pissed and vowed not to take any of their shit. The meeting ended with a notice that they were going to go ahead with 3020a charges, which means they wanted me fired. When you get fired, you lose your pension or at least that's what I was told at the time by a union rep. In addition, they decided to add the allegation that I was absent 13 times during the 2017-2018 school year. That's all they wrote.

A letter that was in my file that discussed my absentees and acknowledged that I had medical documentation to back it up was changed around by the investigator's office. They copied the letter and cut out the part that said, "While we understand you were in a car accident and have doctor's notes, we have to remind you to do your best to be at work". The original letter was supportive. The investigators office only left the dates I was absent and the sentence that said it was important that I be at work. I have the original letter.

I was absent a total of 35 days. I took a nonpaid sick leave for my lumbar fusion surgery on my lower back that I mentioned earlier. I was in a car accident in 2013. I was T-boned and have neck injuries too. I lasted almost 5 years before any kind of surgery; I have 2 titanium rods, 6 screws and 3 artificial discs in my lower back. Somehow along with the missing statement about the girl and the invisible lockers, they didn't have my sick leave papers or the documentation from my surgeon that describes my surgery either. These papers were personally given to my payroll secretary by me to be kept on file. In addition, when this "incident " happened with the girls, I was still getting my bearings back from my surgery. So, any kind of wrestling, horseplay or heavy lifting whether it be goofing with my sons or "assaulting" students would have been difficult and dangerous. In addition to that, they added another allegation, which was 2 years old, where I was taking attendance using my phone on an app called

IO Classroom. When some students would not be quiet, I said (doing an impression of Howard Stern's mother and trying to be funny), "I'm filming you and I'm going to show your mother's that you can't be quiet". Mind you, this was said in a Yiddish/Long Island Jewish accent. Plus, the children know I'm an impressionist, have done voice overs and am asked every day to imitate cartoon characters like SpongeBob SquarePants. A student got up and walked over to me and I showed her my phone was off. This student then yelled to the class, "You dumb niggas, his phone is off! He's just fucking with us!" I was using humor to get the kids quiet instead of showing frustration. I'm quite aware of laws pertaining to music and film given the fact that I took entertainment law classes in college and I know that children under 18 cannot get filmed without a parent's consent. Plus, I don't feel comfortable being filmed while I teach and certainly never film my classes. However, I admit that was a lapse in judgement. It was still better than yelling at students who mostly get abused verbally and physically at home.

The administration also did not like that I was a whistleblower when there were structural things wrong with the school. The school tested for high levels of PCB'S, Polychlorinated Biphenyls (a chemical in window caulking and light fixtures, which if gets into the air, can cause skin irritations and can cause cancer if it's in your blood). I sound like my dad! At the time, I was breaking out in rashes on my legs and my partner in the gym had a cyst that kept returning on his head after having it removed over 3 times. I asked to have the air checked in the school. The principal had a "company" come in and test the air. Their report came out clean. A few days later, my school was on the cover of one of the 3 major NYC newspapers for having the highest levels of PCB'S in the borough. When I called the company, who tested the air in the school, the number was no longer in service. I then started calling news stations and newspapers to share this story. I was pissed that we were lied to, and our health was being compromised. I didn't care who knew I did it. The subsequent summer, construction was done to get rid of any materials containing PCB's. I have photos of the construction. Wait, I thought there was nothing wrong with the building!

In addition to that, the gymnasium was in disrepair: no bell to hear the change of periods, the public announcement speaker was broken so we couldn't hear announcements (like if there was an intruder, lock downs etc), no telephone on my partner's side of the gym, bleachers falling apart exposing sharp metal corners and the dividing wall was so loose, kids could push through and go to either side of the gymnasium. I assume that the administration did not like what I was doing. I was fighting for the health and safety of everyone who goes in that school. This was bigger than education.

I also felt that I was a team player given that I would teach classes out of my license area even though I knew it was illegal: I taught special ed math, special ed reading and health for 3 years. One year, I agreed to teach some social studies classes. I was excited because I like to tell stories and I add in great jokes. That class never happened.

After discussions with the union rep and my well documented anxiety and depression disorders acting up to the point to where I was hospitalized 3 times in parts of the spring of 2019, I decided to retire based on disability. Because of this incident fueling my disorder and the last 10 years of: divorce, car accident, bankruptcy, father's death, SSDI, food stamps, no social life and cutting all my friends off; I became suicidal and was abusing my medication.

Because of The Department of Education's false allegations against me, I lost 2/3 of my pension, I had to take out my tax deferred annuity to live off of, which $15,000 is taken out as a tax penalty, and they destroyed my reputation with their careless accusations. How am I supposed to get a teaching job, or any job if I'm asked why I retired at 19 years, just at the point where I was to hit 20-year longevity with my pay and was set to get a $10,000 raise? As soon as someone hears the word allegations, you're toast.

Chapter 9: Sept 3, 2020, Jacobi Hospital 7A

Today Is September 3, 2021, and I have been here since Aug 21. Since this is my 4th visit to a Psychiatric hospital this year, my Psychiatrist here, Dr P. has informed me that I qualify for Electric Shock Treatment. It's now called Electro Current

Treatment or ECT. Once there is an opening at Elmhurst Hospital in Queens at their psychiatric ward, I will be transferred there and undergo 15 rounds of treatment: 3 times a week for 5 weeks. It seems like a lot. But at this point, I'm willing to try anything.

When I spoke to my mother more and more about the ECT, she started to reveal things about our family's history with mental health that I was just learning for the first time. Mind you, when I started therapy at age 14, this new information could have steered my treatment in a more serious direction than just 2 sessions twice a week with a psychiatrist who would fall asleep during sessions.

Like I stated earlier, my mom's brother, who died of the brain aneurysm was also a diagnosed schizophrenic who went through ECT therapy. My grandmother, his mother, went through ECT therapy after my uncle died. Having spent a lot of time around my grandmother and now knowing this information, I'm quite convinced that she was schizophrenic as well. She couldn't stop herself from talking. Even during conversations, she couldn't stop for another person to be able to speak to her. To get her to stop talking took a lot of work. Also, she would sing and had an awful voice. She would sing melodies that made zero sense musically. They were just random notes put together often sounding flat or sharp which means it sounded disturbing. She was also neurotic about people getting injured, so we were constantly being berated for anything she saw as dangerous. From morning till night when my grandparents would visit from Florida, my grandmother would start cleaning our house and redecorating by moving things around and throwing out things we still needed. For example, she decided to clean out my car and threw away a term paper I wrote for graduate school. Luckily, I had it saved on a disk (remember those?) When things like that would happen, my father would get enraged because he felt that my grandmother didn't know her boundaries. The truth was that she was an undiagnosed schizophrenic. My father would make my mother talk to my grandmother about butting into everything and thinking she could do whatever she wanted. This obviously made my mom uncomfortable. However, the only time I saw my dad yell at my grandmother was when she cleaned out my car. Her response was, "Peter is lucky that he has me to do it for him". I never asked her to do it.

Rumination Warning!

I'm hoping that ECT works to help lessen my feelings of constant existential sadness. It blocks me from being able to be fully present in the here and now.

While I do have more fear currently than ever before, there's also that feeling that I'm stuck in a hole that I dug for myself. It's difficult when you don't like yourself and you're the only one that can make changes happen. You can have the best therapists and drugs in the world, but it still comes down to your decision of getting better or being hospitalized for the rest of your life.

I hate myself for not being able to stay at my job until I was 55. Physical Education is the best teaching job there is to have. And I should have been able to last even having obstacles like an unsupportive, corrupt administration and lack of resources. The school environment was toxic and there was a constant vibe of animosity from the administrators to the staff and vice versa. One feeds off the other and the students suffer because of it. In addition, going to a place like that being a nervous wreck to begin with, adds to the disorder.

Each morning before work (and a lot of jobs before I taught), I would get sick to my stomach like it was my first day ever at my first job ever. I would usually throw up or have the dry heaves and retch in the bathroom sink. Retching is painful because your whole body clenches up as it convulses, and you spit up stomach bile after you have vomited up any food left in your stomach.

After I got divorced and started living on my own again, I would smoke or vape some pot as soon as I would wake up each morning and it would immediately stop the anxiety attacks and the retching. I was able to function normally and not be afraid to leave the house. When I smoke pot or vape THC oil, I feel it puts me to a level of normal where I can concentrate, be more relaxed, and be more available emotionally. I'm able to be in the here and now. I'm not the type of person who smokes to party or who wants to sit, laugh, eat and just be a couch potato. I want an active and full life. Certain strains of marijuana can do that for you.

 Unfortunately, my ex-wife felt that I was smoking to be around her. The truth was I was smoking to be around me. I was smoking pot long before I ever met my ex.

I always found it to be hypocritical of my ex to give me a hard time about weed considering that she is a functioning alcoholic, in my opinion, and had drinks every night at dinner. When I would go food shopping, which I happily did all the time because it's fun, my ex would always call and ask for Corona Lite and ingredients for sangria. While at the same time it would make her mad that I smoked, she would encourage me to drink. She seemed to like it when I was drunk. Alcohol just doesn't agree with my stomach. I throw up easily from alcohol and get terrible heartburn as well. I will only have a drink occasionally. I drank enough in college and in my 30s.

Being a musician, there's always alcohol around. It was never a problem, but I drank my share. I knew when to stop before getting sick which would be about 5 drinks within a couple of hours. I was also never a person to have alcohol in my house, until I was married. I have never sat at home alone and drank.

I first puffed on a joint in the 6th grade when my friend Andy and I found a joint in his brother's room. We were looking in his room for pot and we finally found a joint in his center desk draw. I remember Andy opening the draw and seeing the joint. It was a warm Saturday night, and I was sleeping over at Andy's like I did most Saturday nights. His parents went out every weekend to party and left us at their house with their live-in housekeeper (I told you I grew up in a rich town!) The housekeeper was very nice and left us alone. So, we took the joint and started walking up his street. Andy lit the joint and took a puff; he sucked smoke into his mouth and blew it out like a cigar; no deep inhale, no smoke to the lungs, no getting high. I did the same thing; I sucked smoke into my mouth, waited until I tasted it and then blew it out. I didn't get high. I didn't think Andy did either, although he kept singing this little song, "Heaven on Earth. All it takes is 3 puffs to get yourself high". Ok, maybe Andy was high.

It wasn't until the 8th grade when I tried pot again. This time we were at my friend Jon's house. His family owned a business and were extremely wealthy. Jon's parents would go away for days and weeks at a time leaving 3 teenage boys' home with a maid. It was the perfect place to party.

I was standing in Jon's kitchen with Jon's middle brother, his friends and my friends. They were smoking from a bong, which I had seen before in a smoke shop in my old town: They sold used and new records, cassettes, 8-Track tapes, black lights, rock t-shirts, buttons, patches, denim jackets, lava lamps, posters, pipes and bongs. I loved that store. All the kids in town did.

 So, I was asked if I wanted to try the bong. I told them that I didn't know how, I tried once and nothing happened. Lark, my friend's older brother and cohost of this party said, "You probably didn't inhale", I said. "What do you mean?" He then explained that you must take a giant breath in when you suck in the smoke. Lark then demonstrated on the bong with no pot in it to show me how it worked and then he showed me how to do it with pot in it. One time I saw Lark do such a big bong hit, smoke literally came out of his ears. There are other witnesses. It was hilarious.

Now, being a kid with anxiety, one would think I would be too afraid, but I wasn't. At that point, my knowledge of pot was from watching Cheech and Chong movies. It looked like a lot of fun to me.

I was then handed the bong, a Sawhandle Apogee to be exact. I put my mouth to the tube and Lark lit it for me as he coached me through my first real hit of weed. Lark even handled the carb on the bong so that I could empty the chamber. I don't remember coughing, but what I do remember is that it hit me quick and hit me hard. Everything that is stereotypical about someone that smokes for the first time happened to me: I started laughing uncontrollably and trying to explain how I was feeling to everyone. They were laughing because I was laughing so hard. After about 20 minutes, I got the munchies. Jon's house is the best place to have the munchies. They have everything a stoner wants to eat; leftover Chinese food, cold pizza, mac and cheese and CEREAL!!! My first official meal as a stoner was eating an entire box of Alpha Bits cereal. That's the cereal that is shaped like letters. It was delicious.

The paranoia on the weed came later that night when one of our friends set off the burglar alarm by accident, causing the police to stop by to make sure everything was ok. I was moved from room to room because I was laughing loud and then freaking out that the police had shown up. I was sure that I would get busted. Thankfully, Lark, was a calm and cool character who spoke to the police, assured them that everything was ok, and they left.

I quickly learned that smoking pot as a teenager is like playing Russian Roulette on whether you will have a good high or start freaking out and having existential crises for hours on end. The teenage brain is not developed enough to handle marijuana and even some drugs for depression like Prozac. A person's brain isn't fully developed until our mid-twenties and even people in their 20s can't handle marijuana or psychotropic drugs as well. I mention Prozac because I took it at age 26 and it made me want to kill myself. I took a handful of Xanax to either stop the Prozac side effects or die. Either way, I ended up in the emergency room.

The worst panic attack I had as a teen smoking pot was at another friend's house. We went to his house to get stoned after taking my 11th grade science midterm. We were smoking in my friend's room and listening to Dark Side of the Moon. Note: if you have the propensity to have panic attacks while smoking pot, listening to Pink Floyd only makes it worse. Led Zeppelin is the better choice.

As we smoked, my friend Gordan took out the razor blade that used to do coke with (he stole the coke from his parents), he then turned the razor to the dull side and slid it across his wrist. As the song "Time" played with its depressing lyrics, Gordan then said, "If you slit your wrist, the blood squirts out like a water gun until you die!". Well, that was enough for me! I then started to suffer what was the worst panic attack I have ever had in my life up to that moment. Everything happened; the cold stabbing feeling in my sternum, face numb and cold tingling in my hands and feet. The feeling of fear hit and the reality that I will die one day and that our lives mean nothing in this universe kept repeating in my head over and over. Each time this thought patterned repeated itself, it would get worse and worse each round.

I ran to the bathroom and began to vomit. Along with high levels of fear, I had cold sweats, I was shaking, crying and screaming about how I don't want to die. I was obsessing over the concept of death in my mind at the worst levels I've ever felt.

This same day, which was either a Tuesday or a Thursday, I had my therapist appointment at 7pm like always. This time was going to be different. I never went to my sessions high. I was afraid of getting a lecture and my shrink telling my parents.

By the time 7pm rolled around, I was no longer that high and I had calmed down enough to be able to go to my appointment. I never told my shrink that I was high, and he never said that he knew I was high. After the session, I was glad to be home in my room to sleep it off.

After that experience, at which I was 16, I had a few more bad experiences with pot, and I figured that maybe it wasn't for me. However, if I had a few drinks, I was able to smoke without any issues. But, given the fact that I'm a light drinker, it all began to become too much trouble and I stopped smoking pot completely by age 18. In addition, my interest in being a lacrosse goalie grew more and more and it kept me away from pot. I got to a point with lacrosse where I played for a college in upstate, NY for almost 2 seasons, only to quit to drum for a band, declare a major in Music Industry and focus on becoming a working musician.

At age 28, I was in a bar in Elmsford, NY with my great friend, college roommate and bandmate, David. David and I were in the bathroom, and he pulled out a pipe called a Proto Pipe, which is like the Swiss Army Knife of pipes; it had a poker to clean the bowl, a pot storage container, a sliding cover for the bowl and a resin collector at the bottom of the pipe.

This is the same pipe that my friend Gordan used to have. I got a big kick out of seeing it. David asked me if I wanted to smoke. I told him it had been 10 years because of anxiety. One irony is that between the ages of 18 and 28 when I didn't smoke pot, were some of the worst years in my life with anxiety if you remove college from that equation. In college, my mind was free for the most part.

So, at age 28, there I was, trying pot again. At that point in my life, I found that when I smoked I didn't get paranoid of suffer anxiety attacks anymore.

Since age 28 I have been smoking pot or most recently, vaping THC oil. I personally don't view it as something to party with or abuse. For me, it's the most effective out of all the medications that I have been on, and it's a plant; not some chemical concoction made in a lab.

My current health care "professionals" told me repeatedly that after you smoke weed you become depressed when it wears off, but so do the meds, so what's the difference? I prefer any form of THC because it doesn't have the side effects like most of the drugs for mental illness.

Chapter 10: Medications I've Taken

The following is a list of medications that I am on or have been on at some point in my life since I started meds at the age of 24 in 1993. I'll try to make the list from most recent going backwards in time: Lithium, Cymbalta, Buspar, Seroquel, Attivan, Attarax Lamictal, Halital, Abilify, Klonopin, Wellbutrin, Xanax, Celexa, Lexapro, Trazodone and Prozac.

The last two, Trazodone and Prozac both affected me where I had to go to the emergency room. On Prozac, I was 26 and I was hearing voices and having panic attacks. While I knew it was all a reaction to the drug, I still couldn't rationalize and stop the feeling that I wanted to die yet I was afraid to die at the same time. It's like watching a nightmare.

When I took Trazodone, I was 43. I had similar side effects as Prozac, and my reaction to Trazodone led to the argument with my ex that would cause our finally getting divorced.

The Trazodone left me with no verbal filter. I knew my ex wasn't happy and wasn't communicating that with me. I felt that during the marriage she made things difficult on purpose so that I would be the one to lash out. You see, in my opinion, my ex is a covert narcissist with grandiose episodes who is very manipulative. She always has a plan to try to get what she wants from people. When hugging her, you can feel your life's energy being sucked out.

During this final argument, my parents were at our apartment to take me to the hospital because of the Trazodone. While this was going on, the Trazodone caused me to see everything in three's and everyone's voices sounded muffled. As my ex and I were arguing, and I asked my mother for her opinion. My mother said she felt there was no love there. My ex started to yell at my mother and then I called her a cunt for doing so. Up until that point in my life I never used the word "cunt" to insult any woman that I dated. I did use it for comedy purposes or to insult other people, which is in a different context as calling your wife a "cunt". However, at that point I felt that I had put up with so much, she deserved it. Later on, I regretted saying it.

Since she still wouldn't communicate, I badgered her until she admitted she wanted a divorce. Since the Trazodone left me also acting obnoxious, I danced a jig in the living room when my ex admitted she wanted a divorce. In the marriage there was no intimacy, and I don't mean sex. I'm talking about connecting emotionally with holding hands, talking, cuddling and just having someone to treat me like an equal, instead of an employee. It's a day I wish I could take back.

The drug combination that I've been on the longest in my life was a Lexapro and Klonopin pairing. I started taking those drugs after I had the Prozac incident and subsequently switched therapists in 1996.

At age 26, I switched to a new therapist named Dr. Peart after my parents, girlfriend and I felt that Dr. Sabot was ineffective. Dr. Peart would be the therapist who helped me most in my life. When I started therapy with Dr. Peart, he prescribed me Celexa and Klonopin. Celexa eventually turned into Lexapro after they changed the drug for supposed improvements. From age 26 to age 49, I was on those 2 drugs. After many years, the drugs stop working as your brain gets used to them. I saw Dr. Peart twice a week for 16 years until his death on Dec 7, 2011. He was in his mid-80's and had a recent heart surgery. His death had a tremendous impact on my life; in lot of ways, it was worse than losing my father.

Chapter 11: Dr. Peart and More on My Dad

Like I stated earlier, I started to see Dr. Peart after losing confidence in my first therapist, Dr. Sabot. I started with Dr. Peart in 1996 and went until 2011. After Dr. Peart died, I bounced around between a few therapists, but wasn't really connecting with anyone. In 2015, I stopped going to therapy because I grew tired of talking about myself and I felt that at that point, I learned everything there is to learn. At some point I needed to man up and use everything I learned by going to therapy since 1984. In addition, up to that point, I had completed 36 credits towards a 2nd master's degree to become a guidance counselor (my students were the ones who suggested that I would make a great counselor). I took many psychology classes and learned even more about myself.

The last therapist I went to regularly was a social worker named Mike. I started seeing him in 2013 and stopped in 2015. One of the reasons I stopped was because he was moving his office from my side of the borough to the opposite side of the borough from where I lived. Getting there would require sitting in rush hour traffic or 90 minutes by bus. Combine that with Mike telling me that he may not have room for me in his schedule was enough for me to stop going. When I told Mike over the phone that I would stop going, he became angry. I found that to be unprofessional and showed that he only wanted the money. Back in December of 1996, when we informed Dr. Sabot that I would be stopping sessions, he became mad as well and told my parents that he couldn't afford to lose patients. My girlfriend at the time, Kim, came to my last session with Dr. Sabot along with my parents and yelled at him for not giving me the treatment I needed. Kim became my hero that day and it led to me meeting Dr. Peart

We were referred to Dr. Peart by my father's psychiatrist. Dr. Peart's office was in Woodmere, Long Island. It was a 40-minute drive to get there, but worth the drive to go see him. At that point,

Kim and I had broken up and I moved back to my folks' home in Nassau County in January of 1997. That was a move backwards in terms of my psyche.

Dr. Peart reminded me of a Jewish Robert DeNiro.

Dr. Peart was tall, had grey hair and had a raspy Brooklyn accent. During our first session, he asked me a question about my use of drinking Jack Daniels when I sang. I used the Jack Daniels to numb my throat so I could make it through nights of singing 40 songs. His response to my answer was, "Fuck you, you are full if shit! There's a part of you that's relying on the Jack Daniels". He had no problems challenging me if I gave an answer too quickly and didn't take the time to answer with what I really felt instead of saying what I thought he wanted to hear. Dr. Sabot would just nod and agree with me when he wasn't dozing off. My time with Dr. Sabot was a waste of time because he NEVER asked me any kinds of questions that required critical thought. In fact, I don't remember him asking any kind of probing questions. He certainly never taught me any coping mechanisms.

After my first session with Dr. Peart, I knew I found a special person to help me. Dr. Peart was an ex-cigarette smoker who would chew on pieces of paper during sessions to satisfy his oral fixation of cigarettes. He was also a fun person who liked and owned fast cars and speed boats. He also opened up about himself, his life and his experiences during medical school.

When I started seeing Dr. Peart, he was 70 years old. His death at age 86 left me devastated. I felt like I had nobody to guide me and nobody to have a strong shoulder to lean on. I had my father, but his mental illness ran his life. My father feared anything new or cutting edge in life and met everything with fear, apprehension and always this quote, "I don't know Pete, I don't think that's a good idea".

Everyone has a vice and my dad's vice was poker (like I mentioned in an earlier chapter). In the 1990's there was a movie about illegal high stakes poker games in NYC called Rounders. In that movie, there is a character based on my father. My dad had a habit of talking to himself while playing poker and it was noticeable enough to have a secondary movie character based on him.

When poker came to Las Vegas, my father suddenly lost his fear of flying to go to Vegas. He wouldn't fly to Europe to give my mom a vacation she deserved, but for poker, he would do anything. When poker finally came to Atlantic City circa 1994, my father was going so much that he finally rented an apartment there for him, my mother and my crazy grandmother too. The great part was that they left me to stay in the house in Nassau County. In addition, having a girlfriend at the time made it a lot of fun; we were free to have sex anywhere and anytime we wanted in the house. It's too bad I was very much anti-marijuana at the time, we could have had even more fun.

My parents would stay in Atlantic City for weeks and sometimes a month at a time. When a gambler is on a winning streak, the entire world seems amazing and makes one feel like all their problems are gone. On the flip side, when a gambler is losing, the whole world would seem like it's ending. When he was winning, he would throw me $500 for the fuck of it, but when he was losing, he would literally cry if I asked for $20. It was an up and down cycle that is very unhealthy and eventually messed up my parent's living arrangements, their finances and any money that was supposed to be inherited by my brother and I was lost. I believe I discussed this earlier, so I won't repeat it. One reason my dad started losing at cards was because of internet poker, which you can play for fun or real money. Now, you had thousands if not millions of people playing poker and getting good at it, thus surpassing my aging father with their skills. There was suddenly more competition. I warned my father about it, comparing poker to the Olympic NBA Dream Team of 1992 with Michael Jordan. That team turned Europe and Asia on to basketball and motivated children to play. Fast forward to the present, the NBA has a large population of European and Asian players who worked their whole lives to become professional basketball players. In addition, there are pro leagues in every major country in Europe and Asia. Israel has a pro basketball league too. Their hoops look like giant bagels!

So, More and more Americans were playing poker, getting good at it and beating my dad, who at one point was probably one of the top poker players in the country.

Chapter 12: Sept 3rd, 2019, continued, Jacobi

Hospital, Bronx

So, I'm now currently taking Lithium (which makes you gain weight; I call it Lithium Love Handles Syndrome), Buspar, Cymbalta and Seroquel. I don't really feel that these drugs are helping, only turning me into a bit of a drug zombie. The Seroquel helps me sleep but it makes you gain weight too, so I hate it and like it at the same time. I like anything that makes you relax so you can sleep. Sometimes sleep is the only peace I have. When you're in a sleep so deep where you don't remember anything, that's blissful. I'm lucky that I was wise enough to never do drugs like heroine and ecstasy. I was too afraid. Sometimes it's good to be afraid of certain things like having to use a needle to take a drug. No thanks. Give me a joint, a box of Fruity Pebbles and some Van Halen (David Lee Roth era only), a fun girlfriend and I think that's about as wild as I want to get. Plus, being a busy musician since 1989, I was exposed to and offered every drug under the sun. Like I said, I was too scared to try. Healthy fear works to protect you from danger and knowing it's difference from anxiety disorder is important to decipher.

I still wake up each morning here at Jacobi 7A with major panic coursing through my veins.

Today, my mind is racing about what I must do to improve my life and to stop feeling victimized, being too existential and most importantly, staying alive for my sons. I constantly get a feeling of shock over what has happened to my life and that I'm in a psychiatric ward. "What kind of father have I become?" is a question my brain asks me all the time with the motive of making me more anxious.

I'm divorced and my ex has a boyfriend that she takes on vacations with my sons. I feel like I've been replaced so easily in every way. Living a divorced life can create pressure in the form of trying to be a better parent than their mom and establish my presence as their father, not boyfriend #3.

Today has been a very long day. It's one of those days where thousands of thoughts spin through your head simultaneously like some sort of Brain Tornado; every spinning thought causes fear, sadness, pain, loss and confusion.

I think about how much I miss my sons. I have 3 sons; twins who are 12 and a 9-year-old. I'm the type of person that didn't know I wanted to be a parent until I became one. When I first held my twins and my youngest, this warm buzzing feeling of awe took over. I got to experience the most joy a person can have, and it beat anxiety that day. But for today, I'm ruminating about the past, worried about the future and I fear being in the hospital for a long time. I also try to be positive about some job ideas for when I get discharged; I'm thinking of taking the civil service test and become a postal worker. I'm not interested in having a mail route because it looks like it can be solitary with no coworkers around. I'm quite sure I would meet people on a mail route. I don't know, it's just one idea.

It's about 9pm now and I've been sitting in the Day Room for most of the day. At this point I'm having panic attacks about just being here in the hospital and how everything just spun out of control. It's a good thing that I took my meds.

I get some deep sleep on Seroquel, and I sometimes have vivid dreams about my ex that feel so real that you wake up and you feel hurt in your heart. Have you ever had a broken heart? It feels like your heart physically hurts and you can feel your chest caving in. The sadness builds up behind the eyes and tears flow in with a current that trails down my cheeks. Sometimes I can hear my teardrops hitting a table or the floor.

Anyway, when the nurses close the day room at 11pm, I head to my room for sleep and wait for the drugs to kick in. Drugs like Ativan, Klonopin. Xanax and Valium are the best for relaxation and sleep because they are narcotics and have similar effects as heroine. Didn't I say I was afraid to take heroine? I guess between having prescriptions for all those medications at one time or another since age 24, I have been technically doing heroine.

Those drugs make you feel amazingly calm, and they work fast too. I know why they are so addictive. Did I become a drug addict? Did I do this on my own, or was I made one as an unintentional consequence of trying to fight anxiety?

When my father was diagnosed with prostate cancer, I took a nosedive emotionally. I was having nonstop panic attacks. When one attack would end, I would try to calm down and then another would start again. I would have to deal with the attacks in the bathroom because I would start retching in the sink and sometimes if an attack is bad I may poop in my pants! It's always best to be near the toilet.

It was about 7pm the night I found out my dad was diagnosed and I took my Klonopin a little early to get some relief. The Klonopin was not working. I called Dr. Peart to tell him what was going on. He told me to take 3 Klonopin whenever my anxiety got to this level. So, I started taking 3 when anxiety was bad, which means that you will run out before your new prescription refill and may have to go a day or two without Klonopin. That comes with some withdrawal symptoms like no sleep, headache, flu like symptoms and depression.

The worst times are when you run out: You feel like the Earth is crashing down upon you. The one good thing about having a mentally ill father was that he had Klonopin that he was prescribed only as needed, so, he had a lot. Asking my dad for 3 or 4 pills that would put me back on my correct dosage schedule was no big deal. Who would have thought that my dad would become my drug dealer?

Sometimes there were occasions when I was out of Klonopin where I would wet my finger and scrape the inside of the pill bottle to get the crumbs from the pills that were broken in half. One time I dropped the pill bottle and the Klonopin dust was on the bathroom floor. There I was, with my saliva covered finger, trying to salvage as much as I could. It was like Bradley Cooper in Limitless when he licks his enemy's blood off the floor because it had the same drug that made him super smart.

Does getting to the level of basically licking my bathroom floor for pill dust make me a drug addict? Does it mean I'm just a person who doesn't want to feel emotional pain anymore? Or is it both? I go back and forth with it and have concluded that it's not just one reason and it doesn't really matter anyway. What matters is how you handle your situation.

I got a good taste for valium while in high school: My friend Ike stole about ten blue Valium from his mom's stash, I don't remember the dosage level. I can always Google it. Anyway, he came to my house and we each took 5. We were about 17 years old.
We were in my bedroom when we took the pills. When they started kicking in, it felt amazing because this super drug got rid of ALL my anxiety

both mentally and physically. Holy shit! I was calm and felt like I could breathe and most of all I didn't feel fear.

Ike and I then started to goof around. At this point, I was feeling like the mad scientist from Looney Tunes, floating in the Ether cloud chasing Bugs Bunny and saying,
"Come baaaaack heeeereee you Ra bit". Ike and I started to wrestle, and we fell to the floor. It felt like it took 15 seconds for me to hit the floor. While on the floor, I remember saying that everything felt like it was in slow motion. After that, we went downstairs to the kitchen, ate some food and then I fell asleep on the sofa in our TV room (people in the suburbs call them "dens"). Ike decided to walk home, which was about two miles from my house. Ike was heavy and could drink a lot without getting drunk and take 5 Valium and be fine to walk home. The next day, I called him and asked him why he left. He said he wanted to go home, he felt amazing on the Valium and wanted to enjoy the walk. Ike was a good friend; sensitive, kind and supportive of my mental illness.

I know that these drugs are dangerous, but I was still in enough pain to take about 15 Ativan this past August and not care whether I woke up or not. It's very scary and hurtful of what I put my children through. I put them at risk of losing their father. I grew up around people who lost their fathers and I know how that loss effects them for the rest of their lives. I'm also supposed to be a person who has a constant fear of death and involuntarily obsesses over it. So how does this happen? What switch turned on in my brain that made me want to die? Was it the meds or is it just my genetics? Once again, it's probably a combination of everything. Not many recipes have one ingredient.

I'm punishing myself as well. I think about what I have become and question my intestinal fortitude. I also try rationalizing that you can start a new career at age 50. I'm lucky to be alive and I have a chance to be a big part of my sons' life like I was before I was committed. I'm also thinking about finding a group to sing with for fun. Playing music is a big emotional release and the positive effects last for days. I don't need to be in front of an audience. I'll be happy just jamming at someone's house and have dinner together afterwards.

I'm just now realizing, that from the end of March of 2019 until now (Sept 3. 2019), I have had 5 stays at 3 different Psychiatric Hospitals. I've spent the better part of 5 months in hospital pajamas.

It's both scary and interesting being exposed to a part of society that exists that most people are unaware of; what life is like in a psychiatric hospital, all these drugs, side effects of the drugs and living amongst the legally insane.

My overall everyday level of anxiety has regressed to what it was in my mid-twenties. At that time, I was depressed about graduating college and starting my life in the real world. It was at that time it became so overwhelming, I had to start taking meds; the first being Xanax.

I fear that once I am discharged and get a job, I will return to old form and get sick every morning before work. I ruminate all day and its sometimes impossible for me to be in the present and not have this existential sadness and awareness that life is meaningless when compared to the vastness of time and the universe. I could be running one of my physical education classes and during a game, my mind would be racing about the same thoughts that plagued me like when I played ball with my friends as a kid. When it happens at work, you feel like everyone knows what's wrong with you and it makes you panic more. I then get overwhelmed and must fight it to keep it from ruining my class. After a class like that, I'm wiped out. I would have to nap between classes because I would get mentally spent so quickly. Most people with anxiety and depression sleep a lot because their brain is constantly running at top speed, burns out and needs a rest. You're constantly burning the candle at both ends

 There's something about the ins and outs of a job that gives me anxiety. I feel I must put on a show so that people do not see that there is a problem. I must be at my very best and perform when deep down inside I feel like a loser, a failure, I'm destined to be yelled at, get fired or get looked upon with judging eyes. This is how I ruminate. This is how I've punished myself since I've been a child.

I see the lives of my old friends, whom which I lashed out at, alienated myself from, can't help but be jealous about their good marriages and financial successes. In addition, I feel bad for my kids that I'm not giving them more. Comparing myself to the successes of others is not a good idea because it leaves you feeling cynical. I grew up in a wealthy town and my peers' lives were set for them before they were even born. The wealthy stay with the wealthy. It's not a knock, it's just what happens to a majority. Do I get bitter and angry when people had connections through family and friends to get to where they are? Yes. Why? Because some either didn't earn it or don't have the talent for it. A great example is a guy I went to high school with who wanted to be a rapper. He was good looking, muscular, but not talented. He was also known as being the biggest asshole and bully in my graduating class. He got a record deal with Arista Records based on the way he looked. They never listened to his demo tape or made him audition or do a showcase at a club with an audience. He has the article explaining how he got signed on his Facebook page. He recorded the cd, and it went nowhere. I was pissed because my friends and I hustled to play clubs and were always marketing ourselves. We rehearsed constantly and were out every weekend handing out flyers at clubs for our gigs. Fear fueled my ambition with music because I knew if I could make a living out

of being a musician, my anxiety would lessen a great deal. I used to want to be famous when I started playing in bands at age 19. It quickly turned into, "I want to play music because it makes me feel good".

I also have a bad taste in my mouth with the fact that the friends that I did have for connections for providing instrumental music for commercials and video games wouldn't take "OUR" material seriously or me as a musician for that matter. "OUR" means the musicians who I collaborate with.
These are musicians who went to The Manhattan School of Music, Julliard, Guitar Institute of Technology in Los Angeles, The Berklee Conservatory in Boston etc... Plus these musicians have been playing their whole lives and have gotten to the point to where they have befriended and correspond with some of the best guitarists in the world like Steve Vai (Frank Zappa and David Lee Roth), George Lynch (Dokken) and Paul Gilbert (Mr. Big). I never brag about me, but I will brag about the musicians I know that are extremely talented and more importantly, amazing friends! These are professional musicians; not hacks and not wannabes. It wasn't just me that my friends would be working with to get a finished product. I always felt that because of my anxiety, I wasn't

looked at as a serious or talented musician by the people I grew up with.

I'm confident when I say that I am a talented singer, drummer and impressionist. I have had song parodies played on The Howard Stern Show for a few years, I sang for a band that was one of the house bands for The
New York Islanders and sang with my group at The Nassau Coliseum for two seasons. I have performed in all the top clubs, bars and halls in the tri-state area since I'm 19. I've sang in front of zero people, and I've sang in front of 12,000 too. 12,000 is more fun.

Ugh! My train of thought has just been distracted because Benny just came into the Day Room, so I must observe him and write down everything he says as fast as I can! I find it fascinating and in no way do I find humor in it. I'm curious about what makes him tick. Is he happy? Is he sad? Does he know where he is? Does he know I'm real or am I a hallucination? He's severely

 ill and I do have empathy for him.

Benny asked if he could put on The Disney Channel and those of us in the room said yes. The other patients are nice to Benny as well. As we watched TV. He asked me if I know about The Transformers and gave me the rundown of all the characters like Downer, Beast War, Dynobot and Bumblebee. I have no idea if those are even real characters. I know next to nothing about The Transformers, so I just smile and nod to Kenny when he speaks.

Benny stammers and stutters and finally talks about how the Decepticons put on Halloween masks and copyrighted the parents of children who try to hurt their children. This makes me think he was abused as a child for some reason. I think The Decepticons represent Child Protective Services.

Benny also said he has a cell phone implanted in his arm so he can design his own Transformers on his forearm. He also mentions many other characters and how they transform into one another. Like I said, I have no idea what is true to the movies and the TV shows about the Transformers, and I don't know if Kenny thinks that the Transformers are real or just a TV show. Benny is a little boy stuck in a man's body. He has about a 2nd to 3rd grade mentality yet manages to hit on the nurses as he walks the unit at night. I overheard him saying that he used to work but had to quit because he moved. I want to ask him what his job was, but I am avoiding it because I'm afraid he might get violent. Whether you cause violence or are a victim of violence at Jacobi hospital, you will get more days added to your stay here. I try to stay quiet in terms of how loud I am when interacting with everyone. I keep it mellow unless I'm on a run of making jokes.

Chapter 13: Psychotherapy at Jacobi 7A

 Each patient here has a team that consists of a psychiatrist, psychologist and a social worker. The therapy you receive here is little to none. The psychiatrist sees you for maybe 8 minutes every other day to inform you about discharge, medications or for me, a transfer to Elmhurst to get shock treatment. The psychiatrists experiment with many different drugs and combinations until one seems to work for you. This leaves the patient experiencing all sorts of side effects like body tremors, numbness of the face, numbness of the feet, numbness of the hands, drooling and trouble sleeping. In addition, some of these drugs make you feel suicidal. I've met and read about people who committed suicide because of drugs like Prozac. Like I stated earlier, Prozac made me want to kill myself.

The psychologist sees you for about 30 minutes per session, once a week, if even that much. Group therapy is sometimes twice a week for 45 minutes, on the occasions that it does happen at all.

Group therapy is a waste of time because our problems are not discussed and the same handouts about how to cope with mental illness are given out each session. I'm supposed to start Cognitive Behavioral Therapy (CBT) and so far, I have seen the psychologist once in the last 5 days. At least she has me writing this journal, which was my assignment over the weekend. I was supposed to put in 2 entries, but instead I have almost 60 pages filled up about me and my life here at 7A.

Today in the Day Room one patient was mad at the fact that she couldn't get something mailed and my psychologist gave her the "I'm sorry that you are upset ", line. I was disappointed on how fake and phony she sounded. The patient is not detached from reality. She's just older and gets agitated easily.

The psychologist and psychiatrist must not converse with one another because neither of them knows what the other is doing. I look

forward to my next session because I'm curious to see what the next step is in CBT
. As far as a social worker goes, during my 3rd stay here, I haven't heard from or seen a social worker once. I heard she was on vacation. Usually when someone is on vacation, another person covers for them. Not in my case this time. I'd like to discuss my life and when I'm being discharged. That conversation happens with the social worker. I would also like to meet with an employment agent to help me get a job. I need to find out where my aftercare outpatient facility will be and for how long that lasts for. It seems like none of the social workers have been assigned to this unit. Maybe that's just me being paranoid. Either way there's not much actual therapy going on here. They mostly just want to give you pills so that you are either mellow or asleep. However, there are more good doctors, nurses and
Behavioral Health Associates (BHA) than bad ones.

Chapter 13: September 4, 2021, Jacobi 7A

 Today I did not get out of bed until about 2:30 p.m. I skipped breakfast and hid from the world. It's a bad habit because it's not restful when I lay in bed all day. It's emotionally painful and you really don't sleep that much. You spend most of the time shaking and sweating out your fear. However, I was able to get up and take a needed shower and take advantage of having a single room by being able to masturbate in the shower. There are a few attractive nurses that are easy enough to fantasize about.

I'm hoping that today my doctor will give me some information about when I will be transferred to Elmhurst Hospital in Queens so I can start ECT. Right now, he is walking with a man named Daniel. Daniel is a small man whose legs shake uncontrollably unless he's laying down. The side effects from his medications are the cause his shaking legs. Daniel has salt and pepper hair and is

about 5' 3" tall. He is thin and not in good physical shape. As he was walking with the psychiatrist, he was given the advice to walk more and do pushups. The psychiatrist, Dr. P, is very friendly and likes to make jokes and curses a lot. Dr. P has good jokes which are well needed here. When he was done with Daniel, we had a brief meeting and he told me that Elmhurst is getting all the information they need about me and that I should not worry. That means he does not know which day I'm going to leave here. We met for about 5 minutes, and I don't know what to tell him except that I'm dying for an Ativan so I can sleep until dinner and have the rest of the day to be calm.

As I write this, I'm sitting in an activity room where Lance, an art therapist is playing the keyboard very well I must say. He missed his calling. He's good enough to play cocktail parties for weddings and corporate parties. Lance runs the art class where grownups color like 5-year-olds. It's where I feel I've hit rock bottom most of the time. I'm 50 years old, sitting in pajamas and a hospital gown and I'm coloring in pictures of flowers. Lance also takes groups to the gym, runs the bingo games and other groups as well. I've been here long enough to where the subject matter of the groups is starting to be repetitive. For example, we've been given the stress management hand out twice since I've been here. Sometimes I think they run out of ideas, or they are too lazy to research new and current activities to do with the patients.

Right now, I feel a lot of emotional pain because I miss my kids and part of me feels like I'm hiding here from life. Sitting in the activity room now is Ramon, Kama, and Angelica. Angelica can only speak Spanish and has a deformed extra right pinky toe that sticks out from the top of her toes between her 4th and 5th toes. She also has a bad temper and smacks the medication window and the windows of the rest of the nurse's station when things do not go her way. She also dumped water on Jeanette's notebook which contained information about her house and apartments that were robbed and vandalized. Also, as I write this, Benny is walking his laps around the unit. I can tell it's him without looking because his Crocs make a crunching sound as they may contact with the floor.

Daniel is sitting just across from me; he has a picture of flowers and a vase that he is coloring with Crayola Super Tip Markers. His first choice for the flowers was red. I noticed that his right hand shakes as he colors. As I look under the table, his feet and legs shake like he's playing double bass drums for a thrash metal band.

As I sit here, I go from fear of leaving here to wanting to leave in a matter of seconds. And then the conflicting thoughts battle it out in my head. Part of me is confident about a new job and the other part of me is petrified. I also hear Rosa screaming in the background along with Lance's boom box playing classical music. It's a very odd combination of sounds and vibes that I'm experiencing right now. In a few minutes the art group will end. I look over and see one of Carmen's drawings. Her work is simple but very good. It looks very much of what Picasso would draw during his cubism period. Carmen also took a trip to an assisted living apartment that she is most likely going to live in. I'm happy for her. As I look over at her I really notice that she has thick facial hair and mutilated earlobes. She claims that when she was younger, she dated Eric Estrada, the actor that was on the TV show CHIPS, before he was famous. She keeps her very curly hair up in a bun and walks with a very small gate like a woman in her nineties.

 So, for almost an hour we sat and listened to some live music and Mozart like drugged up zombies as we colored. Jeanette is falling asleep; Angelica is coloring all her flowers pink and Daniel is using black for one of his flowers. It's mellow in here but it's stressful to me because I'm thinking about all that I must get done when I leave here. How do I put everything in my life back together? Everything seems so daunting and scary. I also must try to remember that nothing can be done while I'm in here. I can hear Rosa screaming again. This time it sounds like laughter.

As Carmen talks about the trip to her new apartment, she recognizes the Mozart piece that's playing on the radio and starts moving her arms like a conductor. Everything she does is slow from moving her arms to walking and talking as well. She really comes alive during art group and reacts positively when she hears a song that moves her. But today, Carmen is moving faster than usual. I think it's because she's in a good mood about getting a new apartment. The group is over now so I must close my book and stop writing for a while.

September 4th, 2019, continued.

If Dijon is Lurch from the Adams family, I found his counterpart, Uncle Fester. He was standing behind me while waiting on line for blood pressure testing. He is new and looks as bad as he smells. He is about 5' 7", Latino, curly hair and sounds like a scuba diver breathing with an oxygen tank. He looks crazy and speaks only Spanish. He is wearing jeans that hang below his belly and wears a black T-shirt. The body odor is of piss and shit. Like Dijon, this man does not know well enough to shower and put on clean clothes. He is severely mentally ill. As I sit to get my blood pressure taken, a nurse informs a 2nd nurse that this man needs to shower and change. The nurse also calls over a BHA to bring him to get his clothes. Having this type of experience and being around sick people who don't know about hygiene is good enough to make me want to get out of here as soon as possible and never come back. I don't care about electric shock treatment right now I just want out.

Speaking of treatment, I haven't seen my psychologist in almost a week. Dr. K is his name and since August 21st, I've only had one meeting with him. I don't know how much CBT therapy will work considering I've had it before with Mike, the social worker that I used to see in my neighborhood. I truly believe that my issues are more chemical than anything. Although what I was exposed to as a child was enough to affect me, it's how I reacted to it is what makes me think my brain chemistry is off. This brings me to my brother, Chet.

Chet:

My brother Chet (like the big brother in Weird Science) although nice now and our relationship is much improved, was not nice to me when we were children. He is 5 years older than me, which made me an easy target for daily verbal and physical abuse. The verbal abuse consisted of calling me a pussy, faggot, and a woman. Daily my self-esteem was put to the test as every move I made and everything I said was criticized and ended with me either being punched around or being called a faggot. The physical abuse came in the way of slaps to the face, wedgies, being punched all over, dead arms, Indian Burns, bloody knuckles with a deck of cards, being sat on, being farted on, being spit on and having boogers being put on you. In his mind, he was busting balls as he would to his friends. However, I was too young to comprehend that and lived in constant fear.

The most tortuous moment came when I was in the 8th grade and came home from playing In the snow where I had fallen and broken my right index finger. Chet came into my room to ask me what was going on with my finger. He then held my hand down on my desk in my bedroom with one hand and punched my broken finger repeatedly, making my finger even more swollen and discolored. To make matters worse, my mother didn't believe my finger was broken and that my brother had been punching it. The next day, my finger was purple, and my mother finally took me to the ER, where it was confirmed that my finger was broken in two places. Maybe it would have been broken in only one spot had Chet not added to the damage.

As we got older, he mellowed out, however it didn't stop me from lashing out with nasty emails from time to time when there were arguments or problems. At one point I went almost 2 years without talking to him.

As I look back, I view his ultra-cocky and arrogance as a reaction to my father's neurotic behavior and beliefs. My brother is also very obsessive compulsive when it comes to being clean, he's also very motivated and a hard worker; He is the opposite of my father. When my father had a herniated disc in his lower back, he was bedridden for 6 weeks and refused to get surgery. He was berated by my brother to, "Suck it up!". My brother told my father he wasn't dying, and my father started crying; yelling at my brother that he didn't know what he was talking about. I've been stuck in bed with more severe back injuries than my dad and even had surgery. A back injury shouldn't cause you to cry like you are dying. My back surgery was a blessing!

That was one of many times that my brother challenged my father's anxiety and neurosis. My brother constantly questioned my father's fear and always pushed him to the point where my father would start to cry. It was very strange and heartbreaking to see my dad in such weak positions. Where was his backbone?

I was once watching a documentary about the musician Ted Nugent on the VH 1 show, Behind the Music; Ted was talking about how tough his dad was. He then said it was better than being raised by a jellyfish. Sadly, I immediately thought about my father as being a jellyfish.

As I stay in this hospital, I'm on good speaking terms with my brother. He's generally worried about me. Unfortunately, he recently got fired from an advertising position at a TV network.

Does my brother lose his mind? No. Does he go to the hospital? No. He picks himself up like a man and uses his connections to get interviews. He even had an interview with ESPN. I once asked him how he wakes up every day and deals with the corporate world. I feel like I wouldn't survive in the corporate world. I'm not mentally strong in that capacity or have I matured in a way that would be conducive for me to be working in the corporate world.

So, while there were problems with my brother and myself while we were growing up and while we were adults; we are at a point where we get along. Sometimes I still find it strange talking to him or hanging out with him because I still remember everything that he did to me when I was a child, and it lingers still to this day.

Benny is here!! Benny has once again entered the day room. We are watching ABC news, Channel 7 here in New York. Benny had some interesting thoughts about hurricane Dorian; he said there is no mother nature, only water and the devil. He also said that a hurricane is like if someone came at you with a knife and cut you and put you in the hospital. So, there is no mother nature. In addition, Benny said that President Trump is not the president because he's too busy being in the hospital. I don't comment on politics because I'm not qualified and I don't believe what Democrats or Republicans say, they all have their own personal agendas.

Chapter 14: The Medication Line

The line to get medication twice a day can be interesting and frustrating at the same time because the line gets long. However, the way that people take their pills is quite interesting because they all have different idiosyncrasies that come out.

Each morning, I take Lithium, Cymbalta and Buspar. It is a total of 5 pills because of how the Lithium needs to be given. When I get my pills at the medicine window, I put all 5 pills in my mouth at once, swallow them and then wash them down with Apple juice or water. Most people take their pills like I do. However, most of the people here are afraid of choking on the pills. I have been taking pills for so long that I have gotten to the point where I can swallow them with no water.

Daniel, who takes medication which makes his body shake, puts one pill at a time in his mouth, and practically sticks his whole hand inside his mouth while tilting his head back. He tries to push the pills down his throat. He then takes a sip of water after each pill. He does this while his whole-body shakes. Other patients do the same thing: one pill at a time, and a sip of water or juice. This slows down the process of everyone getting their meds and it's also frustrating standing on the line.

I know I have no place to go, but it is still frustrating, nonetheless. In addition, just about everyone who takes their medications makes loud swallowing noises as they drink their water. So many bodily noises!

Looking at the line of all the patients here on 7A, you will see quite an array of people from all walks of life. Some people are in street clothes with sneakers with the laces removed so that they can't choke themselves. Some patients like me are in pajamas that the hospital gives out. Being in the pajamas is depressing because you really feel like a mental patient and look like one too. In addition, I haven't shaved in 2 weeks. It's hard to find the correct person in the mornings to shave you. They shave you with an electric razor which is fine because that's what I've been using since I'm 17 or 18. Anyway, back to the pills. At 6:00 p.m.

I'm given Lithium and Cymbalta. At 9:00 p.m. I'm given Seroquel and Lipitor. For anyone that doesn't know, Lipitor is for high cholesterol.

I'm jealous of the patients who are sicker than me because they get to take sedatives every day. I feel it's something I want, so I can lay in bed and sleep the days away while I'm here. When I walk past their rooms and see them sleeping, they look peaceful. For the rest of their lives, they will be taken care of, while I must struggle with anxiety and depression and must function in society because technically, I'm not insane, or at least it doesn't look like I'm insane.

Chapter 15: Our Rooms at 7A

The rooms here at 7A are surprisingly nice and clean for what they are. There are single and double rooms: The double rooms have 2 navy blue plastic heavy duty bed frames that are bolted into the floor. They are solid all around and the mattress lays on top of the plastic frame. One bed is by the door and the other bed is by the window. Across from the beds are a sink and 5 storage shelves that are on each side of the counter for the sink that are also navy blue. There is also a light over the sink. Each room also has a bathroom with another sink, a shower and a toilet. The bathroom door is like a saloon door with no knob and a plastic strip on the side that pushes against the door frame so that the door stays in a closed position. The door cannot be locked. The top of the bathroom door is cut at a 45 degree slant so that the medical staff can see inside to make sure that you are safe. The walls in the room are painted white. If I had a dorm Room like this in college, I would have been very happy. The room I'm in now has graffiti written in pencil on the wall. On one wall next to my bed, there are many things written like: RIP= 100, Dripneko, Blood, Nestor, 2Real, Busky, TNC, Shadow Ops, Nigga from TN5.

Above the sink across from the beds, it says a list of names that I can't read, followed by "as here for real". The same names on the wall near my bed are the same names next to the window. And then it says that all those people were here on December 24th, 2018.

The maintenance staff comes in daily to mop and take out what little garbage I make. I don't know why the walls do not get cleaned with a Mr. Clean magic eraser. It's only written in pencil.

I have experienced both a double room and having a single room. I don't mind sharing a room if the person doesn't shit and piss in their bed. I don't think that's too much to ask for. But this is a psychiatric ward, so you must suck it up and deal with things that are going to be very uncomfortable.

Chapter 16: Observing Some Patients Here on 7A

Today at lunch, I happened to be sitting in a position where my chair was facing everyone on our unit. At one table was Daniel and Dijon. Next to them was Edmund. Towards the back was Tyrone, Carmen, Kalida, Kama and Shania; a new patient who hoards milk after each meal.

Watching Dijon, Edmond and Daniel eat is quite the spectacle: Their hands shake from their medication as they spill more food on themselves then what gets to their mouths. They chew with their mouths open while breathing very heavily almost to the point where they sound like they are hyperventilating. At the end of his meal, Daniel blows his nose at the table, Dijon mixes his milk into his soup and Edmond sits rocking back and forth as he hyperventilates very loudly. After their meals, all three men return to their rooms and sleep until dinner and then repeat the same behaviors. While on one hand it is disturbing that these men don't shower or brush their teeth, I don't feel anger towards them. I feel sorry for them because they are truly sick and don't know any better. However, it does not change the fact that they need single rooms because the odor that they bring with them is unbearable.

Another Interesting procedure that happens here is when a patient is having a fit of anger, acting out of control, being violent or just giving the nurses and the BHA's a rough time. When somebody is out of control, a staff member will set off an alarm, which also sets off blue blinking lights. It's a signal that extra help is needed on 7A or on a different unit. The patient will then be sedated by injection and either put in seclusion or allowed back in their rooms.

Some of the incidents on 7A where someone had to be sedated were when: Chris trying to strangle Maria, Shalika trying to attack Carmen multiple times, German had to be restrained from Shalika after she made comments about his dead mother, Shirley was given injections for being extremely loud and cursing at the staff, Shirley was also violent, Barry was given injections because his first 4 nights here he did not want to go to his room and sleep at night.

I was almost given an injection one morning when I was having terrible anxiety attacks. I was laying in my bed screaming that I couldn't take this anymore. I'm quite sure this was a reaction to the many medications I was on. Doctor P came in to see me and got the orders ready for injection.

Then, a cool nurse forced me out of bed to take a walk around the unit with her while she pulled out her phone and played some Led Zeppelin for me. The first Led Zeppelin song that came on was "All of My Love" off their last album in 1980 before Jon Bonham, the drummer, died. That song is about Robert Plant's son who had passed away. I then started thinking about my sons and how I had to get better for them.

During this walk I did receive an emergency Ativan to calm me down a little bit. I was bugging out and I asked for the pill.

Most of the time when the alarm goes off and the lights flash, it's for another patient on another psych unit, like 8D, which has patients with more severe illnesses. My unit, 7A is where people go when they are here for short stays or being prepared to be discharged.

Almost daily, I'm tempted to ask for an Ativan or an injection because being here is horrible on so many levels: I'm away from my kids (although they live 2 miles from the hospital), feeling like I'm insane, being treated like I'm insane, the overall feelings of malaise, and guilt that I feel about how my life has turned out. I can put myself through the same guilt trips every day with the narrative never changing. It's a constant fight to keep those thoughts way.

As I sit and write this, I'm sitting in the doorway to the outdoor roof area next to the tiny gym we go to: The gym is small, has a basketball hoop, ping pong table, three exercise bicycles and the walls are rubberized.

The roof area has fenced in walls and a fenced top so that nobody can get out. As I look through the fence, I can see The Co-Op City apartment complex, Highway Route 95 and a shopping mall. As I sit here on the roof, I can't help but feel like a complete loser and failure. Part of me feels that some people have wished this upon me or maybe I'm getting what I deserve for burning bridges and alienating myself from my high school, college and work friends.

Taking an injection to be knocked out or a pill as a quick fix to avoid reality for a few hours would be nice right about now. I now know why these medications are so addictive. Part of me feels that if I were wealthy, I would be addicted to pills, however another part of me thinks that I wouldn't be anxious because a lot of my worries as an adult are related to finances and those worries would be gone. If I had a better career with better pay, I would be able to have some peace of mind in my life. People say that money can't make you happy. I'd like to try and see for myself.

Chapter 17: Sept 5, 2019, 4:30pm Jacobi Hospital, 7A

As I leave the art group and head to my room to go to the bathroom, the overwhelming odor of piss is wafting into the hallway from Edmond's room. It is obviously he who smells. I haven't seen him since lunch. He is laying in his bed with the door open. He's wearing the same clothes as he was yesterday while waiting online to get his blood pressure and pulse taken. That is when he stunk up the hallway for the first time. The odor is like the odor in any NYC subway station on a hot day. Even though each room here has its own bathroom, people like Edmund and Dijon still urinate on themselves while they sleep.

Whenever there is a line for medication or getting our vitals taken, I make sure that I do not stand near anyone that has hygiene problems and body odor.

I saw my psychiatrist this morning and he had no news about when I was going to be transferred to Elmhurst hospital for shock treatment. In addition, the doctor at Elmhurst is now on vacation. This means I'll be spending at least next week here. This is both ridiculous and overwhelming. Even with the movie Animal House on TV to make me laugh I still feel overwhelmed and anxious. If Animal House can't make you laugh, you know you're in big trouble. Dr. P did say that he would try some other hospitals to see if they could take me. Staying here next week will make almost 3 weeks here. I feel like I'm being taken advantage of by spending so much time here and that the hospital is making money by my being here. In order to get well, I have to attend the group sessions, as lame and unhelpful as they are. Each time you go to a group, it supposed to be a step closer to getting better. As daunting as it feels, I need to get on with the rest of my life. The reality that I have created is a nightmare. I never thought that I would be 50 years old and staying in a psychiatric ward.

Dr. P said the insurance is covering everything, but I'm worried about coming home to bills that I'll never be able to pay. I've been living in hospital pajamas since I got here for my 3rd visit this year. I wish that I never took all that Ativan and put my mother in a terrible position, and worst of all, making my kids worry about me.

When I spoke to my mom about the day, I took all the pills, she said she didn't know what to do and she thought I was dying. When I woke up in the emergency room at Jacobi after I took all the pills, I was put in the psychiatric holding area so that I could be processed and brought up to 7A.

The holding area is two big rooms that have rubber chairs and rubber ottomans that patients sleep on with sheets that cover their entire bodies from head-to-toe as if they were hiding from the world. Which we all are. When I was put in there, I got a chair and a sheet. I spent at least 7 hours curled up in a ball and my head laying on a sheet folded into a pillow. After a trip to the bathroom, I was walking back to my chair, and I fainted. It was probably because of the meds I was on and the lasting effects of the Ativan. Luckily, I did not hit my head on the floor. That's really all I remember from the holding center. I do remember being at the holding center the other two times I was brought to Jacobi.

The holding center smells like pee, shit, body odor and food that is thrown out in large brown paper garbage bags. It's humiliating laying on the rubber chairs too. It makes you feel like you are in a homeless shelter. I can only assume it is one step up from jail. Being in the holding center is a good indicator that you have reached rock bottom. This whole experience has obviously been life changing and I'm still going through this process. The uncertainty of what's going to happen to me next is starting to make me feel worse and I know that I eventually must put the work in to get better. This has been going on long enough.

At one point, it got quiet in the holding area and that's when I really felt alone and institutionalized like you see in the movies.

Natasha, a girlfriend:

I just got off the phone with a woman named Natasha who I see sometimes. We sort of date. Unfortunately, right now Natasha has thyroid cancer, but it's treatable which is great. When I speak to her, my nerves go crazy because she has more feelings for me than I have for her. She's trying to help me find a job.

I met Natasha 7 years ago at a gig while we were both married. Nothing sexual happened while I was still married, and I had only met her that one time. After I divorced, I met her again at another gig in 2013. She was still married, but her husband and her had not been together sexually because of his abuse of pills and alcohol. He had become addicted to pills and drinking after surgeries on his neck and back. He had fallen at work and went on disability. Her husband had decided that he would sleep and live in the basement of their house and live his life taking pain pills and drinking beer. He was depressed over injuries and was still in constant pain after 3 or 4 surgeries. It's very difficult to heal from all those surgeries.

I was divorced, and Natasha was in a loveless and sexless marriage. We would meet at motels to have sex. Each time we would meet I would feel tremendously guilty for a few weeks afterward, however it didn't stop me from doing it for a while. I would immediately have anxiety attacks driving home from the motels. Even though I had not been cheating because I was divorced and single, I still felt bad about being a part of the equation of her failing marriage.

In May of 2018, Natasha's husband went to

Florida to visit his parents. He died in his sleep at his parents' house of heart failure because of 10 years of heavy drinking and abusing prescription pain medication. The eerie part about the day Natasha's husband died was that she texted me before she found out and said she was home alone, and it felt odd. She said it felt like she was single again. About 30 minutes after her text, she found out her husband died. I found out about an hour later when Natasha's friend Pauline called to tell me.

Almost a month after Natasha's husband died, she said she wanted a serious relationship with me and was ready to jump right in. For starters, she lived 50 miles from me and would rely on me to travel to her because she was afraid to drive on highways. I like driving to Long Island, but sometimes a break is needed. The other problem was that we were still going to motels for sex because she had a teenage daughter at home who knew nothing about me. Even though I was divorced and now Natasha was widowed, I still had anxiety attacks after every time we would meet for sex.

Natasha is brave and courageous. She grew up in Trinidad and moved to Queens when she was in her early twenties. She was able to make it on her own, get married, have a daughter and own a cute home in Suffolk County, Long Island. She is a hard worker, and she works for a library and a veterinary office. No matter how many times I've blown her off and have disappeared for weeks at a time, she would still forgive me. She even said to me she doesn't need me to be in a relationship with her and we could just have sex. To most men, this would be an ideal situation. I don't get afraid of being attached to somebody, but what stresses me out the most is when I'm with someone that I'm not in love with. The sex then becomes moot.

One of the most thoughtless things I did to Natasha was in October of 2018 when I hung out with her at a bar in Suffolk County: We had sex in my car in the parking lot. I had agreed to drive her home afterward, so her friend Pauline didn't have to. After we had sex, I had a panic attack. I put her coat that she left in my car into Pauline's car, which was unlocked. I then left without saying anything to anyone.

I texted her to apologize. One would think that after that she would never have spoken to me again. But no, here I am in a psychiatric ward, and she is still calling me here. I should feel lucky. She always asks me if I miss her or if I think about her. I answer her honestly that I don't have the capacity to miss anyone. I should miss her for that she has been nothing but good to me: she spoils me with gifts, brings homemade food to me and openly says that I'm the only one she wants to be with. She's widowed, has a daughter 2 jobs and fighting thyroid cancer. She doesn't need more drama from a person like me.

Chapter 18: September 6th, 2019, Jacobi 7A
Kasey, the tall Jamaican guy with dreadlocks who talks to himself was having a conversation with the wall next to the phones. Kasey said that he was going to go to the corner store, buy a sandwich, candy and a big soda. He said he will pay for it using his food stamps card even though he maxed it out at $240. After that, he said he would spend time at the beach. He also repeated that he pays his rent and that he comes from a small community which he
is there to help grow. I was guilty of a stereotypical thought and was sure he would mention smoking weed, you know, being that he is Jamaican. But he did not. He then continued to speak in tongues in a high-pitched voice and a high-pitched giggle that goes with it. I sort of wish

he talked about weed, this way we would have had a fun conversation.

Random things that happen on 7A:

1. Last night, a car in the hospital parking lot mysteriously caught on fire. We had a perfect view from the day room window to watch the car go from just a little smoke coming out of the engine to becoming engulfed in flames. All the nurses and patients watched the fire and wondered if it would spread to the cars next to it. Since there is a police and ambulance depot next to the hospital's parking lot, the first responders were there in less than 5 minutes. It took less than 10 seconds for the firefighter to put out the fire. The next morning, the car was still there, and you could still smell the burnt tires.

2. Once while walking with her BHA, Rosa started throwing up. She ate some cheeseburgers for lunch and projectile vomited all over the floor and wall next to the telephones. She then began crawling on the floor in her vomit and eventually laid down on the floor and began to make vomit snow angels. One of the nurses thinks that Rosa got nauseous from having her menstrual cycle. If anyone forgot, Rosa is here because she has brain

damage from a fall that she had when she was little. She is about 5' 4" tall and weighs over 250 pounds, so watching her get sick and roll around in her own vomit was in some ways captivating to watch.

3. Daniel was forced out of his room because he lays in bed all day. He was read the same script I was, "Laying in bed all day will make your depression and anxiety worse ". Daniel then made his way into the dayroom to watch TV. He sat and put his shaking feet up on a chair. He doesn't look insane at all except for his shaking legs.

3. Kasey just walked into the day room and started rambling again. Here are some of the things he said, "That's 2 checks of food stamps over $10000. And there's more to come from the woman who I was stepping out on drugs with. Leave it! It's mine! Fuck all who are here. See what I'm saying? You have to appreciate this part of life. How many times must the Jamaican man be in the news? That's a fucking fuse box, magnetic style of fuse box. That's a Camaro from the 1960s. That's real fucking paraphernalia right there. They couldn't even tell if he's alive or dead,

those stupid asses. Let me see what you got. What are you looking for? You see that? You're never going to learn.". He said all those sentences in a row without taking a break or a pause for any kind of context. He then continued more; "I want one with a roof. It's religion that screwed up the park in America. Which one do you think it is? Son, it's an El Camino (a car with a pickup truck bed). Son, I'm an electrician. I graduated at 18 in the form of 19. You can't fucking count on New York to feed you. Fucking bitch, I have been doing it since I'm 9. Arguing and ending up in court. If you argue, you end up in court and you wouldn't believe what you're there for. Budweiser from walking up your block. You'd better stop writing before I pay my bills. I know she didn't stop. I say my time, a man takes off in true religion and makes a shot. A true religion man can never escape. I don't tell everybody, but I'm a Cooper. The first time I told you that I sent you a letter and took your number down. If you don't have her number, you can't get it from me bro."

I don't try to make sense out of what Kasey is saying. I just try to write down everything he says as fast as possible because I find it interesting.

Chapter 19: Weekends at 7A

Rumination Warning!!

On weekends, there aren't any group meetings or individual counselling sessions. The only groups are 45 minutes in the gym and maybe an art session. Other than that, you are left to your own devices. For me, that would be staying in bed all day. All you do is lay there and think about the mistakes you've made in life. Then you think about the challenges that you face, and you start having panic attacks over and repeatedly. I'm stuck here. I can't take it. It's a constant nightmare. I don't know how I'm going to end up. Will I be able to pay my bills? Will I end up homeless and living in a shelter? The psychologist, Dr. K says that I shouldn't ruminate on things that I can't control while I'm here. That's easy for him to say because he doesn't have my problems or the problems of the other patients here. I want to leave here, but at the same time I'm scared of what lies ahead. Right now, my plan is to drive Uber or Lyft while I attend the hospital's aftercare program. That's where you attend an outpatient program for a few hours a day and go to individual and group counselling. My plan also includes meeting with a social worker and an employment agent to help me find a job. On one hand I look forward to a new job, and on the other, I don't know what I'm qualified to do. Let's also sprinkle in my moments where an existential crisis takes over. My adrenaline is pumping so fast right now that I feel like I'm going to scream and jump out of the window. I still have to get ECT, so I hope I'll be different when I leave. I fear this will take another month of being committed before I even go to the next hospital. Each day I feel like I'm getting worse and not better. Making the smallest decisions like deciding to brush my teeth or take a shower become difficult and overwhelming.

As I write this, I can hear Kasey talking to himself in the hallway and I keep flipping back pages to write down what he says. Tomorrow is Sunday, so there will be another day of sitting around the day room and thinking about life.

The first Batman movie is on TV. It's the one with Michael Keaton and Jack Nicholson. Carmen is sitting at the table next to me. She is the only one here. All the other patients are sleeping in their rooms. It's almost 7:00 p.m. and most of the patients have slept all day. Some of the patients like Kenny and Kasey spend their weekends pacing the unit.

This weekend, we got 3 new patients, but I don't know their names: The first patient is a 20-year-old female who is very shy, quiet and kind. It is her first time in a hospital like this because she seems shocked with all the behaviors that the patients exhibit.

The second patient is a woman from India who is in her 50's. She is missing her bottom and top front teeth and walks the unit talking to herself and making hand gestures that I don't understand. She does not speak any English. If she had teeth and did not abuse herself, she would be quite beautiful.

Patient #3 I nicknamed, "Mini Charles Manson". This guy looked like what Charles Manson's son would have looked like. He has the same face and hair. He also has the same psychotic stare and anger. He curses at and threatens to sue the nurses. While he sat and ate his dinner, he was given an injection. He kept eating like it wasn't happening. Mini Charles likes to walk the unit and talks to himself too. One disturbing optic is that Mini Charles wears his gown backwards which exposes his out of shape chest and belly. It's not a good sight. I'm guessing it won't be long before he has a run in with another patient.

Donna:

Donna is a 20-year-old Latina from The Bronx. At first, I thought she had a beer belly, but it turns out she is 6 months pregnant. She doesn't look pregnant. She came to the hospital because of alcohol poisoning. Donna is very pretty so she gets a lot of attention from the male patients. She also has extremely large breasts and I notice all the men whether they are patients or employees staring at them constantly. I must admit that I stared too.

Donna has also spent time in prison, but for what, I don't know. She lost her mom at age 17, her older brother is in prison, and her younger brother is in another psychiatric hospital.

Last night we were watching Monday Night Football and Donna was especially restless and bored. She had a paper clip in her hand that she was using to try to pick the locks to the doors on the unit so that she can escape. She doesn't care about her belongings; like her clothes and cell phone that are locked up in the hospital storage unit. She said she doesn't care if she gets out of here in just her pajamas. While she was trying to pick a lock, she was busted by a BHA For being near the door. The BHA did not know that Donna was trying to pick the lock. He Just told her that she couldn't be near the door and that she needed to either go back to her room or the Day Room. I must say that I am impressed that Donna knows how to pick locks.

Chapter 20: September 9th, 2019, Jacobi Hospital, 7A, Bronx, NY

Kasey got the needle today. During lunch in the Day Room, Kasey was being paged over the announcement system that he could take his medication. He refused to get up to get his meds. When the nurses came in to give it to him, he began to yell and curse at them and became so belligerent that the alarm that calls the hospital police had to be sounded. When the police came Kasey had to be held down near the television, as he was given an injection to make him sleep. He slept from 12:30 p.m. until 9:30 p.m. The medication still didn't stop him from walking the unit at 4:00 a.m. Kasey also farts and burps while he walks. The farts are so loud that you can hear them from your room no matter if your door is open or closed. The man has talent!

Chapter 21: September 10th, 2019, Jacobi 7A, Bronx, NY

Today at 1:30 p.m. I will find out when I'm getting transferred to Elmhurst hospital for ECT. I'll be doing a phone interview with the doctor from Elmhurst.

It's about 2:00 p.m. right now and I just got off the phone with the doctor from Elmhurst hospital. While I wasn't given a transfer date, the doctor explained the ECT procedure. They give the treatments on Mondays, Wednesdays and Fridays. They also do between 8 and 15 treatments in total. That means I might be in the hospital for another 5 weeks. I'm scared beyond scared because there is so much to do like see my kids, get new car insurance and getting a new job. My mind starts to race, and a million thoughts run through my brain which causes fear and confusion. I then start thinking about the meaning of life and all my existential questions that cause me to go mad. Occasionally, I get a feeling of shock because I can't believe that this is happening and that this is what I'm going through. There is so much uncertainty ahead that I don't know how to react.

The doctor from Elmhurst said that about 1 in 100,000 dies during ECT and so far, they have had 0 deaths in their hospital. With my luck I'll be that 1 in 100,000 to die during ECT. The reality is, that I'm not so scared about the actual procedure of ECT; I'm more worried about how this whole episode in my life continues to go on.

I have some money that was supposed to be part of my tax deferred annuity that I have to use now because I have no money coming in besides my small pension and I haven't been approved for Social Security Disability benefits yet.

I also found out from Geico that I can't drive Uber and Lyft anymore because they don't cover ride share drivers that live at certain addresses in NYC because it costs too much for them to insure my car. In other words, they're worried that my car will get robbed or vandalized and they will have to pay for it.

I live in a very cute neighborhood. While I only live in a basement apartment, I can go outside and walk across the street to the water which is on Long Island Sound.
There is a beach club that is across the street from my apartment where I used to be a member.

I cancelled my membership after my sons lost interest in going to the beach club and swimming at their pool. I initially joined when my sons were about 9 years old and 6 years old so that they could have swimming lessons. In fact, by joining that beach club I learned to get over my fear of swimming because I did not want my sons to see that I had a fear of water and that I couldn't swim. So, on the days when I didn't have my boys, I would go to the beach club alone and practice swimming in the pool. This is the one thing that I'm proud of myself for because now I have the confidence to be able to have a good time with my sons whenever we go swimming.

I am hoping that ECT works and the feeling of not wanting to get better, having insecurities about going to work and not wanting to be alive goes away. There's also a big part of me that's afraid of leaving the hospital and facing the realities of life, but I refuse to be hospitalized forever.

Using some perspective, I have to believe that life is not so bad since there are 70,000 people in the Bahamas right now who are with no homes because of a hurricane. They have nothing. I'm just one man with an illness who's letting the illness win. I must fight! Am I just procrastinating by doing this? Do I really want to be here, or do I need to be here for help? It's for help. I hate admitting it, but I need help.

I have to learn how to go with the flow with life and just let things happen. The reality is that staying here another 3 to 4 weeks is no big deal. Right now, I'm freaking out that I will either wind up living with my mother or wind up living in a shelter. Those are obviously irrational thoughts and probably not what my reality will be. However, while knowing that those thoughts are irrational, it doesn't stop my brain from torturing me and my body reacting. At a certain point one must admit that sometimes there just might be something wrong and that it's not just something that is psychosomatic.

The worst thing about being in a psychiatric hospital is all the downtime. Like I've mentioned before, there are groups that meet for meditation, art and music. However, I can't really concentrate or get the benefits of these groups when I have so much worry and malaise on my mind. All I think about is that everyone in the room will die someday.

I have been encouraged to exercise and do deep breathing exercises, but like I said, it does no good right now. I know at some point I will get bitten by the same fitness bug that I did when I was 19 and started taking weightlifting as a serious part of my lifestyle. Once the fitness bug bites, I know I will start to feel better.

I'm not sure whether I have a bad attitude or I'm at the point in my depression and anxiety where they are at their highest levels than ever before. I know it's time that I get my mental illness finally taken care of before I really do kill myself.

Part of me feels with everything that happened with my job and my marriage was all my fault. I've never stuck up for myself the most part of my life. However, in the cases of my divorce and my career, there were extenuating circumstances in which I had to deal with people who in my opinion, are, in my opinion are truly corrupt and dishonest: This would include my ex-wife, whom I will call Julia: I Googled who the biggest narcissistic actress in Hollywood was and Julia Roberts came up as #1. So, I went with the name Julia. More on her later. In addition, there are the administrators from the school I worked at and the investigators for my case at the New York City

Department of Education, who were the most corrupt and dishonest people that I have ever met in my life. Furthermore, the teacher's Union is in bed with the Department of Education and are not supporting me like they are supposed to. This led my attorney to suggest that we sue the United Federations of Teachers as well.

It's Kasey Time:

Kasey is sitting next to me, and he is having reactions to channel 7 Eyewitness news here in New York City. This is what he said, "What you said, you probably didn't tell them it was over a crack pipe. Who saying that? Secretly I'm laughing secretly I'm like wow, and I can't take this anymore ". " All they want is spent in all, then they went down, and they all speak. Don't tell me that's over there. Listen, I'm moving on. I'm not even thinking about you. Wait, I don't have anybody to talk to! "I know that I'm going to have a good time. Fuck it! That's over 8000 pounds of heroin. Europe, based on heroin. Especially when you're drunk and not trying. Tell me I wouldn't see that shit, that's a problem. Where are you from?

Are you from The Bronx? Well then that's the problem yo!". That's word for word. I never understand it, yet it's never boring.

Chapter 22: A History of My Stays at Different Psychiatric Hospitals

Since the end of March 2019, I have been committed to psychiatric hospitals or hospitals with psychiatric wards about 5 times.

The first psychiatric hospital I ever stayed at was in Amityville, New York called Brunswick Hall. The catalyst of my being brought to Brunswick Hall was because I lost my appeal with the New York City Department of Education and my principal over the false allegations that I abused my students. Remember, there were no lockers in the school for me to throw girls into, no videos, no witnesses although there were almost 200 kids in the hallway with their cellphones, School Dean and a security guard; all of which who claim to have seen nothing. That's because I never abused my students. What hurts most is that I pride myself on being a kind and funny man and beating up my students is something that is not in my DNA.

The 2nd stay for me was at Syosset Hospital's psychiatric ward on Long Island. It was recommended that I was to be transferred directly from North Shore Hospital's ER in Manhasset, NY. I told the doctors there that I put an exercise resistance band around my neck, and I started squeezing it as tight as I could to see what it felt like to choke myself. Once I started choking myself, I stopped immediately and became frightened because of what I had been doing. When I first got to the hospital, I feared telling them the truth of what I did because I did not want to be committed again. However, to get proper help or what we perceive to be help, you must be honest, give in and get yourself checked in to the psychiatric ward.

The third time I was committed to a psychiatric ward was for my first stay at Jacobi Hospital in The Bronx. I was home for about a week from Syosset Hospital. I was at my psychiatrist's office, and I was very suicidal, talking about how everything I see reminds me of ways to kill myself; like using exercise rubber bands, knives and pills. My psychiatrist felt I was in danger to myself and called 911 from her office. The ambulance came and I spent almost 3 weeks at Jacobi. Once again, I had recently started new medications (Ativan and Abilify) and I believe the side effects amplified my anxiety because of my past experiences with Prozac and Trazodone, which led to 2 trips to the ER in Dec of 1996 and Nov of 2012.

The fourth time I was committed, I had decided to take a cab to Jacobi Hospital. During this weekend I had abused Klonopin on a Friday night and Saturday night I abused Ativan. The abuse of the pills was prompted by being butt dialed by my ex-wife who was on vacation with my sons and her boyfriend in Florida. There's nothing quite like listening to everyone at dinner having a good time and hearing what it's like to sound like when you have been replaced. Because of that, I spent my 2nd three week stay at Jacobi and was released and set to go to an aftercare outpatient program.

I was home for less than 2 days after I was discharged from Jacobi when I took about 15 Ativan at once after I realized that I had made the mistake of not fighting for my job, retiring too early, that I'll have to use whatever retirement money that was available, and that I would be working until I was in my seventies.

As I write this, I'm well into my third week of my third stay at Jacobi hospital. It's been a nightmare as my life has been put on hold. But I know I'm not healthy. I know I'm not healthy enough to go home and I know that I must try ECT.

Chapter 23: Brunswick Hall, Psychiatric Hospital, Amityville New York, April 2019

Brunswick Hall was my first ever stay at a psychiatric hospital. I stayed for 10 days. Given the fact that I had never been to a psychiatric hospital, I was frightened. I was transferred from Montefiore Hospital in The Bronx after spending the night in their psychiatric holding area because of my suicidal ideations. Fortunately, the psychiatric holding area for Montefiore hospital is quite nice: You get your own little room and a bed and that was fine enough for me. After spending the night in The Bronx, I was taken by ambulance to Amityville, Long Island.

When you are transferred, you ride on a stretcher. This is when you lose your dignity. You're treated as if you are Hannibal Lecter from Silence of the Lambs; I was strapped into the stretcher so I couldn't escape or hurt anyone. I didn't have any plans on trying to escape so I just dealt with it.

When we arrived at Brunswick Hall, you check in at the main desk. After that, I was brought to my unit and sat in a chair while they processed my paperwork. It was there that the reality of being in a psychiatric hospital really hit me. Almost immediately, I saw very mentally ill patients walking the hall who were very medicated and talking to themselves. I was sitting there wearing my hospital pajamas and looking very nervous.

A nurse then said to me, "Just keep your head down and you'll be all right". Great, this must mean that if I look at anybody there will be violence. It's not that I'm afraid to fight or I don't know how to fight it's that I just don't want to get in any more trouble, and now have violence added to my file.

A few minutes later, I was brought into my wing of the psychiatric ward called Legacy. This ward had all male patients. I knew this was going to be a tough place because as I entered the hallway there were already people arguing and yelling racist remarks at each other. About 10 minutes after being there, a guy named Carl punched another man who was very ill as they waited online for their medication. Carl sucker punched the man and he fell to the floor immediately. Like I said the man was extremely mentally ill and he was also in his late fifties or early sixties. Carl is about my height and weighs about 250 pounds, he is African American, and his eyes are always bloodshot from the medications that he takes.

Chapter 24: Tommy and the Others, Brunswick Hall Amityville New York

There was one person who was very interesting here at Brunswick Hall. His name was Tommy. He was a higher up in a well-known gang, he travelled the world while in the military and served over 20 years in prison for something that I never asked about. It's usually impolite to ask someone what they had been in prison for without them talking about it first.

Tommy had a lot of wisdom to share and knew more than the therapists who ran the group sessions. He thought that people who started fights here were cowards because there are nurses, BHA's and police officers assigned to the unit to break up fights. Tommy would always say "Niggas are always brave on the inside because they know they are protected. How come they never fight niggas on the street where they are free to attack and fight a nigga any time they want? " For some reason, Tommy was a magnet for trouble. He could be sitting in the TV Room doing absolutely nothing and somebody would start with him, and he would get pissed. I think these men were trying to prove to themselves to Tommy because he was in one of most infamous gangs in the USA. Tommy was a mellow alpha male that lived here at Brunswick Hall and was just waiting for his time to finish so that he can go home.

The only laugh I had at Brunswick Hall was from observing Tommy and a friend of his while they watched TV in the Day Room: There was a Korean boy named Brian who was in his twenties who claimed to talk to aliens, knew people in the military, the Secret Service and other secret societies whose names slip my mind now.

Brian had a habit of picking his nose and eating his boogers. He would do this all day, especially in the Day Room. One afternoon, Brian was picking his nose. Tommy and his friend were watching him. I was sitting in the back row observing. Tommy then said, "How is a nigga going to pick his nose and then eat the fucking thing?". As Brian picked his nose to retrieve a new booger to eat, both Tommy and the other man started screaming in disgust. They sounded like the 2 old men that sit in the balcony that heckled The Muppets during The Muppet Show. They started shouting "No! Don't eat that shit!". Tommy and his friend then started yelling at him to flick his booger away. I couldn't help but laugh until I came to tears. They were each saying, "Don't eat it! Flick it! You gotta flick that shit!" I think the funniest part was the inflexion in the voices of Tommy and his friend. They were so animated that I couldn't help but laugh and was grateful just to feel some sort of joy even if it was only for a few minutes.

I was only attacked once at Brunswick, and it was by Carl. I was on line to get some hand sanitizer because my fingers were covered with magic marker from an art class. When I asked for the hand sanitizer, Carl tried to push me and said, "Hey man, no snitching!" Luckily, I was big and strong enough to hold Carl's arms and push him away from me while the nurses grabbed him. They gave him a needle because he had been starting trouble all day and felt that he needed to be subdued. So, for the rest of that day, I didn't see

Carl. I wasn't afraid of Carl because it's not hard to fight off a guy who is on so many sedatives.

After my run in with Carl instead of avoiding him, I would say hello and ask him how he was feeling. When I would do that, he would be friendly. I believe that he didn't remember trying to attack me because when we would have a conversation, he acted like I was a person that he never met before. However, Carl is psychotic, violent and can be dangerous when not sedated. You must be aware of that when you're sitting and talking with someone who has severe mental illness because they could snap at any time. But, for some reason I was able to sit in a room with Carl, talk and hang out. Being an empath, I could also feel his pain and anger.

One of the interesting things that they have here at Brunswick Hall is smoke breaks. Most of the patients here smoke cigarettes and the hospital would supply cigarettes for those who smoked. After each meal, a group of smokers were let outside so they could have their cigarettes. I was not allowed outside because I wasn't a smoker. There were no other times that patients were brought outside for fresh air or just to even toss around a basketball. I was contemplating taking up smoking just so that I can go outside. That's a joke for those who don't have a sense of humor. I did try cigarettes once and it was a year after I had tried marijuana. In addition to the cigarettes making me feel sick to my stomach I felt there was no point in smoking cigarettes because there was no effect like THC. The nicotine also made me feel jittery, which would cause anxiety attacks.

Brian, the Korean nose picker was fun to talk to. He was able to tell me that he was brought in because he was throwing rocks at a streetlight outside a 7-11 in Patchogue. This turns out to be a coincidence because the 7-11 he is talking about is the one that I would go to before all my gigs in Patchogue, New York. This gave me a good visual for when I was listening to his stories. I knew exactly where he was talking about.

Brian said that the streetlight was staring at him, calling him names and sending him messages. Brian understands that he is severely schizophrenic, yet the voices that he hears in his head and the hallucinations that he sees still affect him as if they were real. He knows they are not real and can't help the madness that it makes him feel. I can totally relate because while I know that my thoughts which cause anxiety are not real, it doesn't stop me from reacting emotionally and physically as if the bad thing I picture happening to me is real.

Brian also believes he is skilled in martial arts. He has no problem starting fights and calling people the worst names for their race. Whenever he had an altercation with someone, he would first verbally warn them of his connections with The Secret Service and then get into his best "Karate Kid" crane stance. All of this would happen as his shorts would fall down to his ankles, leaving him standing in his underwear.

 The nurses would of course intervene before any punches were thrown and would administer the needle to Brian. Brian got released before I did. I was told he would eventually be picked up again for some sort of public disturbance which would involve him talking to secret service personnel or aliens. Brian also spoke with a stutter, so understanding what he was trying to say could be difficult and took a lot of patience. Brian once told me that he liked to vandalize cars and people's properties by throwing rocks at all the windows of moving cars or throwing rocks at the windows of houses.

Rumination Warning!

It's hard to believe that what I'm going through is real. It's very scary and very sad at the same time. I'm that guy that winds up standing on the bridge threatening to jump. I'm the guy who lost his job, his wife etc. Right now, I'm barely making ends meet and I live in a basement. I collect social security disability and I'm on food stamps.

 I'm the guy who's been pushed around his whole life and never stuck up for himself. When you are that guy, you either end up dead from suicide, in jail for murder, in the psyche ward or you beat the shit out of the first person that fucks with you. I sometimes fantasize about someone attacking me so that I can be justified in beating them senseless.

 I have no idea what kind of job I can get when I am discharged. The fear and hopelessness courses through my veins like ice water.

 I have moments where I really don't know what I'm going to do. I will seek help with an employment agency like I talked about before and hopefully will find a well-paying job. I must work on first staying alive for my sons and I pray that all my psychological incidents don't have a major effect on them. All I can do is hope and when I speak to them on the phone each day, I reinforce the fact that I'm going to be better than ever when I get out of here. I love my sons and I cry when I think about what I did to myself and what that possibly could have done to them. They don't deserve this and the one thing that I wanted to protect them from when they were born was mental illness. I tried so hard to keep it from them. I didn't want them to see me like how I saw my father at his worst times.

Once again, the idea of taking the civil service test and working at the Post Office occupies my mind. However, the stigma of postal workers is that they eventually snap and shoot everybody in the Post Office. So, maybe I should brainstorm some other ideas for employment.

Chapter 25: An Introduction to My Marriage

Life doesn't turn out like you thought it would. We are not guaranteed anything. When I was married to Julia, we owned a home in a nice suburban town on The North Shore of Nassau County, NY. We originally met near my job. Things were great in the beginning as they always are. We started dating in October of 2002.

The first red flag when we started dating was that she had already booked a trip to The Dominican Republic for Christmas break and was going with an old boyfriend who now she says was only a friend (yeah right). She said she didn't want to cancel the trip because she said she was tired of giving up things in her past relationships. So, I must pay the price for things that other people did to her? She eventually went on the trip, and I was pissed. She assured me that it was a platonic trip. Given the fact that I knew she had an STD and so did I; I figured she wouldn't sleep around and be risky. I chose to trust her. She came back from the trip, and we resumed our relationship. If I said I don't think they had sex, I would sound naïve. After we divorced, she went and had sex with the same ex-boyfriend. This is a woman who was supposedly not into sex anymore and could never give a reason. It was probably because I feel she was lying.

By the summer of 2003, I moved in with Julia and in July of 2004, we got married. Our wedding album says 2005 on the cover because the photo album company fucked up the year. In December of 2005, we bought the house in Nassau County.

We lived in the house for 5 years and she didn't want to live there anymore because she was sick of commuting to the borough where we worked. Meanwhile, I was the one that was driving us every day and warned her before we moved there that the commute will suck at times.

In addition, my parents gave/lent us upwards of $75,000 for the down payment of the house, new washer, dryer, dishwasher, kitchen sink, kitchen counter, stove/oven combo with microwave and supplies to do all the decorating that we were able to do on our own. My dad was winning at poker at the time, which is why we got the money. We got lucky. Like I said, my dad had a very generous and loving side when he was winning. I admit it's hypocritical to not approve of my dad's gambling and then take money for the house. However, I wanted Julia to be happy and comfortable living in a new strange town having lived in the city her whole life. So yes, I took the money when it was offered. Part of the money also came from an inheritance from my great aunt. We also spent over $13,000 on a new deck, barbecue and patio furniture. The new deck was needed because the old one was falling apart and needed proper railing to keep the kids from falling off. Other than the deck, all the other renovations were not immediately necessary and could have been put off for a few years.

Not to take anything away from Julia, she did take out $30,000 from her tax deferred annuity to add to the down payment for the house. In addition to putting on the new deck, we had most of the wood floors refinished and we installed a new wood floor in the kitchen as well.

In August of 2009 Julia got pregnant with our 3rd son. One day in October of 2009 we were driving home from her doctor's appointment and Julia yelled, and I paraphrase, "I told you I didn't want to be pregnant; this is all your fault, you should have gotten a vasectomy!"

When Julia was giving birth to our twins in 2007 via C- section, the doctor asked her if she wanted her tubes tied. Julia had a tough time getting pregnant and had to take prenatal vitamins, inject hormones, and have artificial insemination. She said no to having her tubes tied and wanted, and I paraphrase, "God to decide whether I get pregnant again". I guess she assumed that she would never get pregnant again. I didn't think she would either.

About a month after Julia blamed me for the pregnancy, Nov of 2009, she said she wanted to sell the house because she was tired of commuting. That was the point where I had the biggest anxiety attack that I have had since before I got married. I was very upset about putting 5 years of work into the house and she wanted to sell it just because it became an inconvenience for her to get to work. Meanwhile, I was the one driving us. One purpose of buying a house is to have a nest egg that you can count on if you sell your house at a healthy profit. There's also the obvious fact that by owning a home, having your own front yard, backyard etc... is more conducive and fun for raising a family. I feel children need space to run, play and discover things about nature outside. In addition, if you can afford a home where your child can have their own bedroom, you should do it. I also feel that children need a space of their own in order to have some peaceful time alone. Everyone needs a break from too much external stimuli on the brain. Some of my best memories as a child were spent in my own bedroom which I was lucky to have.

Also, at Julia and I's house, was a big basement to play in, a wonderful backyard that was lined with

Canadian Hemlock trees around the perimeter, beautiful garden lights for the nighttime and a cherry blossom tree right in the middle of the yard. The former homeowners had good taste. I fell in love with that backyard immediately. It was our own little world. But she didn't want it or me. In addition, I felt she never considered our sons and what she was selfishly taking away from them.

The things that I was lucky enough to have as a child were set up for our children. However, because it didn't meet Julia's agenda, everybody had to pack up and move.

So, there I was anxious, afraid and mostly pissed off because I did everything that she asked me to do for the house so she could feel more comfortable there. She wasn't from Long Island, she was from the city and she was nervous about being in a new place, not knowing anyone or the layout of our town.

In January of 2010 when we got an offer on the house, I told Julia that I wanted to separate and that when we moved back to the city, I would find my own apartment. Now remember, she is about 4 months pregnant with our 3rd son. How could I want a separation while she's pregnant? The other thing I thought about was, "Why does she want to move now while she's in the middle of a pregnancy, when during her 1st pregnancy she was on bed rest for the third trimester? "

I found her behavior and decisions to be rash, hasty and manipulative. Something didn't add up. And at the same time, I felt completely guilty about separating from someone who was pregnant and that I had sons that were soon going to be 3 years old. About a week or so before I told Julia that I wanted to separate, I saw a story on TV about how Lance Armstrong left his wife when she was pregnant. After I watched the story, I thought about how terrible a person could be to leave a pregnant woman. And now here I was leaving a pregnant woman. This went against everything I believed a family should be.

A few days after I told Julia that we should separate, she said she was contemplating to abort the baby and said she called a late term abortion doctor for a consultation. Whether this is true or not I don't know. I would like to think it wasn't for my son's sake. If it was true, then it's one of the most disgusting things that I've ever heard a person contemplate. She knew there was a boy in there and that we had a name picked already. If it was false, in some ways it's just as bad because she was trying to manipulate me and my emotions, which I feel is her motifs operandi anyway. You don't threaten to abort your child in order to make your husband feel guilty especially when you created the chaos of wanting to move while pregnant in the first place and technically just paid for the renovations for the new owners; we bought the house for $490,000, spent close $75,000 in renovations/furnishing/appliances and then sold it for $514,000.

In my opinion, that was sociopathic and selfish behavior. It goes along with what I believe to be her covert, grandiose and narcissistic/didactic personality. I also looked at her hasty and irrational decisions as a way of making things bad for me so that I would snap and say I want a divorce. All along I felt she wanted a divorce the whole time which is why she was mad about the pregnancy, or maybe she was cheating and she was afraid the baby wasn't mine. Anything is possible with a person who in my opinion, is a narcissist.

Julia is the type that will make things so bad for you that when you snap, she blames you and will play the victim. After a few years, these behaviors became obvious and transparent.

 We separated for about 5 months. In June of 2010 we reconciled, and I moved in with her and my sons in their basement apartment in the city. After I moved in, we decided that we would try couples' therapy. Before we ever discussed therapy, whenever I would talk about psychology, Julia would call me a, "Know it all" or a "Granola Hippie". However, when it was convenient for her to have me find a therapist for us, I became the expert all of a sudden. Narcissists will use you for any resource so that they really don't have to do the work they claim to do.

 I chose a female counselor on purpose so that Julia would not feel like that there were two men ganging up on her. I knew that once she was in therapy, she would have to own up to her behaviors and being emotionally abusive towards me. In my opinion, Julia's mental illness comes from being physically and sexually abused by her older brother when she was about 5 or 6 years old. This was something she told me. Not only was she abused, but she was also blamed by her mother for "seducing" her brother. In addition, Julia contracted a permanent sexually transmitted disease, which I discussed earlier. To me, that was ok to handle, because I had caught warts in college, so we both had something. My question was always; who abused her brother and gave him a sexually transmitted disease?

 I also noticed that Julia also tended to be a pathological liar in couple's therapy and claimed that I didn't do anything around the house, I'm lazy, I smoke pot (Yes, that part is absolutely 1000% true) and I'm not present enough in my son's lives. All of Julia's claims started to unravel as the therapist asked her more questions to find out what I really do, which was quite a bit. The counselor eventually said to her, and I paraphrase, "I don't know what more this man can do for you. What more do you want from him? Sometimes people don't know what you want unless you ask. He's not a mind reader. You also can't play games with people like giving them the silent treatment and not telling them what you are mad at them for. And then you make him try to guess what he did? What is it that you are trying to accomplish?" At that point, Julia wanted to walk out of the session. I know it takes two people to destroy a relationship, but there are exceptions to the rule when one person wants total control of everything and will do anything to get their way: even threatening a late term abortion. I'm sure she'll read this. After all, this part is about her, which is what all narcissists want. A narcissist will also fail to see their shortcomings and constantly deflect the subject back to the other person.

 Right now, Julia is on her 3rd boyfriend that she has brought around our sons. She has been taking them on vacations, out to dinner, day trips etc. I wonder how much this man pays his own way or if she's using child support money for these excursions. It particularly hurts that there is a man around my sons more than I am. I'm paranoid that I may lose visiting rights with my sons when discharged based on the fact that I've been institutionalized. Right now, my twins are 12 and my youngest son is 9 years old. Hopefully they will be young enough to forget about the last few months. I'm extra worried because with all the mental illness history in my family, there's a chance that one of my kids could end up like me. I will do anything to help my sons if God forbid, they develop anxiety or depression.

There's also more about Julia in the upcoming chapters.

Chapter 26: Sept 11, 2019, Jacobi Hospital, 7A, Bronx, NY

Rumination Warning!

I spent most of the day in bed ruminating about my reality and thinking about the human brain. I once read that we don't use most of our brain. I can't help but wonder; what is contained in the parts of the brain we don't use? Are the answers to the questions I have about death and the universe contained there? I know Albert Einstein and Stephen Hawking's brain activity were higher than anyone else in history as far as we know. It leads me to believe that with more brain activity, more about the unknown would be discovered.

One day, I would like to sit with a physicist and ask all my existential questions about the universe: What existed before the universe? What existed before that etc? What is existence? What is oblivion? Is there a God? A Heaven? What happens after we die? Boom! An existential crisis hits!

To my amazement, I got up out of bed, took a shower and brushed my teeth. I put on clean pajamas, underwear, but was too shy to ask for clean socks. It shouldn't cause anxiety to ask for clean socks, clothes or to do laundry; but it does.

It's not like anybody yells at you if you ask for those things. If the machines are unavailable at that moment, the nurses always politely tell me that they will let me into the laundry room as soon as a machine opens.

My underwear that needs to go in the wash has blood stains all over it because I've been scratching my groin and scrotum; causing cuts that are big enough to leave large blood stains in my underwear. When it's my legs that itch, I get blood stains all over my socks like Curt Schilling pitching against the Yankees in the 2004 American League Pennant.

I've developed some odd habits over the last few years: One habit is that when I shower, I take the shower head and I spray my scrotum and groin with the hottest water I can. There is something about the burning and the pain that gives me a sense of relief, like I'm scratching an itch. I basically scald myself with hot water every day. I know that I'm doing this because it's a way that my anxiety shows up in other forms. The result of this habit is my skin feeling dry and tight. My skin then starts to itch, and I scratch until I bleed. It's a vicious cycle.

After I got married, the sensation that my shins were itchy slowly grew from something I noticed a little bit, to being something that took over. Eventually, I was constantly scratching. I would even scratch using my toenails if I were laying in bed. I would scratch until there was blood.

It wouldn't be unusual for me to wake up in the middle of the night and realize that I had been scratching in my sleep. There would be blood all over the bed sheets and dripping down my legs.

I started to go to different doctors to find out what was wrong. I felt that there was something wrong with my skin. Sound familiar? My dad? I tested negative for everything including scleroderma, which is a type of arthritis of the skin that makes you itch, and you lose all the hair in the area where the Scleroderma was affecting. Over the years, I eventually scratched all the hair off my legs.

Since I had been to every kind of doctor possible to test my skin and all tests for everything coming back negative; I started to wonder if my scratching was psychosomatic. Was I scratching to deal with my anxiety disorder and the stresses of being with Julia? I knew that I loved her, but when someone has such an obtuse personality, it will take its toll on you.

I once asked Dr. Peart if he thought that I was psychosomatically allergic to my wife. He responded, "Fuck yes Peter! Fuck yes!". You should have Robert DeNiro's voice in your head for, "Fuck yes!"

For a few years, Dr. Peart had suggested that the marriage wasn't good for my emotional health. In addition to my opinion and the opinion of Dr. Peart and two other therapists who met Julia, I was married to a narcissist who was constantly testing me, criticizing me and trying to instill her will upon me by trying to take away everything in my life that kept my anxiety at a low level: music and fitness.

Julia was the type that liked everything about me when we got together; I was a musician, I enjoyed exercise, I was sensitive, open about my mental illness and was also willing to help her with her anger issues. When we got together, we agreed that we would support each other.

After we got married, the subjects of me giving up music and not going to the gym began to grow more and more especially when we had kids. After the kids were born, I stopped going to the gym and trained at home, usually at night after everyone was asleep. I would get stoned in my basement, train, play some guitar, masturbate to a porn clip (only on Sundays and Wednesdays), or watch Van Halen videos on YouTube. I'll explain my Sunday and Wednesday masturbation schedule later on.

In addition, her verbal abuse began to increase as well. I remember once when she was mad about something at work and was taking it out on me verbally; yelling at me, finding anything to blame me for etc, I said, "I know you're pissed about work, but please don't take it out on me. You can yell to me about it but not yell at me because of me, that's not fair." Her reply was, and I paraphrase, "Sometimes you have to suck it up". No, I don't have to suck it up. I'm not a verbal punching bag and nor should anyone else be!

There were also constant nonverbal negative gestures and looks of disapproval daily, especially whenever I told her that I booked a gig or that I was to record some music. At that point, anything

I did that involved music was based on trying to make money; and I was.

My twins were born in 2007, and in 2008, I enrolled in college for a second master's degree to become a guidance counselor. I had Julia's support at the beginning. When I enrolled, I was worried that maybe the timing to go back to school with 2 babies at home was too much for our plate. Looking back, it was too much going on at once. I was feeding off the encouragement from a large handful of my students that said they had wished I was their guidance counselor. In fact, I used to get called into meetings to help mediate problems between students because they didn't like the guidance counselor there at the time.

On the very first night I came home from class, I was met by Julia at our front door and she was wearing a schoolgirl outfit. She then told me how proud she was of me for going back to school and being ambitious.

Fast forward a year and a half; I was 36 credits into the 60-credit program and Julia wanted me to take accelerated classes so I could graduate early. The problem was my college did not offer an accelerated program. So, Julia wanted me to drop out and transfer a choice of two schools. Both schools charged twice as much tuition. Julia offered to charge the tuition to her credit card, but at that point I had already maxed out my credit card paying for tuition. I didn't want to have the added stress of another maxed out credit card. Plus, I didn't know where I was going to get the money to pay for the tuition to finish. I was not going to take out another student loan either. I already had one from my first master's degree.

I eventually dropped out of the master's program, which was fine because I had just joined a busy group to play drums for. This meant making more money, no more tuition, no more weeknight classes and no more schoolwork. In addition, by joining this new band, I would get carte blanche at the venues we played. This meant I could bring Julia to those venues when we didn't have gigs, get treated great and have some fun date nights. Her view was that every night we were to be home and if we did go out, it should be together. I always liked date nights and rarely saw friends unless it was for music. I used to have to force her to go dancing with her friends.

There's one thing that always bothered me about dropping out of school and that was: When our twins were infants, Julia was enrolled in graduate school to get her third masters so that she could get a promotion at work. So, when she was going to school, I was taking care of the babies, which I had no problem doing. It's just really exhausting. It was ok for me to take care of the kids while she went to school, but when I went to school, she eventually had a problem with it, just like everything else I did.

Unlike Julia's fair-weather support of me, I was always supportive of her and was willing to do anything to help her achieve whatever she wanted to in her career.

After Julia and I separated the first time, we got back together in July of 2010. My youngest son was born in late May of 2010. In the summer of 2010, Julia got her promotion. I was very excited for her and bought her a name plate for her desk that said her name and title.

One of the first mornings after her promotion, I was driving Julia to work. She said that her working late hours was going to be a "test" for me taking care of all 3 boys. On the average, she would work late about 4 nights a week. Being that I had teacher hours, I had the luxury of being able to pick up my children every day from school and daycare. I would bring them home, play, make dinner, bathe them and get them ready for bed. Bedtime with my kids was always fun because I would sing Van Halen songs, tell jokes, or just make up stories where I would take fairy tales and add poop jokes to them. My sons would laugh and ask for more stories. I viewed this as such a wonderful bonding experience because the only time my dad was cool and relaxed was when he would tell me funny bedtime stories about when he was in the army and when he was a kid. I remember how much I would laugh. However, we would then switch back to being neurotic and yell to my mom from the top of the staircase like a talked about earlier.

Laughing like that before going to bed creates relaxation and you fall asleep in a good mood. Plus, it was a bonding experience with my sons.

When Julia would get home late from work, she would complain that I kept the boys up too late by goofing around. This bothered her because she said that when she would put them to sleep, they expected the same routine as me and she didn't want to waste, and I paraphrase, "20 minutes of my time because I have work to do". She would complain that I loaded the dishwasher wrong even though all the dishes were clean and there were no dirty dishes in the sink. She would even complain about how I folded clothes, not her clothes or my sons' clothes, but my personal "wardrobe". I was a gym teacher. I wore sweatshirts and sweatpants. All day I would sweat in these clothes, and they also took a beating. Folding my clothes perfectly as if I worked at the Gap was not necessary because within 2 hours of being at work, I would be sweaty, dirty and wrinkled up. My gymnasium was filthy with no fans or air conditioning.

So, after working late an average of 4 nights a week, Julia would have the nerve to complain if I had a gig on a Friday or Saturday night, saying that she couldn't take it anymore. Julia once had quipped that being a musician wasn't a real job. Like I stated In earlier chapters, I wasn't trying to be a rock star, nor did I think I was a rock star. I wanted the money from making music and I wanted to have the physical experience of playing drums so that I could get the psychological benefits. In addition, the money I made playing music usually went to groceries and other things for the kids. After most gigs, you could find me at a supermarket at 4am doing the grocery shopping for the house. After shopping, I would go home, unload all my gear and put the groceries away. There were many times that the sun was coming up while I unpacked the groceries. All I would ask from Julia was that I get some sleep so that my anxiety wouldn't act up. I would get to sleep but not without and argument or a look of disapproval.

As our marriage started to deteriorate, I started smoking more and more weed and she was drinking more wine and beer each night at dinner. She hated that I smoked pot. Julia had never tried it because one of her brothers died from pneumonia due to his drug use in the 1990's. However, her brother was also an alcoholic and took more serious drugs like cocaine and ecstasy. I never met her brother, so I don't have an opinion on him except that I'm sorry that he is dead. I heard he could be a funny guy.

So, the loss of her brother made Julia very much against marijuana. I guess Julia was worried that I would end up like her brother. There was one time when Julia was complaining about my pot smoking, and I told her that I haven't seen any doctors prescribe their cancer patients medical alcohol. In my opinion, a narcissist never likes when you use facts against them. They will deflect and try to blame you for other things in order to get the attention away from their stubbornness and put the focus back on your "shortcomings" that don't really exist.

 Smoking/vaping oil helps me to get out of bed, exercise, play music, be more attentive with my kids, motivate me to do more each day, do household chores and just be the all-around good husband and father that I want to be. For me, it brings me up to a psychological level of what I consider to be normal.

 Also, THC stops my racing thoughts, anxiety attacks and the retching. What's the difference between that and these medications that make you groggy,
foggy, fat, raise cholesterol and cause liver damage? Somehow these potentially dangerous medications are more acceptable than a plant that is known to stop tumors from growing.

We should ask Chris Cornell's wife (of the band Soundgarden) or Robin Williams' wife about how they feel about these medications since their husbands' suicides. Both men were on antidepressants which had suicidal ideation as side effects.

So, if I need to vape oil or take a few puffs on a joint to have a productive day, I'm going to do that. Yes, there is always a little bit of guilt associated with it. Maybe I use it as a crutch. But aren't all these medications that I'm taking a crutch as well?

After I got divorced, medicinal marijuana became legal and I was able to get my NYS Medicinal Marijuana Card. I would now be under medical supervision and could choose the strain of marijuana and THC level; I don't need to be stoned like a character from Pinapple Express. The THC level I use is enough to take away my anxiety.

If I vaped oil at home before work in the morning, I wouldn't retch or have anxiety attacks. I was able to go to work and be a more effective teacher. I wasn't nervous and I could be more creative with my lessons. It was better than taking a Klonopin which would make me feel like I was drunk or way too sleepy. I would have to drink tons of coffee to balance out the Klonopin's effects.

As irony would have it, the day that the students who claimed I beat them up was a morning that I did not vape before work. Maybe if I did, I would have been relaxed enough to not care if the girls cut class. All I had to do was not care, and my life would have been different: I know for sure that I wouldn't be sitting here writing a journal in a psychiatric ward.

One interesting phenomenon is that I have been having dreams about pot. In the dreams, I'm always surrounded by it, but never smoke it. I never have sex dreams either.

Rumination Warning!

So, as I sit here in the day room, my adrenaline starts pumping hard through my veins. I'm having a hard time concentrating on anything. All I'm doing right now is worrying. I'm regretting the past, fearing the future and suffering in the present.

While part of me wants to die, there is that giant part of me that has the irrational constant fear of death. I've somehow created a paradox. What do you do with that?

I'm still extremely angry about selling the Nassau County house because I feel the chances of me owning a home again are low, considering that I filed Chapter 7 Bankruptcy in 2016.

I'm also upset at the fact that I can't afford to take my kids on vacation while Julia and her boyfriend take my kids all over the country and I can only assume partly on my dime. How much pride can one man swallow?

I don't feel that the medications that they are giving me are helpful. I mostly feel like a confused zombie. If the meds are working, it's hard to believe because I've had episodes where I've felt lower than ever before. I just want peace of mind.

As I lay in bed here tonight at the end of this day, which happens to be Sept 11 (I think about that every day and about how I used to worry about things like that happening as a kid), I wait for the Seroquel to kick in so I can get some sleep. It's my only peace. Over and over, I ruminate about my kids, Julia, a job and wonder why I had to turn out to be mentally ill.

Chapter 27: Sept 12, 2019, Jacobi Hospital 7A, Bronx, NY

For some reason, I got up and out of bed as soon as I woke up this morning. I also decided to skip the morning stretch group because the movements are smaller than Tai Chi and the group leader talks with that phony hippie accent, which is talking like you are from Los Angeles when you grew up in Queens.

In addition, being a former teacher, I can tell that J does not prepare or write up a lesson for the group. She wings it, which makes it frustrating for me because I know what she is doing. I wasn't a great teacher when it came to classroom management and being strict with the children, however, I always wrote my lesson plans, and I knew my content area as good as anyone.

I already talked about Lance and his expressive arts class, which is just us coloring while he plays keyboards. The positive aspect about this group is that the patients talk with each other, we learn about what all our illnesses are and how we allowed them to take over our lives. We also discuss what we can do to better our lives and what our immediate goals should be. Lance doesn't really comment when we talk. He offers no wisdom or opinions. Now there's a great instructor for you!

What a ruse and waste of taxpayers' money that some of these "therapists" are.

There are 4 Psychiatric wards at Jacobi Hospital in which Lance and J run most of the groups. I'm sure it keeps them busy all day. However, an effort must be made to change things up because doing the same thing every day doesn't help anyone evolve.

Oh! I got it! All the arts therapists and some psychologists talk like Bob Ross, the artist with the grey afro that had a painting show on PBS!

For the most part, I feel like yelling at Lance and J that these groups are not working because they have the energy of an Ambien (sleeping pill). There are people here with severe problems. So, doing unhelpful fitness routines, playing bingo to win a granola bar and giving out the exact same informative papers each week does not help.

I just realized that I've been here almost over 3 weeks and haven't seen a social worker yet.

Today I ate breakfast, took my morning meds and I am ready to hide in bed for the rest of the day. I'm bugging out about that I can't take this existence anymore. Instead of hiding in my room, I put my head down on a table in the Day Room to take a nap. However, I got talked into going to the dance group by a new intern who was full of REAL positive energy and support. As I got to the dance class, there was only one other patient in the group, which was disappointing. I feel the more people there, the more you can interact and feed off each other for support. However, once again, the dance lesson was written terribly with dance moves that are made for senior citizens.

After "dance class", I ate lunch and quickly retreated to my bed. I missed going to the gym, getting some fresh air and most of art group. I stayed in bed under self-torture for about 3 hours.

After I got up, I went to art class for the second half. When I got there, I didn't color. Instead, I opened up to Lance about my life. Sometimes I forget that the expressive arts therapists are supposed to be there to talk about your issues and offer support. Like I stated earlier, a snail could offer more support. In this case, the feedback I received from Lance was something a 10-year-old could give: do deep breathing. Not much help and insight there.

After art, I was feeling even more stuck and asked to talk to Dr. P to find out when I was being discharged to Elmhurst Hospital. He told me that

I'd be leaving after this coming weekend and staying at least until October (little did I know that I would be hospitalized for 11 straight months). Although this was good news, I still asked for a pill. Dr. P said he would give me a Neurontin, which is part sedative and part pain reliever. I was hoping for an Ativan. Neurontin sucks!

At this point I'm starting to feel that being in the hospital for this long is getting out of hand. Conversely, I'm unable to function right now in the real world. I really don't know what I would do to myself if I were left alone at home. I would like to think that after this last Ativan scare, I would never try to put my life at risk again. I'm staying afloat for my sons. I will survive for my sons. I will not be like my father ever again to where it affects my sons.

I'm going on 2 months without seeing my sons. I try to rationalize that I should take care of my illness now instead of being discharged and being brought back by ambulance over and over. I think that would affect my kids more than one long stay at the hospital.

I continue to think; How can this experience not influence my kids? If my first memory of life was at a cemetery at age 2, I think that two 7th graders and a 4th grader will remember this.

My sons know about my illness and the episode with the Ativan. The one compliment that I have for Julia is that she is efficient at raising my sons to be strong and do well in school, (but it doesn't come without some gas lighting and shaming them on her part). In my opinion, she is also the type that uses the success of her children to feed her ego. I feel that she wants everyone to see that she is a great mother. To a narcissist, their children are usually used as props to feed their insatiable need to be worshipped.

I worry about what my sons will think of me when I finally get discharged; will they still love me? Will they resent me? Will they fear me?

I have tried for their whole lives to hide my anxiety and depression. Well, there is no hiding trips to the hospital in this case. Being committed to a hospital was always a combination of fear and something that I knew I would eventually need since I was 14.

I'm missing too much of my sons' lives. I missed my twins getting braces. I had braces as a kid and wanted to guide them through the experience. I missed my youngest take ice hockey lessons. I miss picking them up from school every day. I also miss our Sundays together.

As a father that doesn't have any physical custody, I was with my sons 6 days a week: I would pick them up from school on Monday thru Friday. On Tuesdays and Thursdays, I would keep them until 7pm so we could have dinner together and I would also give them showers and put them in pajamas. In addition, I would have them every Sunday. On Mondays, Wednesdays and Fridays, I would keep them after school until 5pm. Each day I would check and sign their homework, goof around with them and have fun. I also helped coach their baseball and soccer teams for 2 seasons. I've done all of this despite Julia's claims that I barely pick them up from school and am not very involved in their lives. She even lied to her lawyer before family court saying that I had hardly picked up the boys from school during the fall semester of 2018. Little did she remember that I must sign the boys out of school each time I picked them up and I had the paperwork to show it. That fall, I picked up my sons from school 66 times. Julia picked them up 7 times.

Luckily for Julia, my lawyer informed her lawyer that Julia was lying. Who knows where that would have gone if it was brought up in court and she was caught lying? In addition to spending so much time with my sons, I was also spending money on them when technically it was her parenting time. She was getting money for not watching the kids while I spent money during that time. It's double dipping. Unfortunately, no judge in family court will take the time to see the actual time I spend with my sons. This is where fathers get treated unfairly and wind up paying more child support than they should. I need that money to spend on the kids when they are with me. Why am I getting penalized for having more available time to take care of my kids than the person who makes about 30k more a year than I do? Especially now! Who knows what she is doing with that money? It's sure as hell not being invested in a proper living space. Julia and my sons live in a basement apartment with 1 bedroom that all 3 boys share.

Before I was charged with false allegations at work in Dec 2018, my depression had gotten worse over the past two years. I burned bridges with my high school friends, I quit playing music and I stopped going out socially. Everything was pointing in the direction of eventually being hospitalized.

One aspect about depression is that it is a very easy hole to fall into. It also feels like you will never climb out. Depression talks to you and convinces you that it is easier to stay in the hole even if it makes you feel like shit. Feeling like shit fuels the depression. It feels like you're being held down there against your will.

The feeling is so strong that you become paralyzed with fear. You literally can't move. My brain then begins to test my sanity by creating any kind of morbid and depressing scenario so that it can feed off me like a parasite.

 The nights I get the deepest sleeps are following the days when my attacks were at their worst and lasted the longest. I guess my brain burns out and I literally pass out instead of drifting to sleep. I'm convinced that mental illness is a form of brain damage and can get worse if it goes untreated.

When I was married and before my sons were born, I had contemplated having myself committed. Things were going well, and I changed my mind, I had a stable teaching job, was making extra money playing drums, was married to who I perceived to be a loving woman and owned a house. Plus, I had a retirement annuity plan that I invested in with every paycheck and so did Julia. With all the positives, I still had anxiety attacks and vomited in my bathroom sink every morning before work. No matter how good things were, the existential thoughts about death or constantly being worried that my sons will die would not stop.

After dinner tonight on 7A, I went to bed immediately. I woke up after about an hour with the overwhelming fear of death and all the unanswerable questions that come along with it. Its beyond my comprehension. I can literally feel my brain feeling fried as all these thoughts consume me in The Brain Tornado. I know I'm not the only person who goes through this. Most notably, Robin Williams and Jim Carrey (who thankfully is alive) have/had similar issues. Unfortunately, Robin Williams killed himself like I mentioned earlier. I wasn't surprised. I cried deeply for him but wasn't surprised. I could always see-through Robin Williams' eyes, look into his soul and pick up on his depression.

Chapter 28: Sept 13, 2019, Jacobi 7A

It's Friday the 13th. All I need is a black cat, a broken mirror and a ladder to walk under to make this day complete. It's been a shitty day so far based on nothing and a thousand things at the same time. I forced myself to go to morning stretch, our 7A community meeting (this is where we complain about what is wrong on our ward) and Bingo.

After all the morning activities, I made a terrible decision to go back to bed and skip lunch. I tried to sleep but my mind was racing way too much. Once again, I laid there ruminating.

As late afternoon approached, I felt like I was starving. It's my own fault for skipping lunch! Luckily, I won a Nutrigrain bar at Bingo to hold me over. Yay!

This will be my last weekend here at Jacobi. I plan on never coming back.
On Monday, Sept 16th,
2019, I will be transferred to Elmhurst Hospital in Queens, NY for another leg of this journey. I

haven't been notified when I will start ECT. I assume I will find out when I am settled there. I wish I could be transported today so that by Monday I would be able to start ECT a few days earlier.

We just got called to do vitals and give blood to test the levels of medication in our system. Rosa is on the line before me. She is singing and dancing in her own world with her BHA, Hal. Hal is new and is a great guy. He gets it. He understands us here and has a way of giving you the same advice the doctors give you, but he says it in a way that makes you want to follow what he says. I believe that is a result of having a positive aura.

My psychologist, Dr. K was not around again today, which means that I have only seen him twice in two weeks.

The group meetings continue to be repetitive, and I have 3 to 4 copies of the same handouts sitting in my room. It's rare that you have an untimed one on one session so that you can really get everything out of your system. A short session ends just when you start getting warmed up and have your thoughts organized in the order that you wanted to discuss them.

Today is the first time I'm meeting with my social worker since I was admitted here in August. When I mean I saw her, I mean I saw her in the hallway and was barely able to ask her a question because she was working on discharging another patient. I quickly wanted to ask her about employment agencies. She said, "Well, you are leaving Monday and I've been working on your after-care plan and that will transfer over to Elmhurst with you". I know that I will have to attend an outpatient program, I just hope it is near my apartment. The nurses assured me that my program would be in my neighborhood. Nurses know more than everybody here. Nurses are the greatest people in the world.

I am just now noticing that it has been quieter here on 7A since Kasey was discharged 2 days ago. We now have a second woman named Donna; she is 59 years old but looks like she's about 70. She told me today that she was a Hassidic Jew but does not practice the religion anymore. What's interesting about Donna is that she talks like she is a rapper and is missing most of her front teeth. She walks using a walker and talks back to the television constantly. I've heard her say she teaches Islam, went to Northeastern University in

Boston, met Mike Tyson and once met Barry White in a parking lot in Las Vegas. It's obvious that she's done a lot of drugs if I were to just go by her appearance. She claims she grew up in Boston and has 7 sisters who are all retired bus drivers. As a member of the tribe, I do not think she is Jewish.

 My thoughts quickly turned from Donna to thoughts on therapy and medication here at 7A.

Once or twice a week isn't enough. The patients need therapy here every day. If there isn't enough time for psychologists or psychiatrists to see their patients, then the hospital needs to hire more. The therapists have a script that they go by with lines that match what you say about your feelings. Some of these contrived lines are: " I know this must be very hard for you ", "I'm sorry you feel this way" and "Over time, things will get better". Even Daniel, the man with the shaking legs and who happens to be very quiet, blurted out, "You all say the same things to every patient. I do 3 things here: eat, sleep and take meds".

I bet that Daniel is on the drug Abilify, which is why his legs shake. When I took that drug, my legs shook so much that there were some days I needed a cane to walk. Everyone else I know that took it had the same reaction. Your medication is a crap shoot. You never know how you are going to react. My mama always said, "Life is like a box of medications; you never know what side effects you're gonna get".

As dinner arrives, all the patients emerge out of their bedrooms like feral cats in an alleyway. We line up by the meal cart and wait for our names to be called to take our trays into the Day Room to eat.

Sometimes when we are having meals it reminds me of when I was in grade school: At lunch, kids would trade food and desserts with each other.

If for some reason I get extra milk, I give it to Carmen, who never gets milk. She's not lactose intolerant, so I don't know why she's not getting any milk. Maybe she has high cholesterol.

The food here is perfectly fine, better than any public-school cafeteria food and much better than prison food, so I'm told.

Like I stated earlier, most of the patients go back to sleep after each meal. Some of the patients will come out of their rooms at 8:00 p.m. for snack. Snack consists of sandwiches, cookies and juice. Sometimes there is fruit salad and granola bars.

I eat my snack in the day room and wait till medication is given out at 9:00 p.m. After that I pray the Seroquel knocks me out quickly. After meds are given out, I'm usually the only one in the day Room watching TV, like right at this moment.

I'm watching Impractical Jokers to try to get some laughs, but it's hard to change my frame of thought with all that is weighing on me. I mostly start to think about ECT and the movie A Beautiful Mind where Russell Crowe plays, Dr. John Nash, a Princeton math professor who had schizophrenia and underwent ECT. The scene where he gets ECT is disturbing; electrodes are attached to his head, a mouth guard is inserted so that he won't bite his tongue and he is mostly sedated. When the shocks are administered, his body convulses because mini seizures are being induced. In the movie, Nash's wife looks on from an observation window with a psychiatrist who says, and I paraphrase, "I know it may look painful, but he is sedated. Imagine going through life thinking that certain things or people were real, only to find out they are not; that's where the real pain is". I start to picture myself as Dr. Nash: will I look like that when I'm being shocked? The only difference between me and a schizophrenic is that I know my thoughts are not real, yet I still react as if they are. The switch in my brain that controls fear is stuck in the "On" position.

RUMINATION WARNING!

I'm starting to think about how I missed the entire summer. I've spent most of the summer here at Jacobi hospital. I watched the 4th of July fireworks from the day room window, and I spent Labor Day laying in my bed.

If I'm correct, I was home for a total of 2 days over this summer and only saw my kids once.

I start to worry again about that I will have no chance of getting a good job when I am discharged. I was so used to being a teacher. It was supposed to be a secure job, but it wasn't. I feel I was part of a witch hunt. Why else would they bring up absenteeism from a year ago (my back surgery) and bring up that I told the children that I was filming them because they didn't stop talking and I couldn't start my lesson? Apparently using psychological techniques like that are frowned upon. In my humble opinion, it's better than yelling or standing there waiting for the kids to be quiet. Sometimes you must do something interesting or funny in order to get the attention of the students.

One of my other theories about why I feel I was pushed out of the Department of Education is that I was getting to the stage on the pay scale where I would have gotten a $10,000 raise at either the beginning or end of my 20th year teaching. Sometimes schools want to trim their payrolls and find ways to get rid of older teachers and their higher salaries, which they earned! The school can then hire a recent graduate with only a bachelor's degree and start paying at the minimum salary. I have seen it happen to other teachers, but never thought it would happen to me. They chose to believe outlandish lies and ruin my career. Not to mention triggering this major nervous breakdown as well. What do I say at a job interview when they asked me why I retired early?

As I sit here in a psychiatric hospital, another man will be with Julia watching my son play hockey tomorrow and buy him a soda at the snack bar. Another man gets to spend more time with my sons than I do. This is my worst nightmare coming true.

I know that I am their father and that nobody can replace me, but it still hurts. As I picture all these scenarios, my body starts acting up with panic. I feel sick to my stomach.

All I do is over think things wherever I am, whether it be in bed, watching TV, eating, shitting or shaving. This is my life. Are people that are truly insane lucky in some way? I would think that there is some level of anguish that they feel or that there is a part of them that knows that they are not living an ordinary life.

It's evening now and snack just arrived. All the Stray Cats have emerged for one last bite before they go back to sleep until tomorrow. As fast as the other patients eat is as fast as they leave the day room to go back to bed.

Instead of going to bed, I stay in the dayroom to watch TV and try to change my state of mind even if it's for 15 minutes. I usually stay in the dayroom until they close it for the night or if I start getting tired. Either way, 11pm is technically lights out, although we have night walkers doing laps around our rectangle shaped unit.

Unfortunately, I spend most of my time ruminating about mistakes in life, missing my kids, my divorce, my conflicting feelings about Julia, future employment and of course, existential questions that have no answers. It is possible for a person to talk themselves out of their self-confidence and leave themselves feeling that they are destined to fail at everything.

RUMINATION WARNING!

After I take my meds, I go back into the dayroom and start Watching American Ninja Warrior, an obstacle course gameshow. The contestants are in great shape and have a "carpe diem" attitude towards life. They are successful and have fulfilling lives. I then question why I am not living a successful life. At this point, successful to me is keeping my illness at a point where it's not ruining relationships with family and friends.

I am envious/jealous of those people I know that are naturally happy and have financial success. In addition, I do get hateful/angry of those who only got to that level because they inherited a family business, or their parents had great connections for them to get into college and then step into a great career two days after graduation.

Over the years I developed a high level of animosity towards former childhood friends that wouldn't consider my music, which was recorded with talented musicians. This music was geared towards video games, TV, film and radio. I had friends in all those industries. I had one friend who edits TV commercials tell me that she didn't know anyone in advertising. Huh? You edit commercials and you don't know anyone in advertising???

It seems that none of my friends would refer me to any of their business connections. I couldn't understand why; I have a music degree, I've had opera training, I've had comedy songs played on The Howard Stern Show, I can MC events, I do impressions, I play drums, I'm a very talented singer and I'm an even better mimic and I know talented people to create things that I cannot. In addition, I've performed at just about every high-end venue in the tristate area and have been a busy musician since 1989.

In or around 2015, after a get together dinner with all those friends, I sent the meanest group email that I could think of. Now mind you, to my friends I was meek, kind and never argued with anyone. This email was certainly out of character. Only one friend, who wasn't even at the dinner called me to see if I was ok; that was Jon. He knew this was unlike me to behave to this extreme. I was the funny, nice and sensitive one in our group of friends. I have since apologized to everyone. Two friends accepted my apology and said they understood that I was going through a rough time. One friend did send me nasty texts out of nowhere after she read a comment I made to another friend on social media: he was a DJ and couldn't get his close friends or family to come to his gigs. I commented that close family and friends are sometimes the least supportive of your passion because they can't see you in a new and different light that they aren't used to. So, this friend decided to continue the war of words that I thought was over. She was being mean, and I dropped the atom bomb of all insults on her and her husband: She is unable to have children, so I started ripping into her about that: I said, "Is it you that can't get pregnant or is your husband shooting blanks? Maybe you guys did too much acid and cocaine in college!" She then wrote that I crossed the line. If you invite me out of the blue to play in the mud, don't think you're not gonna get dirty.

In the original email to my high school friends, I aired my grievances and held nothing back as I ripped into them for acting like they were self-made, but really their families hooked them up and paid for everything to give them a gigantic head start in life. Some friends married into rich families and got jobs with their father in law's business.

One friend did nothing but party throughout high school and college. He literally did nothing but get lucky by marrying a rich girl. His qualifications include being able to do a bong hit and chug beer at the same time. Furthermore, to act like he is some sort of Jewish Tony Soprano made him even more animated and disturbing to be around. You can also include his cockiness and constant bragging. He was the narcissist of my group of friends.

Some therapists told me that maybe my friends couldn't see me as a professional adult because they still saw me as a neurotic teenager.

I'm starting to shake with anger and am seething. Time to change the subject: who is in here with me?

I've decided to watch some TV with a patient that I've never mentioned before, Tyronne. Tyronne has been here for 2 months and is awaiting

Section 8 housing; government paid housing. It turns out that Tyronne has been watching me as he says, "You think too much. Life is what it is, and you must accept that. You can't think too much, and you have to keep fighting." I then admitted to him that he was 100% correct and that I have been over thinking/ruminating my entire life. Tyronne told me that he was the same way as me and that it can be a constant battle. My instincts tell me that Tyronne has had it worse than me. Tyronne always has food or juice with him. He must be hoarding food in his room. In addition, I don't know if Tyronne has made improvements with his mental illness or if he is just mellow from the meds. Either way, I like his message and appreciate where he comes from.

Chapter 29: Sept 14, 2019, Jacobi 7A

Today is the day that I am supposed to be transferred to Elmhurst Hospital at noon. It is now 12:15 pm and Dr. P has come to tell me that today is the big day. He then offered me an Ativan because he could see that while I wanted to go, my face became even more pale than normal because of fear. All I have been thinking about for the last 3 days was getting out of here. It has left my nerves shot. Part of me feels like I've gone even further down the rabbit hole and this whole experience is defining what my life has become. I have to remain vigilant to the fact that this journey isn't finished yet and more help is on the way in the form of electric shock. At least this Ativan will give me some peace of mind today.

As I sit waiting to be transferred, I start to think about my parents. I have mentioned this earlier: In 1984 when I started therapy my parents knew that my uncle and grandmother both had ECT and were both schizophrenic; why did they not inform my first psychiatrist, Dr. Sabot? In addition, they knew all of this when I was 9 when my mental illness truly surfaced and never acted on it. They knew I was suffering worse than I led on because I told them I was. I asked for help. My father, who had been in therapy his whole life couldn't tell I was suffering? Having two close relatives with mental illness and getting ECT is a huge detail to not mention to a therapist. Am I wrong? If that had been mentioned, maybe these issues could have been treated differently. Maybe I should have been hospitalized back in 1984 or even in 1978.

Still, I somehow managed to graduate high school with an 83 average and got into college despite my illness. I did bomb the SAT exam due to anxiety. It's hard to take a test while holding in nervous diarrhea. Back then, a perfect score was 1600 points. I got an 890, a horrible score!!! The second time I took it, I had worse anxiety and got an 850!! I even took an SAT course twice a week and broke 1000 on their practice tests numerous times. I must have felt more comfortable at the SAT course location. It may have been because at the course location they had an unlimited supply of chocolate Twizzlers and Smarties.

Back to the present. As I'm still waiting to be transferred to Elmhurst today, two new patients arrived at 7A: Martin and Gary.

Martin is an interesting character: He told me he has Multiple Sclerosis. Martin has a very raspy voice and when he talks, it sounds like he is gargling on mouthwash. As soon as Martin got settled in, he started walking laps around the unit as he talked and sang to himself. Martin was transferred here from a homeless shelter, lives on disability (I don't judge because I get it too) and is on food stamps (me too). In December of 2019, he should be moving into Section 8 housing. Martin is excited because he will now have a few months to save money before he moves into his new place. Any kind of prejudices or preconceived notions I had about the homeless have changed by 180 degrees. Once you spend some time, meaning weeks and months on end with someone who is mentally ill and homeless, the stigma disappears, and you find the real person and the old person that they used to be trapped inside. It is heartbreaking.

Gary:

Gary happened to be my first roommate during my first stay here at Jacobi. He has returned. Gary is African American, about 6' 3" tall and is very skinny. He looks like Bill Russell, The Boston Celtics center who has 11 NBA championship rings.

In my opinion, Gary has extreme schizophrenia and multiple personality disorder. He lives in an imaginary world that is all his own. Gary is only slightly aware of the real world. Gary talks to different people in his head and even has different voices that he uses for each person that answers him back. Gary is a one-man act. He does most of his talking in the middle of the night as he stands near the shelves that hold his belongings. As he talks, he has a deck of cards that he likes to shuffle at the same time. He would ask a question in his own voice, "Did you see what happened over there?" and then answer with a completely different voice like he was Mel Blanc from The Looney Tunes, "Yeah, I see what is happening. They are doing drugs". Other conversations involve drugs and women's breasts (which would make me laugh as a laid there in the dark watching and listening). Gary does not and has never talked to me. I say hello. Either he doesn't understand, doesn't know I'm real or he just doesn't want to talk to me or anybody. When Gary does sleep, he farts, a lot. Luckily it stayed in his Dutch oven most of the time. Occasionally, the odor would waft over my way and I would either cover my head with my blanket or breathe from my mouth. Gary would sleep all day and only come out for food and meds. He was also very neat and clean. He would shower at least 3 times a day. It's better than Dijon who would shit the bed.

Chapter 30: Oct 2, 2019, Elmhurst Hospital, Psychiatric Ward, Queens, NY

I have been at Elmhurst Hospital for about 2 weeks and have done about 6 sessions of ECT. The preparation a patient undergoes for ECT is simple: an IV gets hooked up, they start the anesthesia drip and I fall asleep after about 20 seconds. I must say, the 20 seconds of anesthesia you feel before you fall asleep is blissful. No wonder people do heroine. Anyway, after you fall asleep, the medical staff puts the electrodes on your head, put a bite guard in your mouth and shock you with 12 volts of electricity that causes mini seizures that are supposed to stimulate your brain to a level where you are less depressed than before. In addition, the seizures do not cause violent convulsions like in the movies. Medical technology has improved to where the actual procedure is not scary. However, you still feel like a slab of meat or science project.

After 6 sessions, I can't honestly say whether I feel any different. I most definitely didn't expect to be cured overnight as well. I do feel a little clearer in terms of not feeling as much like a zombie lately.

Chapter 31: Music

The one thing that I am forever grateful to my brother for is giving me my introduction to hard rock, heavy metal and progressive music. My brother loved big speakers and was always being yelled at by my dad to turn it down.

By the age of 6, I knew that I could sing and play drums. I could picture in my head what the drummer was doing and was able to copy the parts as I used oversized chopsticks to bang on my desk and pillows.

The first band that did it for me was KISS: My classmate in the first grade brought KISS Alive 1 to class for everyone to listen to (his dad was the original Tony in West Side Story). Anyway, I got my turn to listen to KISS for the first time on headphones. This was my first profound moment with music and planted the seed for what I wanted to do in life. The first KISS song I heard that day was Cold Gin. As I listened, I stared at the album cover and the picture magazine that came with it. I was in awe: 4 guys in makeup and crazy costumes. To me they were beyond human. After that day in 1975, all I wanted was KISS until 1978. It was in February of 1978 that THE most important day of music happened for me. I was brought to a place where a band literally took away my anxiety, fear, worry, sadness and made me feel primal and alive for the first time in my life. That was the day my brother brought home Van Halen 1 the week that it came out.

On the back of Van Halen 1 is a short thank you to Gene Simmons of KISS. Gene Simmons helped Van Halen record a demo that eventually got them signed to Warner Brother Records. Anyway, there was a rumor that Van Halen was KISS without make up and that they wanted a 2nd band so that they didn't have to wear the make-up. However, once my brother put on side 1 and Running With the Devil came on, I knew that this was not KISS. I was hooked before the first chorus. I hadn't even heard Eddie Van Halen solo yet on the song. Between the guitar riff and David Lee Roth's screams in the introduction, I became immediately affected. The 2nd song is Eruption, Eddie Van Halen's most famous guitar solo and probably the most famous guitar solo ever. I also figured rather quickly that this was not Ace Frehley. I love Ace and always will, but this was a being from another stratosphere. I knew Eruption was played on guitar, I just never heard anything like that before.

Soon after listening to Van Halen 1, my brother decided he had enough of me for the day and kicked me out of his room.

When I asked my mother to buy me the Van Halen album, she said no because my brother already had a copy and that we should share. Sharing never happened, only humiliating beatings and teasing.

 I was left with my brother playing his music loud and I was able to learn the music of Van Halen, Rush (mostly Rush), Yes, Black Sabbath, Iron Maiden, Judas Priest, ELP, Molly Hatchet, etc…but it was Van Halen that I wanted to hear. I was too young to find them on the radio and there were never any concerts on TV (no MTV yet). So, I was at the mercy of my brother's mood for when he wanted to listen to Van Halen. Also, I think I may have been the first 8-year-old in history to know the song Karn Evil 9- 2nd Impression by Emerson, Lake and Palmer. That's the song with the lyric, "Welcome back my friends to the show that never ends……."

At the end of the summer of 1982, MTV became available on Long Island, and we finally got it. When MTV started in 1981, most bands did not have music videos and would submit their live performances for content. At this point, the closest thing to seeing anything live from Van Halen was just from pictures in rock magazines.

Then it happened; it was August of 1982 and I just got home from sleepaway camp. Van Halen's album Diver Down was very popular, but it's the album Fair Warning that is the masterpiece. That album came out in 1981 and featured the song, Unchained; THE song that sets me free emotionally. Anyway, like I said, it was one of the first weeks we had MTV and finally I saw the infamous video for Unchained live from the Oakland Coliseum on June 12, 1981. This was the first time I was ever seeing a video of Van Halen. The video starts out with the greatest riff ever as David Lee Roth stands on the drum riser and yells, "Everybody up!". As the drums and bass come in, David Lee Roth jumps off the drum riser and does a perfect split and lands on his feet. They were like nothing I had ever seen. The stage presence and charisma that all 4 members had blew away every band in the world. Van Halen is famous for making

Black Sabbath look like fools when they opened for them in 1978.

After seeing Unchained, I knew I wanted to be a part of that. I wanted to be a part of them. My bedroom became a Van Halen temple with posters and pictures covering every inch of every wall, literally. I couldn't wait to get home each day after school and escape into my room and play my Van Halen albums. I would play them in order; however, the album Fair Warning is the music that saved my life. They gave me hope, energy, laughs and of course listening to the greatest guitarist of all time and watching the greatest front man of all time.

 At that time, I knew I could sing and drum but had no drum kit and didn't know any kids who wanted to be in a band. When I was 17, my parents finally rented me a drum set and offered me lessons after I had been asking since I was 6. I took the kit but didn't want lessons. When I got the drum kit home and set it up, I started playing it; and I played it well. My mother couldn't understand how I knew how to play. I was born with it, but my parents already knew that and never guided me in that direction. My brother took guitar lessons and quit after 2 years. My parents told me that they thought I would quit as well which was why they never got me lessons. So, I did it on my own.

During high school, the only thing that mattered to me was Van Halen. They were keeping me alive. On March 30, 1984, I got to see them at MSG. I remember most of the show. I was 14 and I said to myself that one day I would be on stage like David Lee Roth, in great shape, long hair, shirtless and the girls would scream for my band.

By age 20, a little less than 6 years after seeing Van Halen in concert, I was singing for a band and sold out a 300-seat movie theater. It would be my third or fourth time on stage as a singer. At that show, I was in amazing shape, my hair was getting nice and long, I wore ripped jeans and for most of the show, my shirt was off. And yes, the girls screamed, and they screamed loud. Another part of my wanting to be on stage was to prove to an ex-girlfriend that I was special. Now suddenly, dozens of girls wanted to sleep with me and the band. In the later chapters I discuss in detail about being treated like a non-famous rock star with anxiety disorder.

Chapter 32: Oct 2, 2019, Elmhurst Hospital, Queens, NY

RUMINATION WARNING!

If my pets' heads were falling off, I'd be the 3rd lead in Dumb and Dumber. I really have zero idea of what I'm going to do next. I get too many ideas at once; I then get overwhelmed and go back to having no ideas. I know that the one thing I'll have to do is post hospital care. I'm not up for spending all day in a hospital and then going home at night. I need to start working immediately.

Given the way my teaching career ended, it leaves people curious of why I retired 5 years early. In this world, You are guilty until you are proven innocent. I keep thinking about that all I had to do was let the girls cut class. All I had to do was not care. That split decision changed my life. I keep going over all the details like the fact that there are no lockers in the school to throw people into, the dean and security guard were standing there, there was nothing on video from the school's video camera and from any camera from the 150 to 200 students that were travelling to their 2nd period class. I keep thinking about my 2nd disciplinary hearing where it was apparent that the Department of Education was going after my job. So, like a scared moron, I retired, not realizing that I would be getting less of a pension because I did the arithmetic incorrectly. I was also afraid that if I got fired, I would lose my pension. I've gotten conflicting facts of whether that really happens or not. I know I wrote about this a few times earlier, but this is what rumination is like. It's exhausting to think about, write and read about. I feel like telling myself to shut the fuck up already.

What I should have done was to keep my reassignment at the district office with full pay and wait to see how my final disciplinary hearing would go. I should have been brave and stuck up for myself. I felt I saw the writing on the wall: Getting rid of an older teacher by accusing him of corporal punishment is more economical for the school because my salary equals the starting salary of just about 3 recent college graduates who have yet to earn their master's degree and can be hired at a lower salary. The school would be saving money by getting rid of me. Especially a gym teacher. We are a dime a dozen. Good academic teachers are hard to find.

Like I said, I've seen it happen before and have had many conversations with my former union representative and friend who knows about other cases of teachers that went through the same thing that I went through.

So, here I am in the psychiatric Ward at Elmhurst Hospital and it's been just about 5 months since I've been hospitalized. I have been to 4 different hospitals since April of 2019. To make matters worse, my father passed away in April of 2019, just over a month shy of being married to my mom for 60 years. During those crazy months in the Spring, I still wanted to do something outrageous for my parents like call the news and have them do a story about a couple being married for 60 years. That's rare these days because the divorce rate is currently at about 70%.

Chapter 33: October 3rd, 2019, Elmhurst Hospital, Queens, New York

Today has been a horrible day of way too much thinking about the future and what I'm going to do about money to live and help raise my kids and be a great father. What happened to me?

Everything today is hitting me harder than usual. Maybe it's because I'm in yet another hospital and this nightmare doesn't seem to have an end in sight.

My parents, while giving me love, didn't prepare me to be anything. They never pushed me in one direction or to strive in some sort of profession like being an attorney, stockbroker or even a psychologist. They knew I liked music, so they rented me that drum kit and they figured that was it. I just existed.

I can honestly say and with a sad heart that my father was a lazy man or terribly ill who got lucky with the job he had for most of his adult life. Like I stated earlier, his job was selling advertising for a fashion trade newspaper. My father claimed there wasn't much to do in his office. If advertising orders came in, the secretary would take them, process them and basically do the jobs of all the advertising salesmen. So, these guys and my dad barely showed up for work. My father's behavior and attitude showed that he didn't like to work. Each morning I could hear him in the bathroom having diarrhea and passing gas and attributed it to him being anxious about going to work.

I looked back on my relationship with my father with mixed emotions: On one hand, he was loving, funny and generous to a fault when money was good. He put me through college, I grew up in a nice house and had my own bedroom. We spent a lot of time together playing sports and he took me to tons of basketball and hockey games at MSG.

The other side of my dad was obviously his mental illness and showing fear most of the time. My father never taught me to be brave or tough. I learned from his behavior to be afraid of just about everything. So, I grew up afraid and what I thought was lazy. That's not a very good combination.

Chapter 34: Being a Musician

Like I talked about in earlier journal entries, the one thing that saves me or saved me from anxiety is music. I'm a singing drummer, and in college I was singing in a band that had some interest from John Bon Jovi's distant cousin, Tony, who owned a famous recording studio in Manhattan called The Power Station. We were slated to do a demo with Tony Bongiovi (the real spelling of their name), and he was going to work with us and help us improve our songs, my singing and songwriting. In addition, we also had some interest from the road manager of Metallica. This was in March of 1990 and Metallica's album, And Justice for All was doing great on MTV and The Billboard Charts.

 I knew that the music that we wrote was good enough for a record deal. However, I knew that deep down inside that my voice was not developed yet, and these were my first attempts at writing lyrics and melodies. The trick is to be original and different. You can't try to be different; it just has to happen organically.

In addition, we also had some interest from an artist and repertoire assistant from PolyGram records. She had attended one of our shows, which was the theatre that our band sold out.

The interest in our band stopped immediately the day that radio stations started playing Nirvana, Pearl Jam, Soundgarden and my favorite of all the Seattle bands, Alice in Chains.

 My college professor who had hooked us up with all these connections was the one who broke the news to me in her office after she got off the phone with Tony Bongiovi. I asked, "No more Tony Bongiovi?", She said "Correct", I said, "No more

Walter O'Brien, the road manager for Metallica?", She said, "Correct". I then asked, "Everybody went to Seattle, right? ", She answered, "Yup, there is a major music scene going on there". Indeed, there was. Within two weeks, the music industry turned upside down. All the hairbands like Poison, Motley Crue, Warrant, Skid Row, Def Leppard etc. were all pushed to the side because that type of rock music got saturated very quickly with bands that were just copying each other. Something new was desperately needed. While at the same time I was extremely disappointed that we weren't going to get the chance to develop ourselves with a professional producer, I was excited about how these bands from Seattle sounded. Most of the bands had vocalists who were baritones, which was my natural range. The bands that we were trying to sound like had singers who were tenors which made it difficult for me because I was straining quite a bit to hit higher notes. When I heard singers like Eddie Vedder and Layne Staley, I became inspired by the fact that singers with low voices were now popular. My problem was, I wasn't different, and I wasn't original. My singing voice is technically very good. However, that does not automatically translate into writing songs that are different from everything else.

Our music was good enough because our guitarist Darren, was a guitar prodigy. I met him when he was 17 and I was 20. He was from Oneonta, New York, where I was going to college. I had just switched my major to Music Industry when I met Darren and joined his band. Darren had won many national music competitions and acknowledgements from the press. When you start playing music with a person of that caliber, it was very easy to think that we would get signed someday. When I saw Darren play for the first time, it didn't seem real. I never saw a person play guitar AND piano like that up close. He was something out of Masterpiece Theater. The rest of the band consisted of Darren's cousin Shane, who played rhythm guitar, Tim the bassist and Rob the drummer. Darren, Rob and Shane were still in high school, and Tim was 21 at the time and worked at McDonald's next to The Southside Mall in Oneonta.

One day when Tim was working at McDonald's, a man came into the restaurant, pulled out a shotgun and pointed it 6 inches from Tim's face. The man demanded all the money in the cash register. Tim managed to stay calm and survived the robbery, however it messed him up for a while.

The other 4 members of the band lived in or near Oneonta. I was the "mysterious singer" from the city to all the teenagers in the surrounding towns that followed Darren and rest of the guys from their old bands. The greatest part about being in this band was the bond we formed.

When I joined the band, it was an exciting time. We called the band Vicious Angel. I wanted to call the band Amethyst, because I think it's a beautiful crystal, the name sounds cool, and there's a lot you can do visually with purple crystals. However, the guys in the band thought the name was too heavy for the type of music we were writing and playing. We were a combination of Van Halen and Bon Jovi. We weren't particularly glammed out.

Our usual stage clothes consisted of ripped jeans and T shirts. Visually, the goal I had for myself was to be in great physical shape, take off my shirt on stage and get as primal as I could. Before each gig, I would tell myself to be as confident as David Lee Roth even if I didn't feel that way deep inside. However, when I would get in front of people, I would become calm without trying. This was the reality I had been searching for. Every aspect about being in a band was exciting and kept me driven. I loved rehearsing, writing, making flyers for the band, promoting shows, playing shows and even carrying equipment.

This proved to be one of the most exciting times in my life. We were very popular in Oneonta and among the surrounding towns and counties of upstate New York. Once we started to get popular, I began to really believe that music could be my profession. My goal of achieving some sort of peace of mind was starting to come true at some level. On any given day I could be driving in my car and our songs would be playing on the local radio stations and the college radio station.

I also started to receive attention from women like I never had before. My theory was to grow my hair, lift weights and sing in a band with my shirt off; and that would be a good way of attracting women. Little did I know that it would work. On one hand when you are a 20-year-old man with a high libido and women are throwing themselves at you it's something that you can't resist. On the other hand, when you are a person who suffers from severe anxiety, depression and then you add on the AIDS epidemic at the time, sleeping with women would cause anxiety attacks that would last for days on end. I would wonder who else these girls have slept with and that I would catch AIDS. It was a double-edged sword; I wanted to get laid but it scared the shit out of me afterward.

While the band won every music competition we entered, we would also receive fan mail, six packs of beer constantly being left at my front door with a red ribbon on top, articles in regional newspapers, being followed by girls in public and like I said, airplay on local radio. I never developed an ego about it. I don't know if it was because I had low self-esteem or because my goals were not ego driven; it was for emotional stability. However, it is nice when you get off stage and immediately a girl tells you how much she wants to fuck you; and in less than 5 minutes you're fucking.

While at college I never had a steady girlfriend. It was partly because I wanted to sleep with as many women as I could even though it caused anxiety a good majority of the time. At the time, I wanted new experiences to make up for my depressed high school years. In addition, I was still deeply in love with my high school girlfriend, and I wasn't letting myself open up to someone new. There was one girl, Stacey, who I let get away.

Anyway, my career in music never really took off in terms of being an original artist, however, I managed to stay busy and have fun for the better part of 30 years. Like I've stated before I've played in front of 0 people, and I've played in front of 12,000.

I was also in some interesting bands; an Italian wedding band, and a reggae band for 7 years as a drummer and was in cover bands that were managed by the top booking agency on Long Island. We played all the top venues and clubs in Nassau County, Suffolk County and all those crazy clubs on the beach in The Hamptons and Montauk. Lots of steroids and vodka mixed with Red Bull in those club crowds.

After I had my car accident in 2013 and subsequent back surgery in April of 2018, I lost interest in doing the one thing that I loved the most, and that was playing music. Not only did I stop performing, but I also stopped playing and practicing on my own as well. I was under the notion that I was older and didn't want to be a middle-aged man trying to hold on to his youth and perform on stage with my gut shaking around under my shirt. Some people call this "dad rock".

 The only interest that I really have with music would be to record instrumental music for TV, movies and radio. I would also still like to do voice overs. Having a hit song is not important to me nor is it very realistic. I get great joy in going to a studio and being creative, it's just as good as performing in front of an audience. Who knows what the future will bring in terms of making music for a project or just sitting at home and playing for my own joy and relaxation.

RUMINATION WARNING

 While writing about music my train of thought gets interrupted because suddenly, I got a huge anxiety attack, and my fear of the future is somehow amplified to levels like I have never felt before. I wish I felt as strong as all the staff here tell me that they think I am. Right now, it's about 3:00 p.m. and the adrenaline is pumping hard. I feel like I don't want to live and that I won't survive in the real world. I then start to pace the hallway waiting for an Ativan to give me some relief from all this. I spoke to the social worker earlier and he tried to give me deep breathing exercises to do. I have had 8 sessions of ECT and I think this huge anxiety attack is happening because of the sessions. I was told that there would be periods of adjusting to the treatment. Sometimes you have to feel worse in order to start feeling better. I'm choosing to look at this panic attack as my body purging negative thoughts and experiences.

I decided to go to my room to ride this episode out. My roommate is in bed, and he is crying. I don't know what he is crying about but it's just adding to the madness that I'm experiencing. He is a nice man and is from India. He has a very thick accent so it's hard to understand what he's saying. When he talks, I just nod my head in agreement, and it usually goes smooth. I can't take his crying, so I decide to go into the hallway which is very busy and loud.

 A part of me has learned that these negative thoughts are just that, thoughts. In addition, you can't stop them from happening. When you try to fight them from happening, you wind up feeling worse. The best thing to do is ride the wave of these negative thoughts until they subside and start to understand that it's a process. Once you can give your thoughts a label or an identity, it's easier to align them in your brain so that you can get a mental picture of how to navigate your

thought process. This doesn't mean that you're never going to have bad days and that your anxiety or whatever your mental illness is, will go away. I believe I've said it before; there is no cure there is only learning to live with it and keep it at a level as low as possible.

HALFTIME BREAK!!!
Various Photographs

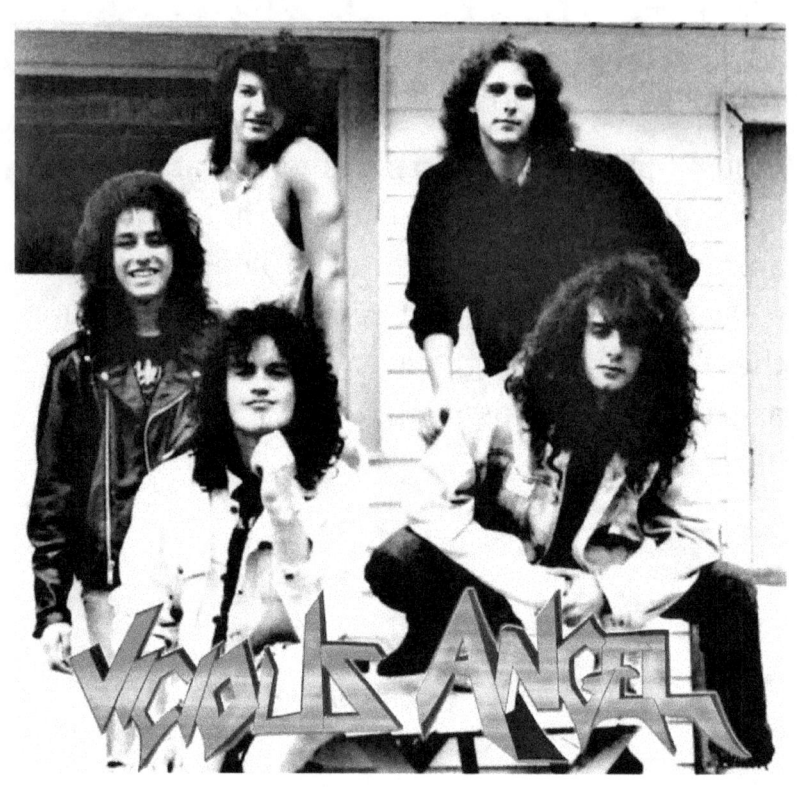

Band Promo Shot Spring 1990

Darren Wilsey and I at Polygram Records, May 24, 1990

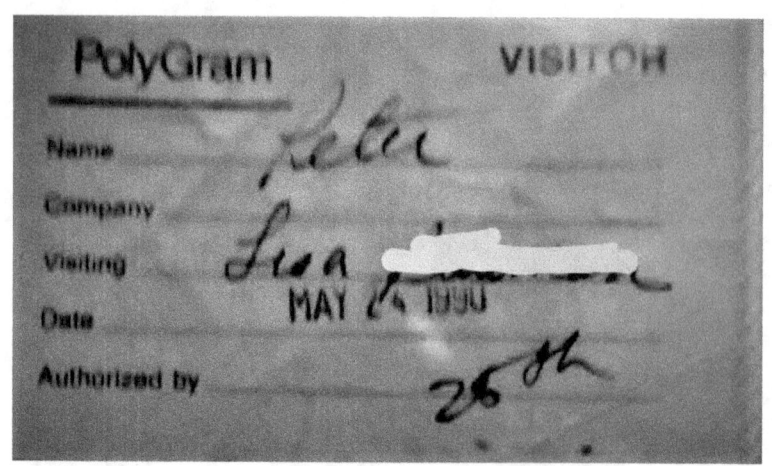

Polygram Records Visitor Pass

June 10th, 1990, Oneonta Theater, SOLD OUT!

April 1991, Oneonta Theater Show #2, SOLD OUT!

My band, Purple Bejesus 1994

NY Islanders Band Pass

Band Promo Headshot 1993

Drumming in Fall of 2017

I was a child model from 1976-1980

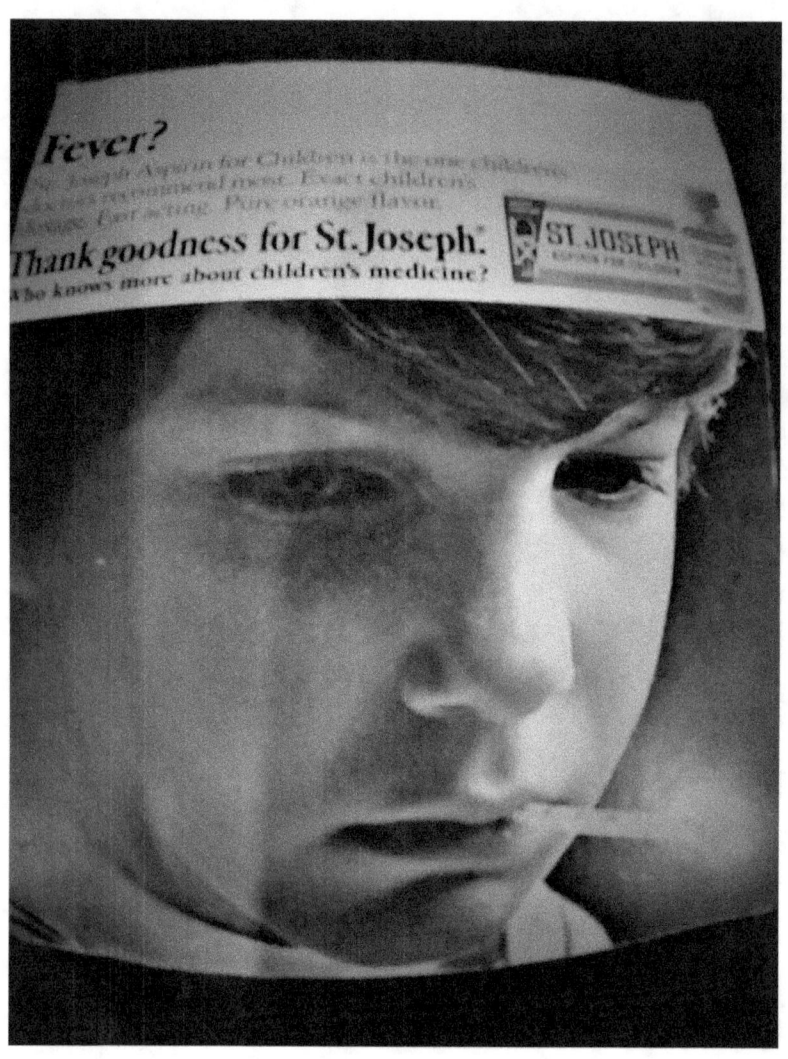

My first job!

Burger King Playhouse Promo Poster (displayed at every BK in the USA)

Donny and Marie Osmond Record Player, Circa 1977

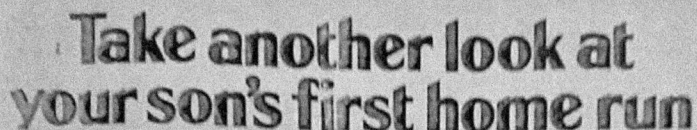

Ad for JVC's first ever "portable video camera"

Fall 1988, SUNY Oneonta Lacrosse Goalie

My Grandfather Lewey and I

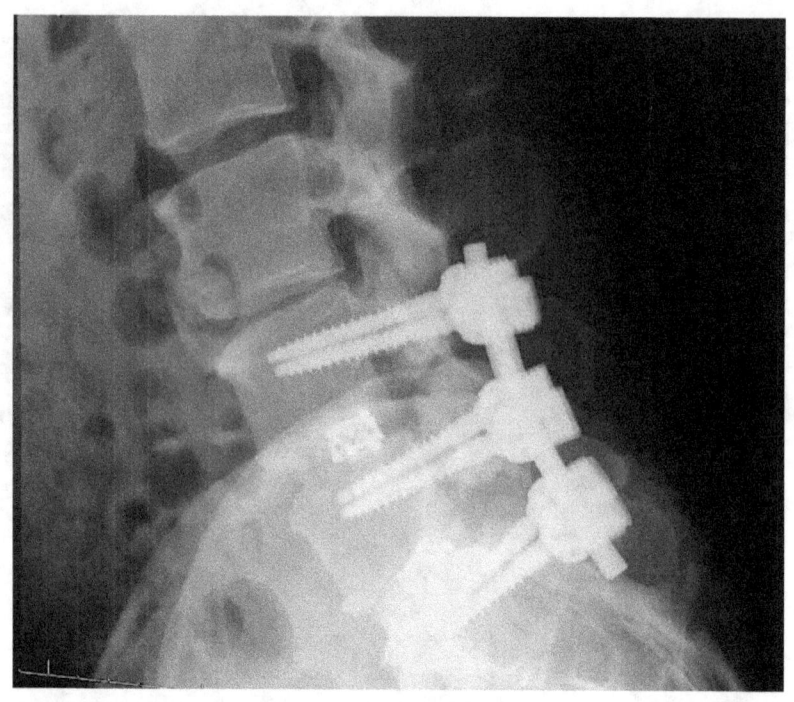

X Ray of my Lumbar Spine hardware, post-surgery, May 2018

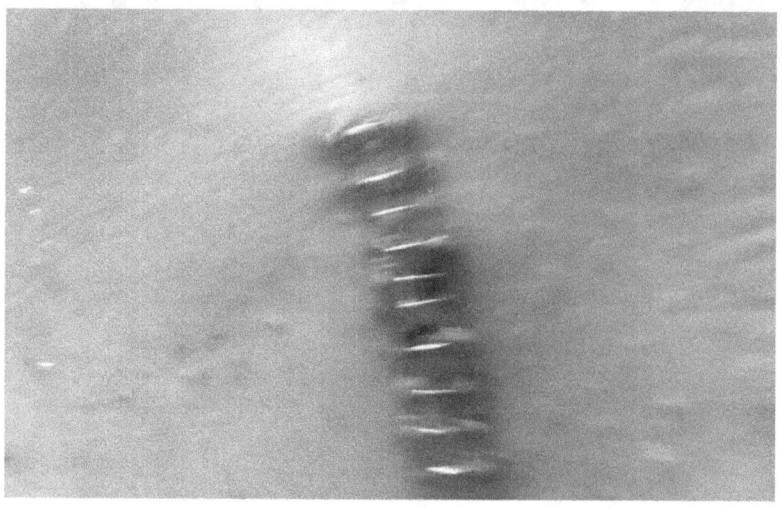

The staples that closed my surgery incision: 33 total

My old job location: Inappropriate gymnasium conditions. classes were still being held in the gym while old bleachers were slowly removed over a 2-week period. Circa Spring 2019.

More bleacher removal left incomplete; classes still held in gymnasium regardless.

Bleacher separation from gym wall. This was left like for at least 2 years.

My work partner's intraschool phone. Finally fixed after almost 7 years of requests.

Broken gymnasium dividing door. Very big safety hazard. Was still broken as of May 2019.

Loose wood panels and double wood beams starting to lean.

Exposed wires. I was told there were not live. It still needs fixing. Unprofessional.

More exposure to electrical system.

Construction sign for Polychlorinated Biphenyls (PCB) removal that we were told did not exist. Summer 2008

PCB removal in the "arcade" of the school. Summer 2008

PCB removal at school's main entrance, Summer 2008

The home I owned with Julia

Backyard of home. The Cherry Blossom tree is on the left.

Living room of house.

Kitchen

Samples of Original Artwork from Psychiatric Hospitals:

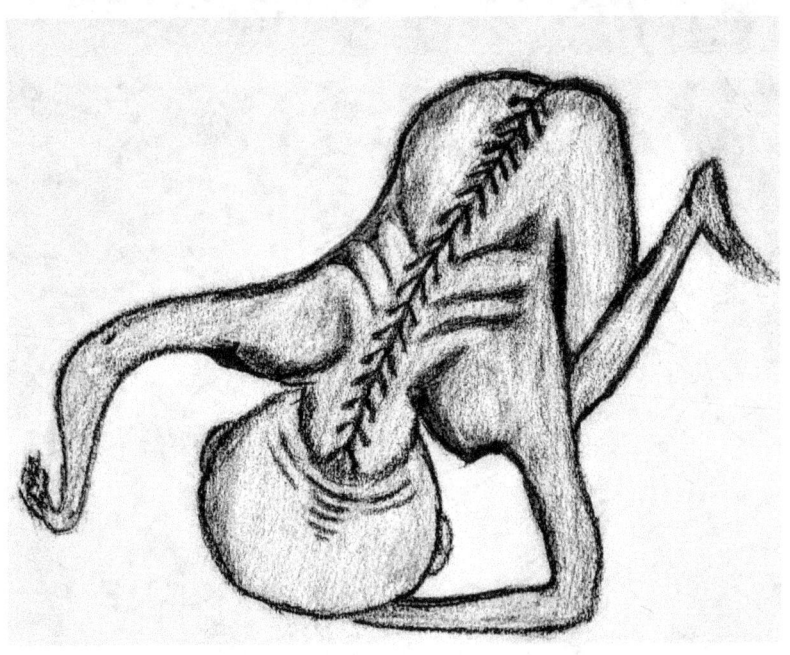

Sorry! No more pictures!

Start of the 2nd Half

Chapter 35: The Psychiatric Ward at Elmhurst Hospital, Queens, NY

The psychiatric ward at Elmhurst Hospital occupies two floors or more. On the floor I'm on, which I don't know, along with the ward name, is one hallway that is about 40 to 50 yards long. Each room is set up for 2 people and has a bathroom with a shower, toilet, and sink.

In the middle of the hallway is the nurse's station and the medication station. Across from that is the day room where we eat, watch TV, and have our groups. This unit is very small, so it makes you feel a bit claustrophobic.

When I do walk the hallway there is an Asian man who walks too who wears a knit hat and a hoodie.

Every time we pass each other, we do fist bumps. It's amazing how something so simple as a fist bump can make you feel connected to a person. And it's also something to cherish while you're locked up because of all the loneliness that you feel most of the time even though you are surrounded by people all day.

Well, I just took my Ativan and now I'm deciding whether to lay in bed or sit and write. I guess I'll sit and write. What does one do when feel trapped on the edge? I'm sitting in the dayroom. There are 3 other patients in here. It's a little cold in here. I was told that hospitals are kept on the cold side so that bacteria and germs can't spread as easily as they would in a warm and humid environment.

As I sit here writing and watch channel 7 (ABC) I'm forced to watch General Hospital. If there's one type of show that I dislike the most is daytime soap operas. The old nighttime soap operas like Dallas and Dynasty were awesome. Daytime soap operas are just terrible. Until today, I had no clue that General Hospital was still on the air along with The Young and the Restless. None of them are young and they're too old to be restless. They have the same actors as they did when I was a kid.

I'd love to lay down and sleep, but then I have to wake up and realize where I am and start that whole cycle of rumination all over again.

I'm not particularly scared of being alone, it's the heaviness and sadness of being alone that causes heartache. When you are alone and you have depression and anxiety it takes extra effort to get out of bed, wash yourself, go to work, make money, take care of your kids and do things that are good for your health.

When you're amid a terrible anxiety attack it feels like it will never end. There is a part of you that knows that it will eventually end, but the anxiety beats that rational thought to a pulp at times. You still have to ride that wave in order to survive.

While in the day room today I was sitting at a table with an older woman named Lucille. She is a patient here. Lucille is older and reminds me of Penny Marshall in the way that she looks and the way that she talks with that thick Brooklyn accent. Unlike Penny Marshall, Lucille has constant thoughts of killing her mother with a knife. She says she feels guilty about wanting to kill her mother because she loves her mother. That's quite the paradox. She also feels that God will punish her if she does kill her mother. There's a pretty good chance he will if she kills her mother. Lucille said she went against God, and now God is punishing her because she is here at Elmhurst. Lucille is doing a word search and is asking me questions about shock treatment at the same time. Lucille also told me it's the voices in her head telling her to kill her mother.

At this point at my stay at several hospitals and meeting quite a few people that suffer from schizophrenia and I've learned a few things about the disease: Some people have schizophrenia where they hallucinate, see people, animals or monsters that don't really exist. In addition, they hear voices in their head. Severe schizophrenics don't know that these hallucinations and voices are not real. This will cause them to be violent, anxious, depressed and suicidal.

Other people that I've met with schizophrenia hear the voices in their heads, hallucinate and they know that none of it is real. However, even though that they know they have schizophrenia, and they understand what it is; it doesn't stop them from suffering.

After talking about the different ways that we can kill Lucille's mother, the conversation gets livelier thanks to the BHA, named Chandler.

Sometimes you meet a person in your life that you know that you should be listening to everything that they say because everything they say is important and is meant to help you. Chandler is this type of guy; he has the wisdom of 1000 lifetimes. Today's conversation with Chandler is not so deep and was mostly about nostalgia and the TV shows and comedians that we watched as children. Because Chandler and I are the same age, I feel a great connection to him.

I'm in a good mood right now because I had fun talking to Chandler and I even had fun talking about killing Lucille's mother because we started goofing about it and I was able to make her laugh. Making people laugh puts me in a good mood and Lucille is a pisser. I like hearing her talk. I feel like I'm on an episode of Laverne and Shirley every time we have a conversation. Should I be Lenny, Squiggy or Boo Boo Kitty?

I don't want my good mood to become manic because when you become manic your energy level shoots to the sky like you just snorted a giant mountain of cocaine like the one Al Pacino snorts in Scarface. Your energy level shoots sky high and then you crash. When you crash, you end up lower from where you started in terms of your mood level. That's exactly what cocaine does, and it is why people get addicted to it because they want to stay "up".

Cocaine was a drug I tried once and was never interested in doing it again. I was in high school, and I stayed up all night doing lines and talking about music and cats. I woke up the next morning with a bloody nose and a large case of guilt. After that I never touched it again.

Like I feared, I just crashed from my good mood and start to ruminate about Julia and how she is with somebody else and has created a family around him with my children. When we were married and would have arguments, Julia would threaten to leave me and take the children. I believe that after we had our twins and before she got pregnant with our 3rd son, she had already made up her mind that she wanted to eventually leave me. Many mental health professionals will say that women make up their minds about leaving their husbands about a year before it happens and then they start to grieve the marriage as it starts to deteriorate. As the marriage starts to deteriorate, all the positive aspects of your marriage start to disappear one by one including: sex, friendship, emotional support, sticking up for one another, working as a team and raising the kids together. I believe that this is a passive aggressive tactic used so that the other person eventually snaps because they have been cut off emotionally. The person that is being cut off is then looked at as the person that instigated the divorce.

Chapter 36: October 07, 2019, Elmhurst Hospital Queens, New York

Today is Monday, and I had a horrible weekend that was filled with anxiety and fear. I feel extra anxious today after my 9th ECT treatment. The nurses gave me my favorite pill, Ativan, to take off the edge. In addition to making me feel relaxed and calm, Ativan takes away my suicidal thoughts. Eventually I will be taken off it. Today more than most days, my thoughts of doom and gloom are hitting me hard right now. I don't wish I was dead, it's more that I want to be in that coma that I had mentioned in the earlier chapters; warm, peaceful and safe.

Today I also met with my new psychologist, Dr. C. He is a good therapist and is very nice. He also notices right away that I have a lot on my plate. He wants me to handle one thing at a time and not ruminate so much on what kind of job I will get. I can't control that while in the hospital.

Dr. C says treating anxiety is possible but it's a long journey and takes hard work and that I won't be able to solve everything at once. If you overwhelm yourself with trying to solve everything at once, you make your mental illness even worse.

The Ativan has worn off! Hello fear! Hello anxiety! Hello sadness! Hello Julia with your boyfriend and my sons!

On an interesting note, we have a patient named Mr. R who is a Latino man that looks like a heavy George Lopez. R stays up all night and squawks like a bird. He does this while walking up-and down the hallway, keeping everyone awake; just like Barry did at Jacobi! Yesterday he needed the needle to knock him out because he was out of control, being loud and starting to get violent.

At dinner, Mr. R had just woken up a few minutes earlier and was still falling asleep in his food tray.

Mr. R also likes to invade people's personal space as well. In addition, last night at 3:15 a.m. he was looking for paper, so he started knocking at everyone's door asking for paper.

When Mr. R does act up, he likes to do it at meals. He shovels his food in his mouth which reminds me of John Belushi in the cafeteria scene from Animal House where his character, Bluto, is shoving entire hamburgers in his mouth and stealing food. Belushi was also great at raising one eyebrow to show he was about to do something mischievous.

As Mr. R eats, he insults the staff. After he eats, he then walks up-and-down the hallway and crows like a rooster in some sort of ritual. Mr. R is in rare form tonight and I wouldn't be surprised if he got a second needle. Sometimes I wouldn't mind getting the needle just to see what it feels like. It's got to feel great on some sort of level. Knowing me, I would like it too much.

Chapter 37: Oct 8, 2019, Elmhurst Hospital, Psychiatric Ward

I just met with doctor C again. I'm having a rough day today. I ruminate about that there will never be an escape from anxiety and depression. The one major issue that I have mentioned numerous times is getting out of bed in the morning and not being able to start the day without it feeling like that it is an impossible task. I've mentioned before that my anxiety attacks come with vomiting, having the dry heaves and spitting up bile. If mental illness has a taste, it's stomach bile. I'm surprised that at my age and how long I've been getting sick every morning, that I haven't given myself a stomach ulcer or any intestinal disorders.

I've decided to take my notebook with me and sit in the day room where we have open group. Open group is where we get to listen to music, play cards, read the newspaper, talk to each other or write down thoughts.

 As I sit here in the dayroom, a new patient gets admitted to our ward; his name is Victor. Victor is about 22 and is Latino and either doesn't speak English or he is unable to speak. Victor has the word DEAD tattooed on his fingers: The tattoos are on his left hand and each letter from the word "dead" starts on his left pointer finger and ends at his pinky, leaving his thumb blank. So, when he makes a fist, you see the word "dead".

As I fight for a change of thought, I contemplate how hard making changes in life can be for people. How did I get this so far gone? I'm distracted right now because there is salsa music playing and a few people are dancing. It makes me think of Julia and how much she likes salsa dancing. You would think that by me being a musician and a singer that I wouldn't feel self-conscious about dancing on a crowded dance floor where nobody is paying attention to me. However, I don't feel that I'm a good dancer and when I do dance, I feel like everybody's watching me and making fun of me. I can't help but think that if I fought harder to put that silly idiosyncrasy aside, it would have been a piece of the puzzle that would have helped fixed my marriage. I also should not forget what she did that caused to the marriage to fail.

Once again, my stomach is empty because I skipped breakfast. I was stupid and stayed in bed. When you repeat the same behaviors repeatedly with no change, that is the definition of insanity. That old adage still rings true. Fear kept me in bed this morning. I kept letting it win. I must remember that it is just one part of me and that I have a lot to offer the world. However, when you're in a deep hole like this, it feels impossible to get out of. I feel like crying right now, so I will. I miss my kids and I miss my old life. I had a house, a wife, and was living the American dream. I know I was no angel in the marriage. There was the pot smoking and the infidelity during our last month of marriage that she doesn't know about, until now if she is reading this.

I have thoughts about infidelity, what it means and what it does to the person that commits it (I discuss my feelings about it in a later chapter).

Like I talked about in the earlier chapters, Julia told me she was molested as a child by her older brother.

I read in graduate school that victims of sexual abuse go in one of two directions: they either wind up living a very sexually promiscuous lifestyle and have trouble keeping relationships or they become the opposite and sex probably reminds them of the times that they were abused. Thus, having sex can be traumatic. There are also a bunch of behavioral disorders that can develop because of sexual abuse. In terms of Julia, in my opinion, she became a narcissist who must have things her way, be in charge and wants to be constantly praised. It's either her way or the highway. I feel she is obsessive compulsive about cleanliness, has anger issues and is a functioning alcoholic. I have recordings of my sons saying that Julia had been too drunk on more than one occasion to give them baths. In addition, I believe she is always manipulating or planning ways to take advantage of people over the most minute and mundane things. Also, like I shared earlier, Julia would take out her displaced anger on me and would expect me to take that verbal abuse daily.

Sometimes Julia would get violent: One occasion, which I witnessed, was when we were driving in Queens to visit my parents. We were on the exit ramp to get off the highway. The exit ramp had traffic and was moving slow. So, Julia was driving the car slow. An older woman who was about 60 years of age was in the car behind us and didn't like that we were going slow and pacing with the traffic in front of us so that we didn't have to stop and go constantly. When the traffic on the exit ramp came to a standstill and we had to stop, the woman behind us bumped us with her car on purpose. Julia then got out of the car and started to shake the woman's driver side window which was open about halfway as she screamed at the woman. Then Julia smacked the woman in the back of the head with an open hand and knocked off her hat. I was completely shocked that she did that and at that point started to question whether being with her was a good idea or not.

Another violent incident that occurred was when Julia was driving on the main road near our home in Nassau County. According to what Julia told me, a man in a black BMW cut off a landscaping truck which then swerved and almost hit Julia. Julia then raced after the BMW, pulled in front of him and stopped short, causing the BMW to stop. The man got out of his car and so did Julia. She told me she started to yell at him and then punched him in the face.

The last incident that I will mention is the most troubling: One day I was picking up my sons from school. My youngest son who was about 7 at the time met me in the main hallway first. He was crying. I asked him what was wrong. He answered, "I got a zero on my homework because I forgot to do it and I don't want mommy to hit me AGAIN!" As I processed what he said, the principal of their school came out of his office and asked my son what he just said. He heard it loud and clear because his office is adjacent to the main hallway. My son repeated that he had gotten a zero for no homework and that Julia smacked him in the head before for the same reason. The principal then asked to speak to me in his office. He told me that he had to call Child Protective Services because he heard a child claim to be abused. I told him to do what he had to do.

Child Protective Services first came to visit my apartment because my sons were there and needed to be interviewed. While my older sons claimed they were never hit, my youngest stuck to his story and I believe him. In addition, my older sons kept yelling at my youngest that, "Mom never hit you!" Maybe they were protecting Julia. I was also interviewed and was treated like I was the accused party. I had to remind them that this was about Julia and not me. After investigating Julia, they concluded there was no abuse. No abuse? How about the fact that she makes a lot of money plus child support yet makes 3 boys share one bedroom in a basement apartment. According to any divorce settlement, the children are entitled to a lifestyle that is equal or close to what it was before the divorce took place. That means my sons deserve to live in either a house or large enough apartment where they are not constantly on top of each other. None of them get any privacy.

In addition to what my opinions are of what mental illnesses Julia has: I believe it left her not interested in sex, although she would not admit that. She would just say she wasn't into sex and not give any reason why. I knew why; she was broken by her brother and was blamed for it by her mother!

At the beginning of our relationship, we had what I would call a normal sex life. However, there were certain things about our sex life that I found odd: She couldn't self-lubricate so we had to rely on her saliva or KY jelly. She wouldn't let me touch her vagina in a sexual way or touch her clitoris in order to give her an orgasm. I can count on one hand how many times she let me give her oral sex. Eventually, our sex life came down to having sex about once or twice every 2 to 3 weeks.

For me sex and intimacy are important. It's how I convey my feelings for someone the most. In addition, I enjoy putting my partner's pleasure before mine. I'm a guy, I know during sex that I will eventually have an orgasm, so I don't worry about it. When I was younger, I was trying not to have orgasms so quickly so that the sex would last longer. The trick is to masturbate the day you know that you're going to have sex. When you eventually do have sex, you last a long time, your partner gets satisfied and you grow closer.

Having a connection both mentally and physically with Julia was very important to me because I feel that intimacy between two people keeps the relationship strong.

Unfortunately, my sex life with Julia came down to her asking me if I wanted sex and if I did, I should make it quick. The next step would be for me to go to the bathroom to get the KY jelly while she got a towel to put on the bed so that after I came, there would be no wet spot on the sheets. That part I get. No one wants to sleep on the wet spot.

After we had been to couple's counselling for a while, I felt comfortable enough to ask her in a non-threatening way what her views on sex were and how she felt about it with me. I also wanted to make sure that when I asked her it was during a time when we were not fighting, we were relaxed and in a friendly mood toward one another. One Saturday morning while she sat in the bathtub, I walked in and sat down on the toilet (with the lid closed obviously). I then told her that I was concerned about our sex life because we were only having sex about 3 times a month. I asked her if it was me because of all the cuts that I had on my legs from my scratching. She told me that it wasn't the cuts on my legs and that it had nothing to do with me. She then told me that she's just not into sex and not interested in it. I asked her what I can do to help her feel more comfortable and she said there was nothing I could do. I didn't know what to say after that, so I just left the bathroom and contemplated whether she was completely damaged from sexual abuse, or she was lying and was cheating on me. If she was cheating, she would never tell. I was left not knowing what was going on. If you're not fucking your wife, somebody else is. In my opinion, I think she was cheating.

 About a week or so after the sex conversation, we were cuddling on the couch and I was massaging her feet, calves and shoulders like I did every night. By the way I can also count on one hand how many massages that I got during the 8 years of marriage. But I digress. During this cuddling session I tried to initiate it going further with the hopes of being romantic, having sex, making sure she had an orgasm, was happy and it would keep our relationship going. I was quickly rejected. I asked her what I was supposed to do. She told me that I would have to use my hand. It was at that point that I realized that whatever sex life I had with Julia was officially over.

I wasn't against masturbation, in fact, I have kept the same masturbation schedule that I had when I was 13 and realized I was able to masturbate. I mentioned this earlier and I promised an explanation, which to me, makes sense.

Starting in 8th grade, I would usually masturbate on Sunday nights and Wednesday nights. The reason for that was; if I skipped a few days between orgasms, I would have bigger orgasms on Sunday and Wednesday nights. So that's the schedule I would keep. When the Internet became available and free pornography became available, I didn't masturbate more. However, it took more time to find the right video that I wanted to masturbate to. If you haven't looked at internet pornography lately, you'll find that each free pornography website has hundreds of categories to choose from. The choices go from normal sex to the ridiculous.

When I was a kid, I had a few magazines hidden in the closet and the choice of material was easy, and the whole process took about 5 minutes. With free porn on the internet, it takes 15 minutes: 12 minutes to find the video that turns you on and 3 minutes of actual masturbation time. In the 12 minutes it takes you to find the video that you like, you may click on 15 to 20 videos to see if it's something that you want to fantasize to. When searching the menu on the pornography site it shows up on your browsing history on your computer. So, when Julia checked my browsing history one time, she saw links to about 50 videos. She then began to accuse me of being addicted to porn and that she did not want me watching porn on the internet and that she only wanted me to watch porn on DVDs. She also didn't like the fact that I looked at videos that had Black women and Latino women. I found this strange because except for me and one other boyfriend in her life, Julia only dated Latin men.

I started to feel like I was in a George Orwell novel, and she was The Dream Police whose job it was to control my thoughts. I felt that she was trying to take control of every aspect of my life. I said to her, "You don't want to have sex, yet you want to control my masturbation material? That's crossing a line that is very inappropriate. In addition, you think I'm addicted to porn when you know I have the silly masturbation schedule. What do you think I'm doing, watching the entire movie to see how it ends? You've slowly closed the walls in on me. You don't want me to be a musician, you don't want me to go to the gym, you don't want me to work out when I'm home, you don't want me to smoke pot, you give me the silent treatment for days on end, you don't want sex, you're OK if I drink, everything I do is wrong. What sort of life do you want me to have?" She basically said she wanted me home all the time and to do the things that she wanted me to do that fit her agenda. In my opinion, that's what Julia is all about. She has T shirts that say, "boss lady" and other shirts that have sayings which show her as a bossy person. It became quite apparent that she didn't want a husband, she wanted an employee.

So, infidelity.

When Julia and I separated for the first time I was still teaching at the middle school in the city. It was April of 2010 and on Tuesday and Thursday afternoons I was able to take my physical education classes outside and have class in the schoolyard. On one Tuesday, I was with my class, and I saw a woman walking her 2 dogs on the opposite side of the street as the school yard. I looked at her, she looked at me, we both smiled, and I knew that something was going to happen. I wasn't looking for it, but I knew that something was going to happen. At the end of the class while I was walking my students back inside the school, the woman, named Marisol was still walking her dogs. I told her from across the street that I would be out here the same time on Thursday afternoon. Maybe I was looking for it after all.

When I brought my class outside on Thursday afternoon, Marisol decided to walk her dogs on the same side of the street and sidewalk as the schoolyard. We started talking through the fence. Now, there have been times in my life when I've met women and right away the sexual chemistry was overwhelming. This was one of those overwhelming times. As we talked through the chain linked fence, it was very apparent that we were going to hook up. When I got out of school that day, Marisol was waiting for me, and we planned on going out. At this point in my life, I'm separated, I'm still married, and my wife is pregnant with my 3rd child and here I am making a date. Why was I doing this? In terms of beauty, women can't really match the beauty of my ex-wife Julia. When she walks into a room you can't help but notice her. There is a charisma and a way that she carries herself like a Pollyanna, which I feel is a false persona. During our marriage, I never stopped trying to be amorous with Julia. I wanted physical closeness because it made me feel secure. I never felt secure. I always felt that I did something wrong. Every time she called my name and wanted to talk to me, I assumed I had done something wrong. I was walking on eggshells, and I was a wreck and was vulnerable. None of it is an excuse because I'm a grown man and can make my own decisions. However, I was experiencing anger and rebellion, which are emotions that are very rare in my personality. I reached a point where I had compromised my integrity and was planning on ruining the sanctity of my marriage even though I was separated and wasn't sure whether we were going to get back together again. It's still no excuse and it should not have been done. She was pregnant and it doesn't matter at that point how neglected I felt.

So, I went out with Marisol only a few weeks before my 3rd son was born. When you are separated and your wife is pregnant, and you're on a date with another woman, it's a new level of low. During my date with Marisol, it didn't take long until we were all over each other and having sex in my car, and then at my apartment. She knew I was still married, was separated, had twins and that a new baby was coming in late May. Marisol didn't seem to care about any of that and wanted to continue our relationship. I couldn't do it because I truly loved Julia. I only wanted Julia.

One night Julia accused me of smoking weed, and I hadn't. I yelled in her face to look at my eyes to see that I hadn't been smoking. She said she felt intimidated and that I was going to hit her. I told her I was sad to hear that after all that she supposedly knew about me and what my illness was: fear, depression and wanting to hide. Violence was never an issue with me, only in fantasy.

When Julia and I started couple's counselling, the first thing I said to the therapist was; I know in my heart of hearts that Julia is supposed to be my wife and my family. It just felt this was the way it was supposed to be even with the problems that we were having. I didn't think that they were too big to fix. It was just a matter of us communicating to each other in a healthier way. I would be remiss if I left out the point that the counselor stressed to Julia that she needed to work on her temper, letting go of control and being more patient with me and other people too. There is a list of incidents where Julia had problems with people at work, her friends and my brother (that wasn't a surprise). Julia put some effort into changing, but we all know people don't change, especially when it's contrived. When it's forced, there's a point where the person snaps and becomes their old self again. That's what happened with me and Julia in terms of trying to follow the techniques of getting along better given to us by our therapist.

I feel like I wasn't given the chance to love Julia like I wanted to. I blame myself partially because of my imperfections as a human being and I partially hold her responsible for not being able to let go of control for a while and let me run the show. And by running the show I mean romance, letting me plan our day together, looking into each other's eyes, saying" I love you", being able to touch her all over and make her feel wonderful, going for a bike ride, walking a nature trail or even playing a sport together. I was never too shy to tell Julia that I loved her all the time, but when she said, "I love you too", it sounded like she was almost asking a question or how someone would say it to a distant cousin.

 The relationship, if you want to call it that, with Marisol only lasted a couple of weeks. I ended it because I knew I had made a terrible mistake and was making decisions based on what I thought might make me feel better emotionally. It did the opposite; I have now become the dirt bag that I read about in newspapers. For example, I had mentioned that Lance Armstrong left his wife when she was pregnant and Alex Rodriguez, the baseball player, left his wife Cynthia when she was pregnant because he was having an affair with Madonna. When I read these stories, I was still married. At that point I was happy being a father and being married regardless of how exhausting and tough it could be. I viewed separating from your wife when she is pregnant has got to be the cruelest thing that you could do to somebody. How do you leave someone that you supposedly love? How do you do that to the children that you already have?

When I did it, I fell back on the reasons that Julia blamed me for the pregnancy of our youngest son, and then about a month later wanted to sell our house, and then when I freaked out and said we should separate, she said she called the late term abortion doctor for a consultation

This was a culmination of her making rash decisions. Like I also stated earlier, I don't know whether she really did call a late term abortion doctor or whether she was lying to get me to not separate from her. And like I stated, either way it doesn't matter because I feel she was enough of a sociopath to make up the story so that I would feel guilty.

At that point I didn't know what kind of person she was. I understand that I put her under pressure for suggesting we separate, however, this entire situation started the day she blamed me for the pregnancy when she knew full well that she could have gotten her tubes tied when she was giving birth to our twins.

According to research I have done, Narcissists do not like to take responsibility for their mind games, hidden agendas, control issues, cruelty and consistently trying to keep people at a lower level than they think they are at. Narcissists will hold themselves with high self-esteem that is held up by extremely weak legs. I believe that I also stated earlier that when I was blamed for the pregnancy it triggered the belief in my mind that she wanted to get divorced. I believe if we hadn't separated the first time, we would have moved back to the city together, had the baby, and then at some point I would have been told that she wanted a divorce. If she had never gotten pregnant with our 3rd child, I believe that she still would have wanted to sell the house, move and then eventually tell me she wanted a divorce. Either way we would have gotten divorced.

After I stopped seeing Marisol, I felt that any innocence that was left in my life was destroyed at my own hands and irrational thinking. Did I cheat? Some people say yes, and some say no because I was separated. I know that Julia went on a few dates during that time as well. She will tell you that she never did, but I saw a text on her phone that said she needed "testosterone infused attention". I was guilty of looking on her phone and she was guilty of snooping on my Facebook account and browser history long before I ever even thought of snooping on her phone, which was wrong too and I take responsibility for that. By the way, "Testosterone infused attention"? That doesn't sound like a woman not interested in sex.

Either way, I slept with another woman even though deep down, I only wanted Julia. I thought it would make me feel better. My penis told me it would make me feel better. The penis can be a fool sometimes. To me, I cheated. I know I was separated, but I still consider it cheating.

I never told Julia that I was with Marisol. To be totally honest, the biggest reason was that I didn't want to ruin the possibility of getting back together. Don't forget that she dated too, and I figured we both were in the wrong: That's called rationalizing one's own bad behavior so that you convince yourself that you did nothing wrong when you really did. When our youngest received his baptism in July of 2010, we reconciled and soon after, I moved back in with Julia and the kids to that basement apartment which I hated because my sons didn't have their own rooms and we could afford a bigger place for them. For some reason, she won't move. As I write this, they still live in that basement apartment.

Things went well until Nov 2012 when I was on the anti-psychotic drug, Trazodone. The drug was given to me for sleep. However, it made me feel arrogant and I was seeing everything in triple.

The last time Julia and I had sex was in our bathroom. In the middle of it, she started to cry. I asked her why and she wouldn't say. I knew at that point that the marriage was over. I also felt like I just raped my wife and it caused an anxiety attack. She was completely shut down. Looking back, I feel that she was seeing somebody else. My reaction to that was to start meeting Marisol for sex in addition to my high school girlfriend as well. I felt I had nothing to lose. I felt that I gave Julia everything; I faced my biggest fears in life by getting married, buying a house and having children. In addition, I felt I gave her everything that I could emotionally, economically and physically, meaning that every time I had sex with her, I risked getting an STD. I had already caught one in college and didn't want to catch her's and I didn't want her to catch mine. When we first started dating, we had to have a conversation about her venereal disease and mine. We had to make the decision of whether we wanted to be with a person with a venereal disease. I knew that

I loved her and that someday I would marry her and that was bigger than any venereal disease. I also figured if I caught it, it would be no big deal because she would be the only person that I would be having sex with anyway. She must have loved me at that point because she knew she was at risk too. I may have mental illness, but I didn't let it stop me from trying to live the American dream, falling in love and being in a marriage for the rest of my life. I know that during the marriage that my first reactions to change were always met with fear, however I always managed to put it aside and be there for my family, at least up until I got committed. That will haunt me for the rest of my life. I know the hospital is a place where people are supposed to get better, but the experience is traumatic in its own way. When you do leave, you are affected for the rest of your life.

If you have a spouse that you truly love and is the only one that you want to be with sexually and you cheat; there is no chance at all it will make you feel better or in any way solve any of your problems. Furthermore, your broken moral code can never be repaired, and you have to live with the mistake for the rest of your life. No matter what you do you can never ever get back the innocence of your marriage and the innocence that you had of once being a pure husband. I accept my mistakes.

Julia's sister in law:

Julia's sister-in-law, April, who we rented our apartment from, also worked at the same school as me. One day she yelled at me in front of the staff, "When are you moving out?" She yelled at me because I forgot that I told her that I would share a staff parking permit with her so that she would be able to use it every day, park in front of the school and not have to walk to the building from a couple of blocks away. I didn't need or want a permit because I would park about ¼ mile from work because I liked to have a little walk before work to calm down.

The union representative, who oversaw the permits knew that I would never be using the permit and forced Julia's sister-in-law, to share the permit with another staff member. This pissed her off which led her to yell and embarrass me in front of the entire staff. April would only have to find a parking space twice a week. On Wednesdays, alternate side parking is not in effect on the block where we worked, and we can park wherever we wanted. And on days she worked late, she could park her car in front of the school after 4pm, so, it wasn't as much of a convenience for her as it was more a case of laziness OR being totally depressed. In my opinion, she became

a hoarder that developed anxiety and depression because she lost her husband, Julia's brother, to a brain tumor and leaving a young daughter. Yet another widow! That adds up to about 7 or 8 people I know who were widowed before the age of 45. One tragedy after another again. I did get to meet and live with Julia's brother at their house/apartment. Unfortunately, he was already sick for a few years and his mind wasn't what it used to be. I was told that Julia's brother was funny, smart, kind, he could cook, a computer whiz and knew how to play guitar a little bit. The man I met couldn't remember his daughter's name. It reminded of my childhood all over again and I knew I was going to see a wife lose her husband and a young girl lose her dad. Regardless of that, Julia's sister-in-law and I didn't see eye to eye on much except that we both love the band U2. After Julia's brother died, I made attempts to call April to come stay at our house in Nassau for weekends. She turned the invitations down. Our twins had just been born and I thought she would like to be around her nephews. She was probably too depressed and it was too soon to be playing with babies. After a while, I would ask Julia if I should ask April and her daughter to come stay and visit for some weekends. Julia would tell me not to and would say "no" if I asked her to call April instead of me. I was doing this because my mother was THE support system for all of my relatives and friends that lost their spouses. I spent a good part of my youth visiting grieving widows and trying to make them laugh. I wanted to help at the time.

But I digress. Somehow Julia could have empathy for April's mental illness, but not mine. The irony is that April was instrumental in getting Julia to go out with me. She even warned me that Julia was a difficult person to live with. I never listened to her.

On the day April yelled at me, I called Julia and told her what happened. Julia then started making excuses for April and wouldn't let me speak. Being that I was on trazodone, I yelled so loud for her to shut up and let me talk, that I blew out my vocal cords. This was the Friday after Hurricane Sandy. The next day, the rent was due, and Julia gave April the rent money and didn't stick up for me. This is what led to our final fight and divorce.

To give proper perspective about why I was pissed that Julia didn't stick up for me is based on the following incident:

When my nephew was born (my brother's son), my parents, Julia and I drove to Connecticut to see the baby at the hospital. Given that my brother had my 3-year-old niece at home, we decided to go in shifts to the hospital to see my nephew and sister-in-law; this way someone would stay at the house with my niece and our twin sons who were 2 years old at the time. Julia volunteered first to watch my niece and our twins as my parents and I went to the hospital. The plan was to drive my parents back after their visit and go back to the hospital with Julia so she could see the baby. But there was an issue. When my parents and I went for our visit, we saw my nephew and then went to see my sister-in-law in her hospital room. She seemed to be very tired as she talked to us. Then, she started to turn very pale, gaunt and said she didn't feel well. She asked us to call a doctor and for us to leave the room. She did not want us seeing her get sick. Apparently, my sister-in-law was bleeding from her uterus and had to go back into the operating room. She was losing blood a little too fast and it was dangerous. My parents and I were asked to leave the hospital to go back and take care of my niece and the twins. My brother stayed at the hospital and asked that we come back after we knew that his wife was out of danger.

When we arrived at my brother's house to get Julia, my mother started whispering something to my father about my sister-in-law. My mom could never be smooth enough to whisper something to somebody because her voice sounds like Edith Bunker.

Julia noticed the whispering and asked what was going on. I told her that my sister-in-law was bleeding from her uterus and that we all got asked to leave the hospital and come back in a couple of days to see the baby. Julia somehow got it in her mind that my sister-in-law did not want her to come see the baby. When I repeated to her that my sister-in-law was in a dangerous situation, Julia still saw no reason why that she couldn't go see the baby. I then told her that it would be inappropriate for us to go see the baby while the doctor is trying to stop my sister-in-law from internal bleeding.

We left my brother's house and Julia felt slighted. Four months later she emailed my brother and told him how insulted she was that she was not able to see the baby. It sounds like a Seinfeld episode. My brother responded with a nasty email to Julia before informing me that she had sent him a nasty, self-centered email which obviously showed that Julia only cared for herself and that she missed out on seeing the baby. Clearly, in this case Julia was in the wrong. However, being that she was my wife, I was extremely angry at my brother for not informing me first about her email, going over my head and getting into an argument with my wife and making things more uncomfortable than they already were. Below is the email that Julia sent to Chet. I added some notes in BOLD lettering to remind you of the context of the letter. While there are parts of the email where she defends me; it's my opinion that those parts of the email are to make herself look like a martyr:

From: Julia

Date: Fri, 18 Dec 2009

To: Chet

Subject:

You know, Chet, I've done a lot - a lot more than you know - to help bring you and Peter closer, to help keep our families together. However, it has gotten to the point where I have had enough myself. I have been slighted enough. I have endured enough. At this point, I leave Peter's family, to Peter. When he is ready and when he feels it is possible for you two to have a normal relationship, then maybe he'll pursue it. I will not stand in the way, nor will I push him like I did the last time.

I know that you and your wife are oblivious to some of the things that you do that upset us, and for that reason, I have pushed and pushed Peter telling him that your behaviors are not intentional - but rather, just a function of your personalities - which are, to say the least, very different than ours. I won't do that anymore, because as I stated, I have had enough myself. There have been many instances in the past when you two have hurt me – your wife announcing in Atlantic City that you chose the name Daisy for the baby, after I had told you two over dinner at your mother's that that was the name Peter and I had chosen for our daughter*(Note that this was in 2005 and we weren't sure if Julia could even get pregnant, our twin SONS were born in 2007),* your wife turning down my invitation for you and her whole family to come over for Thanksgiving just because she wanted to show off the addition even though I had stated that I wanted my whole family together for the first holiday since my brother died *(Note that her oldest brother died in March of 2007 and she wanted Thanksgiving of 2007 to be at our house which was something I wanted too),* or your whole family not visiting Peter when he had pneumonia**(Note: the first morning that I knew I was sick and it was more than a chest cold, Julia accused me of faking)** and all of you being pissy at me because I asked mom to come over and help me with the boys while he was sick. For God's sake, I was working full time, taking care of twins and the house, and Peter wasn't even contagious! But somehow, I was wrong for asking for help? Each time, I sucked it up and continued to push Peter to his family.

But most recently, I was deeply offended by not being allowed to see my new nephew the day he was born. I sat for one and a half hours each way squeezed between two car seats just to come up there. I entertained my boys in your house while everyone was at the hospital. I endured weird looks from your mother beginning the moment I arrived, and her pulling your father to the side to repeatedly whisper in private about God knows what though I couldn't help but feel it was something about me. And then, when Peter was getting us ready to go to the hospital, to be told by your mother that I couldn't go? I understand that your wife had issues. I understand she was tired **(Note Julia was told that my sister-in-law had *internal bleeding in her uterus*)** But I didn't have to see her. I could have seen the baby and wished you well and sent a message to her through you. To put it mildly, it was rude and mean-spirited to not let me see him. And for me, this was the last straw.

I'm not angry anymore. I'm not even frustrated or even bothered. I just feel done. I'll respond to your emails. I'll respond to your calls. I'll see you at family affairs. But for now, that will be about it. I know on some level; you love your brother. I, of course, wish that you two can someday have a great relationship and my sons can play with their cousins. When that will happen, I won't even pretend to know, but I will hope that someday it can.

Julia

At first, I tried calling Chet so that I could yell at him and threaten to beat the shit out of him if he ever talked to her like that ever again. I got his voicemail and instead of leaving a message, I sent him the nastiest email that I've ever written to anybody. The email covered my resentment towards him since childhood and the way he treated me and beat me up. In addition, I said he should search out a therapist now for his children if he decides to treat them the same as he treated me when we were children.

This is the email that I sent to Chet:

From: Peter
Subject:
To: Chet
Date: Friday, December 18, 2009, 11:38 AM

You want to hear from me? Fine. My email will not be filled with me's and I's. It will be filled with plenty of you's. You are a cocky, arrogant, vain, elitist and a narcissistic person whose personality has changed very little since adolescence. God forbid somebody has a different opinion then yours. You feel you need to be right ALL of the time and provide little if no room for any ones' point of view or input to a normal conversation. You are condescending to those around you whether it be family, friends or even strangers. You are an embarrassment as well. An example would be yelling at an old woman after you bullied your way into the toll booth line at our parent's apartment complex by cutting her off. You belittle our parents and your wife in front of mixed company. You criticize those around you at a concert for having tattoos or dressing in their style of choice. Don't forget you have something in common with those people and that would be the music that you enjoy. You and your wife give advice on raising children when you have a nanny, maid, landscaper and car service to and from day care. And lest you forget, I have almost 10 years of teaching some of the toughest children in this country. You would not last 5 minutes at the school where I teach. It's not jealousy or even envy to that matter, it humorous. Your sense of reality and values are clearly skewed. Maybe mine are too but at this point I could give a fuck.

I have been pushed by Julia and our parents to have a relationship. When I have made efforts, I always find our time together to be fruitless, disappointing and empty. To be even more honest, I never felt that I had an older brother: I had a bully who lived in the same house as me who referred to me as faggot throughout my formative years. These memories do not go away. You do not treat me as an equal, but instead as some weak and helpless child. I have seen more and been through more than you can ever imagine. Your "little" anxiety attack that landed you in the emergency room was only a taste of what the mind can do. Maybe you have spent too much time in a suspended state of adolescence and are just now coming back to Earth and your subconscious is just now catching up to you. And finally, you just genuinely lack common courtesy for others. The best time in my life was when you finally moved out of our house and left for college.

Start looking for therapists now for your children if you plan on staying a prick your whole life. I do feel sorry for our parents, they don't deserve this, but this is my time and I do not need to be around people I genuinely feel uncomfortable around, brothers or not.

Any emails sent by you will not be read nor will any phone calls be accepted.

Fuck You,

Peter

PS. Trying to belittle my wife is useless, she's smarter than you think you are.

After I sent the email, I called Julia to tell her what I did. I also sent her a copy of the email. At first, she was very impressed that I tried to call him and talk to him live to let him have it before writing an email. After reading the email while on the phone with me, Julia got sexually turned on. She absolutely loved the email that I sent my brother and said to me, and I paraphrase, "I can't believe you tried to call him first and then sent him this email. You're going to get some tonight!" She also got turned on once because I learned how to use a power washer and cleaned our deck and the siding on the house. Sex was given as a reward if she felt that I had done enough around the house or if I displayed my alpha male side.

I was disappointed for a few reasons: Julia was clearly in the wrong and could not see it at all. I was upset because my relationship with my brother at that time wasn't so great and now Julia managed to make it even worse. Lastly, and the most disturbing was that Julia was sexually turned on at the fact that I was fighting. Is this what makes her attracted to me, melodrama? In addition, I also started to realize that Julia thrived on having conflicts with people or she is usually plotting or planning something where somebody always gets the short end of the stick. I wouldn't know what it feels like to be turned on when your spouse sticks up for you because I was rarely afforded that sort of emotional support from Julia. It was ok if I did it for her even if it meant becoming more estranged from my brother.

So, going back to the story with April and how Julia didn't stick up for me: It set off our final argument that would end with Julia saying that she wanted a divorce after I had to point out all the things that she had cut me off from emotionally and physically. I believe I told this part of the story before, but after my mother told Julia that she didn't see any love from her towards me, Julia then started yelling at my mother. This pissed me off because my mother treated Julia better than her mother ever treated her. My mother would go shopping with Julia, help watch the boys with Julia and became Julia's biggest confidant. My mother had done nothing less than treat Julia like she was her biological daughter. In addition, look at all the money my parents gave us to make her happy. When Julia started yelling at my mother, I yelled at her to stop and called her a "cunt"; that's when Julia said it was time for me to leave. After all the terrible things that were said and done to me, our marriage ended because of just one word that I said? Before that, the worst thing I ever told her was that she was being an asshole (during the divorce, both of our verbal gloves came off and the insults over text messages were ugly from both sides) I had badgered her into telling me what she really wanted because she had been keeping quiet for so long. I think she was doing it on purpose so that I would snap; This way she looks like the innocent party here, when she was manipulating the entire situation. This is what narcissists do: They make things so bad for you that when you snap, they then blame you for the problem.

Chapter 38: October 8, 2019, Continued, Elmhurst Hospital Queens New York

If I sit for too long, my lower back where I had my surgery starts to get stiff. I can't complain about my surgery because it was a complete success and rarely do I get any back pain or leg pain. Sometimes I get stiff, and if I stretch for a little while, I loosen up. One of the dumb things that people do after having lumbar fusion surgery is thinking that they could go back to the exercises or the fitness regimen that they were doing before they got injured.

When I had my follow up appointment with my surgeon about a month after my surgery, he mentioned that I was cleared to do any activity that I wanted. He even told me that I could run a marathon if I wanted to. I was never one to want to run a marathon even before I got injured in a car accident. After a surgery, there is no way I'm going to start taking up running as a hobby. I was always a person that hated running which is why I was always the goalie when I played sports. I hated running up-and-down the field.

The point of this right now is that my back is stiff and that I have to stand up and continue writing while I lean on the counter. It's freezing in here because one of the windows is open and its cold outside.

My mind continues to race and it's hard to see a future with the way I'm feeling and behaving. It's hitting me hard right now for no apparent reason. So, like I said, one of the ways to learn to fight is to just ride out these feelings until they subside and take them for what they are worth, simple chemical reactions in your brain. Sometimes you have to break it down to be that simple. The reason is so that you can have a better perspective and be able to control your emotions more. It's always a good idea to read as much as possible about whatever mental illness or other problems that you have. With some knowledge comes improvements in your moods and behaviors.

I have energy right now and I don't know where to go. I don't want to go to my room because it's quiet and lonely. I don't want to walk the hallway because I start to feel like I'm a mentally ill zombie just wandering aimlessly in a hallway in a cold psychiatric ward. I'll stay in the day room and wait for lunch. Even though I'm not hungry, I will force myself to eat.

It is now after lunch and I wound up eating my entire lunch which was delicious: Salisbury steak, potatoes, gravy, bean soup and vanilla pudding. I love pudding. I don't care if it's vanilla or chocolate. When it comes to pudding, I don't see race, just a delicious and fattening snack.

The food here is good except for the breaded flounder. I am not a big fish eater except for sushi, and that has to be smothered in a lot of soy sauce and wasabi.

As I sat eating my pudding, I started to think about what I'm getting out of being hospitalized. During this experience I've realized that if someone is considering killing themselves, it's a signal that they have run out of ideas on their own about how to help themselves and it's time to ask for outside help. Asking for help is better than being dead.

Sometimes for a few moments, I have the capacity to live in the present and when that happens, everything feels OK. From those times I get a taste of what life would be like without mental illness. My living in the present does not last long and it fades quickly, and I go back to worrying. As if worrying wasn't enough, it comes with surges of negative energy which is full of a chemical called cortisol. Cortisol is the chemical in your body that makes you feel anxious and continues to flow through your body as your anxiety level gets higher and higher. Even though I've experienced anxiety attacks hundreds of times, when they hit, it always feels like the first time I have ever had one thanks to cortisol. When you add adrenaline to the mix, you feel even worse. Adrenaline surges while in a great mood keep the endorphins pumping. I do believe that is the "Runner's High".

The nurse just announced that its snack time and Mr. R screams it while crowing like a rooster. Here come the Stray Cats.

No matter how bad a person feels, they must keep trying. Even though sometimes I don't believe it, staying consistent with trying to get better will work. It takes a lot of patience because improvements only happen in baby steps. Remember, Rome was not built in a day but was destroyed in one. Rushing things will make you crash and burn.

As I sit here in the day room and have conversations with Chandler and Lucille, Mr. R gets called by the social worker for his meeting and he decides to leave the room by galloping like a horse. I've learned not to question why people exhibit certain behaviors. I accept that everybody is different and that everybody here has a different severity of mental illness. I know that I suffer, and I've met people who suffer way worse than I do. It then gives me some perspective about the things that I have going for me. I'm not an idiot, it's just that I have this issue that holds me back. Once I get past my issues, there's nothing I can't do. I graduated high school, I graduated from college with a bachelor's degree, I have a master's degree, I was a certified personal trainer, I can sing, I can drum, I'm funny, and I'm a sincere person. There's one thing that I do take pride about myself and that is being a nice person. Have I been nice my whole life? No. Nobody is perfect, and we have to learn to not be so hard on ourselves when we make mistakes.

I know that admitting that I was unfaithful while separated and the last month of my marriage will permanently end any chance of reconciliation; not that there was a chance anyway. I'm admitting it now on purpose to give myself no choice but to move forward.

If you are in a bad marriage and trying to fix it isn't working, DO NOT CHEAT. Break up and get separated ASAP before you start screwing around with other people. Never underestimate the value of a clear conscience. I certainly wish I had one.

In addition, if you feel that you want a divorce based purely on the fact that you think you are missing out on something in life, talk to some divorced people before you do and hopefully you learn that you aren't missing a thing. If your marriage is flat, you have to try, no matter how much you resent the person for all the petty things that couples bicker about. Both parties have to put pride aside in order to put the focus on the fact that you really love each other, and those feelings need to be a priority.

I was once listening to a talk show on the radio and the topic was how to keep love alive in a relationship. There was a male and female host for the show, and they discussed the one simple thing that you should do to keep your love alive and that is: consider first what your spouse needs before taking care of your own needs. More simply, it was a lesson on how to be thoughtful.

Simple gestures like: If you are stopping off at the pharmacy to pick up your medication and you notice that the facial cleanser that your wife uses is buy one get one free, buy it for her. When you get home with the cleanser, lots of things will happen: your wife will appreciate that you were thinking of her, you saved her a trip to the pharmacy, you just made her feel more secure about the relationship and the bond you share becomes stronger. All that goodness from facial cleanser!

The important aspect is that it's supposed to create a relationship where both people give. The more you give, the more you'll get back, which only works with two willing participants.

Chapter 39: Dating After Divorce

After I got divorced, I felt like I was shot out of a cannon and felt I was ready to date, which was more like I was ready to have sex with someone different. The first person I started to see was Marisol again. As I started to get to know her better, I quickly realized that she was not a nice person.

Marisol would get pissed if I was taking care of my sons and was only available to see her after I was done. I was free every night and every Saturday too. She would ask in a sarcastic tone, "When are we hanging out? After you see your kids? You're with your kids too much!". Those statements started the road to the breakup rather quickly.

The final thing that Marisol said that made me decide that I was done was that she said that she didn't care about Sept 11th because she didn't know anybody in the towers. Well, I did: the nicest guy in my high school graduating class, Doug was killed, my classmate Susan's two uncles were firefighters and died in the towers, another classmate, Lisa, lost her husband, my friend Michael's older brother Alan was killed (he was also a classmate of my brother) and of course I know a lot of people who lost someone and have met many people who were in it. I also know first responders who stayed around for the cleanup who are now getting cancer. After all that, I was done with Marisol.

After Marisol, I started talking to my high school girlfriend, Rita. Rita was my first love and who I lost my virginity to. I was lucky to be in love with the person I lost my virginity to. It made sex an extremely deeply emotional experience for me and it also showed me right away what connecting with the right person is supposed to feel like.

During the last month of my marriage, Rita and I hooked up a few times after finding each other on Facebook. She was divorced and I knew it was a matter of weeks before my marriage ended. We had sex a few times. Most people go back to an ex usually after a divorce for rebound sex.

Julia had rebound sex with her ex-boyfriend after we divorced. I was upset that she told me a lie about her views and feelings about sex; and now here she was having sex. If you're not fucking your wife, someone else is.

Anyway, Rita and I were under the delusion that our teenage love would reignite and that the feelings that we were each other's soul mates would come back as well. This did not happen. Rita and I realized that we weren't soul mates anymore and did end up staying friends. Having a friend like Rita, who knows everything about me and doesn't judge is a positive thing. Plus, I knew Rita since I was 7. In high school when I first fell in love with Rita, it was so intense that it would cause panic attacks. I would throw up every time before going to see her. I also couldn't eat in front of her because of nerves. I believe it's called being Lovesick.

I tried to date Natasha too after my divorce, but that didn't work because we were still meeting in motels, her husband was still alive and that whole dynamic gave me anxiety attacks too.

There were also a handful of women who I dated that I would break up with and ghost if I felt they were trying to control me or say something nasty that reminded me of Julia. When that would happen, I would experience flashbacks about my marriage and was concerned that they would treat me like Julia did.

There was one woman who I went to high school with that I dated on and off. Her name was Pamela. She survived 9/11, an abusive marriage, 3 miscarriages and the death of both her parents within one year. She had PTSD and was bi-polar at this point. She also liked taking the drug Mollies.

When we hooked up, she had just gotten out of another abusive relationship.

One night in June of 2013, Pamela and I went out to dinner and came back to my apartment. We smoked some weed and started cuddling on my bed as we watched the NBA finals. I felt very relaxed with Pamela and was under the impression that this night was going wonderfully. Out of nowhere Pamela sat up and said, "You don't like me". I said, "What?", she repeated it again. I asked her what made her think I didn't like her, when in fact, I thought I was falling for her. I then said to her," I don't understand what's wrong; we had fun talking at dinner, our sex life and intimacy is strong (Pamela loved to rub every part of my body except for my feet; I think feet are gross and don't want to subject anyone to my feet) we just smoked some good pot and now we are holding each other. I thought tonight was going great. I don't understand ". She just continued to say that she knows that I don't like her and was not willing to elaborate more. Maybe the pot made her bug out.

After a few minutes, Pamela grew angrier which triggered my bad thoughts of my marriage and prompted me to ask her to leave my apartment.

She said, "no". That went back and forth a few times until I said I would call the police. After that threat, she grabbed her overnight bag and left. When she got to her car, she called me and asked to come back because she was stoned. I became mean and told her that if she was too high to drive, she could take an Uber home and I would pay for it. She decided to drive home and made it safely. She sent me a phony text message that she had gotten into an accident on the way home and that it was all my fault.

When you get involved with someone who is bipolar and is abusing pills, you never know when they will flip on you. Pamela and I tried a few more times to be together, but the day after every night we spent together, she would have a psychotic episode either by text or phone and would yell at me for not doing things for her that she never asked me to do; like drive her to New Jersey to look at an apartment she was interested in. When I said to her, "How am I supposed to know that you want me to go with you to New Jersey when I had no idea that you were looking in New Jersey and had no idea that you wanted to go?". After I said that, she became defensive and tried to accuse me of other petty things that simply never happened. When this behavior became constant, it felt like the worst part of my marriage, and I stopped seeing Pamela. I had to block her too from my phone because she would text disturbing messages accusing me of being like her ex-husband and boyfriend who were mentally and physically abusive. Getting completely away from Pamela was tough because the sex was good and she loved foreplay, heavy petting and she was very lustful. I still care for Pamela, but her problems outweigh mine in the way that she becomes abusive which is bad for me.

When you are single these days, online dating is the main way people connect. I've tried just about all the major dating sites like Match, Tinder, Plenty of Fish and Bumble. I was kicked off Tinder because I would just swipe right on every picture just to see who I matched with. I guess they caught on and kicked me off. I don't suggest that people swipe right to everyone because sometimes it's good not to know who likes you. I try not to be a snob or judgmental about looks or appearances, but some of the women who I matched with made me feel worse. In addition, after Julia, the only direction is down in terms of women being attractive (physical beauty does not matter if you have a horrible personality), which leads me to Patricia:

I met Patricia on Match. Patricia was born in Mexico, moved to San Diego with her family when she was a toddler and stayed in San Diego until she moved to New York in the early 2000's. After living in NYC for a while, she got married and moved to a cute town called Dobbs Ferry and had 2 sons.

Patricia was very attractive, exuded an amazing amorous vibe, funny, liked to smoke weed and was into eating healthy foods that tasted amazing. She was special. In addition, our sex life was off the hook! The day we met, the chemistry was so instant that we drove to my apartment and had sex. Whenever I would see her, we would have sex before even having a full conversation. Her usual line when I got to her house was, "Ok, get those pants off mister!".

Not only did I meet someone great, but I also started to feel that I was starting to heal from my divorce and could move on. I didn't want to get serious right away with Patricia; however, I did want a monogamous relationship and friendship to grow at a natural pace, which was what Patricia said she wanted too. Things with Patricia felt right, and I was happy until a few things happened: during one day in the summer of 2016 when we started dating, Patricia was at a mall with her sons and saw Julia with my sons. Patricia called me and said, "I just saw your ex-wife and your sons. You never told me how beautiful she was. Even my sons think she is prettier than I am". I told her that Julia's level of beauty is only exceeded by her level of evil. Patricia started to become insecure and whatever I said to make her feel more secure did not work.

A few weeks later, Patricia decided to get breast implants because she had lost some weight and one side effect was that she lost her breast size. After her surgery I helped her out a bit and was supportive.

When August of 2016 came around, Patricia told me that she was going to visit her family in San Diego. Her father, a Mexican immigrant who came to San Diego and worked hard enough until he owned two auto body shops and enough land where there was a house for him, a house for each of Patricia's brothers, and an extra 4th house.

Patricia's visit was to last two weeks. When she first got there, she called me for the first few days. After that, I never heard from or saw her again.

During our last conversation, Patricia told me that her brothers had become marijuana farmers who also made edibles and had a booming business going. They offered her a job, the 4th house on their property to live for free and obviously a good school for her sons. I told Patricia that I was supportive of her and whatever decision she made. Like I said, after that phone call, I never heard from her again.

One day in May of 2018, a few weeks after my back surgery, I started to think about Patricia. I still had her old work number from when she lived in Dobbs Ferry. She worked for a commercial real estate agent. I called the number and asked to speak to her and was very surprised to be put on hold while they told her that there was a call waiting for her. She never moved! Maybe she will want to see me again.

When she got on the phone she said, "Hi, this is Patricia", I said," Hey, it's me, Peter". She then said, "Peter who?". I slumped in my chair as I said," You know, Peter Vox? We dated for 3 months. One of our sons have the same name, we were having a great time until your vacation to San Diego and I never heard from you again. I called to say hello". She repeated that she didn't remember. I then quickly said goodbye and hung up as I felt like a complete idiot. I used a butt plug/vibrator combo on her and she doesn't remember me? One of my therapists told me that she probably blew me off because she was intimidated by Julia's beauty and probably felt that I would leave her for someone "prettier". I was attracted to Patricia as soon as I met her, and she became even more attractive and sexy as I got to know her better. After that, I never tried to call her again. The one positive aspect that I learned from that brief relationship was that I could care for somebody else and that getting over Julia could be possible.

I dated a lot of women since my divorce and Patricia was the only one who I grew feelings for. Also, Patricia felt like a friend too and we would giggle together like Howard Stern and Robin Quivers do when they laugh over an inside joke. Since I know that Patricia still lives here, I sometimes think about trying again. I'll just assume she doesn't remember me and leave it at that. Maybe I blew her mind so much in bed that it caused her brain to reset. Ya think?

Like I mentioned in earlier sections of the journal, I'm a musician and no matter how old you are or your level of talent, women love musicians. Especially singers. Eddie Murphy does a famous comedy routine about singers, and I paraphrase, "There's something about singers that make women lose their fucking minds. All you have to do is sing. You don't even have to be good looking…..because….Mick Jagger is one ugly motherfucker, and he gets all the pussy in the world. And, he has big ass lips. Even black people say it, "Dam! He's got some big mother fucking lips!" If you've never seen Eddie Murphy "Delirious" or haven't seen it in a while, go back and watch it and it will reaffirm that he is the greatest comedian of all time.

Back to being a musician:

When I moved from drums to being a lead vocalist, the attention from women was immediate: from teenage girls (which was weird) to college girls, to older women. After each show I would either hook up or find out from a girl that she had a crush on me. I took advantage, and like I said earlier, it was scary sleeping around because of AIDS even though I was using condoms.

As irony would have it, like I mentioned earlier, I caught genital warts during a time when I hadn't had intercourse in a few months. The campus doctor explained that intercourse wasn't the only way to catch warts. I caught them from a girl that I fooled around with but never had sex with. I had touched her vagina with both of my hands and touched my penis at some point while one of my hands must have still been wet with vaginal fluid. That's how I caught them. Yup, they're that easy to catch. That was December of 1990 and genital warts were running rampant all over Oneonta. I lived in a house of 8 guys and 4 of us caught warts. I got them treated at the college medical center and thank God they never came back. That was 31 years ago and I still worry!

At one point, I started to make a list of all the girls that I had slept with; this way I could keep track in case I caught something. As the list grew larger, there was a part of me that was proud of my sexual conquests and parts of me that felt like I was diminishing the value that I originally placed on having feelings for someone you sleep with.

After I graduated college, I kept adding to the list up until I got married and continued it after marriage as well until I realized that I had slept with over 200 women. If you talk to an average person, 200 sexual partners is an astronomical number. However, if you talk to a musician, 200 is a drop in the bucket. I have met musicians that have had over 600 to 700 sexual partners which even made me feel overwhelmed.

Does sleeping with too many people lower your capacity for love? I don't know the answer to that. I do know that I blew off a lot of great women who I could have been in relationships with but was too caught up about the excitement of experiencing new and more women.

I even got the point where I accidentally discovered a great way to hook up at a gig: it was the beginning of 2002, and I was in a cover band called Those Meddling Kids. We were playing at a club in Bayside, NY called which is no longer there. Before the gig started, I was standing on the dance floor about 4 feet from the stage. I wasn't dressed in a way that it was obvious that I was in the band. I was wearing a plain black dress shirt.

I started talking to a beautiful woman named Liza. Liza was with her friend who was rude. As I talked with both, I was getting one-word answers and Liza was not interested. At that point, I never mentioned that I was in the band. I didn't want to come off as being cocky. Then, something interesting happened; my keyboard player reached down from the stage, tapped me on my head and said, "Hey man, it's time to start". As Liza saw this she asked, "Time to start what?", I answered in a coy tone, "Oh, I sing for the band, and we are playing here tonight". I smiled and then climbed on to the stage.

Our opening song was Corduroy by Pearl Jam, which I happen to sing very well. That night, my voice was in great shape. As I sang and looked down at Liza, I could see the change in her demeanor immediately.

After the set was over, Liza immediately walked over to me and asked, "Why didn't you tell me you could sing like that?" I answered, "I usually don't walk up to people and say, "Hi, I'm a good singer!"" The next thing I knew, Liza was starting to touch my arms and giving me hugs. Other surprise guests that night were 2 ex-girlfriends and a woman I had met while loading my car with gear the week before. It was very strange.

Liza was so attractive that when I walked with her to the bathroom, every guy and girl couldn't help but look at her with jaws dropped. One guy even asked me, "How did you get her? "I laughed and said, "I don't know". After that night, I only went on one date with Liza. It turned out that she was married and that her husband was in jail for being a member of an organized crime ring.

I found out she was married when we went to her house after our date and saw a gigantic photo portrait of Liza and her husband. I asked her who he was, and she told me and said that he would be in jail for a long time. She also said that she had other boyfriends while he was away. This didn't sit well with me because guys like that have friends on the outside looking after their wives. I did not want to be involved in a situation where I could get jumped or even worse for being with Liza.

 Before we were supposed to have our 2nd date, I called Liza and explained why I couldn't see her. She made fun of me and questioned my manhood. She said, "You're not a real man. My husband is in jail!", I answered with a joke; "If I'm not a real man, what's with the penis, chest hair and unwanted nasal hair?" She hung up and I never heard from her again. Consider that a bullet dodged. The disappointment of not having sex with Liza didn't last long. There were plenty of single women around with no husbands in jail.

Chapter 40: My Brief Stint as a Nudist

As I've mentioned, my final separation from Julia was mid-November of 2012. Before end of the month, I had already moved into my apartment and wanted to go out and do new things. Little did I know that a new thing would happen right away.

I wound up meeting a woman named Sharon on Facebook. She was a life coach and had two female clients who I went to high school with. She was attractive, cool, loved musicians, smoked weed and was a nudist. She was also a quack in terms of being a life coach. It wasn't until we met for drinks did, I find out that she was a nudist. We first met in a bar near my hometown on Long Island. We had a great time talking about music. She had claimed to know Robert Plant and Bono. She also said she fucked Robert Plant and that she liked to go to sex clubs for orgies along with being a nudist. This night started getting more interesting by the second.

Sharon then told me that her nudist friends were meeting at a hookah bar and asked if I wanted to go. No, it wasn't a nude hookah bar! So, we went to the hookah bar and a met her friends. One nudist friend was Paola; she was 25, from the Dominican Republic and was stunning.

After talking with the nudists for a while, they invited me to a nudist event the next evening that they were having at a health club in Wantagh, Long Island. I asked what would be going on. I was told there would be drinks, swimming, hot tub and volleyball, all nude. I accepted the invitation. I had no problem being naked because there were many incidents in college, including graduation, where I could be seen either running around the streets of Oneonta naked with my friends, singing in my underwear on stage or trying to enter a bar with no clothes on.

The next night arrived and as I drove closer to the health club, I started to get a little nervous. After I parked my car, I entered the health club to check in for the event. The people at the desk were in their 60's and naked; not what I wanted to see. In fact, most nudists are people that you would rather not see naked. Nonetheless, the couple at the desk were very nice. They then told me I could choose either the men's or women's locker room to store my belongings. I was also told that it was my choice to be naked and that the only thing I could wear was a towel and then I could take it off whenever I felt comfortable. This put me at ease a little bit, but I was still nervous.

As I started to undress in the locker room, I noticed that my penis was hiding like a scared turtle. I became concerned because I didn't want to walk out there and not have a good hang. First, I went to pee. After I peed, I started to pull on my penis to bring it to its regular size when flaccid, which looks like a normal penis; not huge, but not a cocktail wiener either. As I pulled, I started talking out loud to my penis saying, "Come on buddy! Wake up! We gotta put on a good show out there!". After a few moments, I gave up on my penis, wrapped my towel around my waist, headed out of the locker room and met Sharon, Paola and the other nudists. This one particular "woman" was extremely attractive. She was topless and was wearing her towel. She looked like the former Miss USA, Vanessa Williams. I will refer to "her" as Vanessa. There's a reason I am putting quotes around all the pronouns for Vanessa. That explanation is coming up. In the meantime, turn on Lola by The Kinks. And, by the way, when I saw Paola naked, the problem with my shy penis was cured. My towel became a teepee. My little engine suddenly could!

After a few beers, I decided to take off my towel and be nude along with everyone else. As soon as I took off my towel, Vanessa Williams started giving me a lot of attention and became very touchy feely. I began to think that this night was a pretty good idea (La La La La Lola!). As we drank more, we went into to the pool, the hot tub and even played a game of nude volleyball which is disturbing to both play and watch. I don't need to see dicks and balls flopping all over the place.

After a while, some of the guests and I kept drinking and started making out with who they thought was attractive. I was led into the women's locker room where I was met by a girl in her 30's who was nude, and she started to kiss me. We both walked into the shower room where Vanessa Williams was, still topless and still wearing "her" towel. I stood in the shower with Vanessa and started kissing "her" and feeling her amazing looking breasts. This was at the end of the event, and we soon had to leave.

After we left, Paola, Vanessa Williams, and another guy and I went to The Wantagh Diner. Vanessa and I stayed in the car to fool around. She gave me a blowjob; however, I did not have an orgasm because we planned on going to a motel after the diner and I was holding off. When we first got to the diner Paola started acting strange and was trying to pull me out of the car to come eat. It was if she was trying to stop me from being with Vanessa. After Paola and her friend finished eating, I drove them both to their cars.

Vanessa and I went to a motel. I was excited because I was going to have sex with a beautiful woman. As we fooled around on the bed, I was trying to move things along and decided to reach down Vanessa's pants. On my first try, I was blocked. A few minutes later, I tried again and was blocked by "her" hand.

Every clue that I ignored about Vanessa like; being tall, having big hands and being physically strong all started to make sense at the same time. Vanessa admitted that she was born a man. She started her transformation about 15 years earlier when she started hormone therapy. She looked like a natural born woman.

When I found out, I said, "Now everything makes sense! You know, you should be honest with people from the beginning if you're going to get involved sexually with them", she then answered, "We can still have fun". I said no and reminded her again to be honest because there have been incidents where transgendered people have gotten beaten up because of situations like the one we were in. I told her that I prefer someone who was born a woman and told her that she could have the room as I left to go home.

I wasn't as much freaked out as I was disappointed that she wasn't born a woman and that I didn't have the wild night I thought I would have. There were no anxiety attacks, and I accepted the fact that I got fooled. I also looked at the whole night as a funny experience to tell my friends. She was hot, LOL!

The next week, I was invited by the nudists for comedy night in Manhattan. Their organization rented a theater on the lower West Side of Manhattan. The activities for the night were to watch 3 or 4 comedians as we sat naked in the crowd, eat at the buffet and play Naked Twister after the show.

The first 3 comedians were great; one of them even did his act nude. The 4th comedian was a surprise and someone that I was a fan of, Dave Attell. So, there I was, sitting naked in the front row of a theater watching one of my favorite comedians at the time. After the comedy show, everyone convened in the main lobby of the theater, naked. Paola asked me if I wanted to meet Dave Attell. I told her yes, but not while I was naked. Instead of meeting the comedians, I walked upstairs to the party room. The staircase was in the front of the building and was enclosed in glass, meaning that everyone on the street could see me climbing the stairs. At that point, I didn't care. I went to the party room where I ran into Vanessa Williams who apologized for our incident. I told her I was fine and that we were friends. After that, Paola said, "I was trying to tell you last week at the diner that she was born a man. That's why I was pulling you from the car!". I said, "You could have told me at the beginning of the night". I couldn't be mad at her because she was naked and had the sexiest body I've ever seen. After we had some food, the event hosts set up the Twister tarp. I sat with Paola while waiting for my turn. Paola switched from sitting next to me to sitting in between my legs. She asked for a shoulder massage.

As I massaged her, she leaned further into my body until her beautiful ass was pressing up against my groin. She began grinding her hips slowly and pushed against me more and more. I got hard of course and was extremely turned on. I thought for sure that I would be hooking up with Paola.

As I was trying not to have an orgasm in front of the group, Paola and I got called for our turn of Twister. We were playing against another woman and man. I didn't want my ass to be in everyone's face and I certainly didn't want another guy's ass in my face. After 3 spins, I was the first one out. Thank God! Who knows what could have happened; I could have been tea bagged by a stranger!

After the event at the theater, we went to a club to drink and dance. When we got to the club, I took my wallet, keys and phone out of my jacket and put them in the pockets of my pants. I then put my jacket down near everyone else's that we were with.

I started to not enjoy the club because at this point in my life, I had been working clubs for the last 30 years and was tired of the crowds, the loudness and drunk behavior. In addition, it was impossible to get Paola alone to have a drink or even to dance. There were men all around her and I quickly realized that she had narcissistic tendencies like my ex, Julia. As soon as I saw that red flag, I decided to leave the club.

I mentioned my keys, wallet and phone because when I looked for my coat to leave, I discovered that it had been stolen. I was lucky to have put my stuff in my pockets.

I left the club and walked about 15 blocks in 20 degrees to my car. I drove home with the heat on high, and never spoke to any of the nudists ever again.

The one annoying aspect about nudists is that they feel they are freer emotionally than other people because they don't wear clothes. They feel that you are missing out on being truly free unless you're naked. It couldn't be further from the truth. It's not a big deal and it's really all about sex even though the nudists will tell you it isn't. I don't need to have my penis showing in order to be free. I wanted the experience and I got one like I never expected.

Chapter 41: Oct 8, 2019, continued, Elmhurst Hospital Queens, NY

Lucille is talking to me about Mr. R and all the noises he makes. She says, "Who needs a zoo when you got this guy?". Lucille has a good sense of humor and can laugh at the jokes we make about how to kill her mother.

Right now, it's cold in the day room. When I get cold, I get panic attacks because I feel as if being cold is a sign of being vulnerable and weak. Part of me wants to punch holes in the walls and break anything that is made from glass. However, destruction and vandalism aren't usually my way.

In order to stop my anxiety, I go to the nurses' station to ask for an Ativan. To my disappointment, I get told that I can no longer have Ativan because of my abuse of it in the past. Instead, they give me an Attarax, which is another pill for anxiety that I've never heard of. This medication does not work on me. No wonder I've never heard of it because it sucks! Like Joey Ramone said, "I wanna be sedated".

As I sit and pray for this new pill to work, I fight the fear of what lies ahead of me in the real world. I'm starting to follow the rules of Cognitive Behavioral Therapy and try to focus on something different in order to change my current state of mind.

I've mentioned earlier that the choices that one has in a psychiatric ward to keep busy are limited to; TV, drawing, cards, listening to music, reading or trying to get motivated to start exercising again.

Luckily, a group is starting. I'm thankful to have the BHA's and Chandler who are with us because I look forward to talking with them, hearing about their life experiences and their thoughts about mental illness.

As the group starts, Mr. R. starts chirping like a bird as he plays ping pong with Chandler. Lucille decides to put on the radio, and she tunes to the station Z100, which only plays top 40 music.

I don't know any of these songs and never heard of any of these artists. I used to pay attention to what was new and popular to try to gauge what direction I should take with writing my own songs. I guess falling out of touch is what happens when you age and stop giving a crap about new music.

As this open group continues, Mr. R continues to play ping pong with another patient named Lilian. Lilian quickly learns that Mr. R isn't fun to play ping pong with because he just hits the ball across the room.

There is another patient here who I call Lola because she looks like how Barry Manilow describes the woman, Lola in the last verse of Copacabana: tattered dress and dead flowers in her hair. Lola wears the same dress every day; she wears a frizzy wig and carries old magazines. She also wears all the bracelets that she makes in the art group.

Victor, the kid with DEAD tattooed on his left hand enters the day room and sits right next to me. He reads the activity calendar that is printed on a piece of paper. I have still not heard Victor talk, even when he was my roommate for a few days.

A cold shock of reality suddenly hits me, and I start ruminating again about my divorce, my kids, my career, bankruptcy, SSDI and food stamps. Am I becoming a person that lives off the system? Am

I that sick that I need to? I don't know. I do know that I feel like a complete loser since I am relying on the system right now.

I tell Chandler how I'm feeling, and he reminds me that nothing is permanent and that one day I won't need the system. In addition, he tells me if I truly need the help, there's no reason to be ashamed. He then reinforces to me that I'm obviously not faking it and that I am an example of someone who truly has an illness and needs some help for a while.

I've also been crying a lot today. I don't cry heavily because I think my meds stop certain emotions from being expressed. But today, I cried a lot. Maybe the shock treatment is working and feelings that were repressed for so long have started to come to the surface. Maybe it's part of the healing process.

I then start to think about all the people in my life that died too young; Uncle Wayne, Aunt Beth, my cousin Paul, my step cousin Terry, my neighbor Teddy, my mother's best friend Sheila, my classmate Stuart (what a great kid he was. He was so brave. He was diagnosed with cancer in 1982 and died in the summer of 1986).

Another kid in my school named David killed himself when he was in 10th grade, and I was in 9th. He lived 2 houses down from my friend Mark. Unfortunately, David's mother died of cancer which subsequently led to his older brother killing himself. I became friendly with him, and he exhibited the same kind of loneliness that Sylvester Stallone shows in the original Rocky. He even looked like Stallone a little bit except David had reddish brown hair with natural auburn highlights. He was a great athlete and was strong. However, he was in pain. He would constantly talk about how his mom died and how his brother killed himself. This obviously left David's father a mess as well. While I never talked to his dad, I would see him from a distance and assumed he was living in despair. How could you not?

I also grew up with a friend named Philip. I've known Philip so long that I can't remember not knowing him. We went to school together, took tennis lessons together with his brother Alan, and we even went to college together, were roommates and fraternity brothers.

I met Philip because our mothers were friends. Like my mom's friend Sheila who died of cancer, Philip's mother had cancer. She lived with it for almost 20 years before dying when I was 23. If you want to talk about courage, Phil's mom was the epitome of it. No matter how sick she got at times, her spirit was never broken. She always had a positive attitude and tried to keep her sons in control while her husband, Martin worked as an engineer designing weapons for the military.

When we were in college, Phil's mom went into remission for a while, but the cancer unfortunately came back which eventually led to her passing; leaving her husband widowed with 2 grown sons.

Martin, Phil's dad became good friends with Sheila's (mom's friend who died) husband Fred through a bereavement group. I was happy to see them become friends because I felt bad for both of them. Philip's dad never showed much emotion, while Fred was funny, kind and loving. After Sheila died, that spark in Fred went dark. While he put on airs that he was ok, I could look into his eyes and see that look of hurt and loss. After all, I started to be able to identify that look by age 3.

As I sit here, I continue to ruminate about the past and the future. I get just as tired writing about it as I do talking or thinking about it.

My thoughts then switch to thinking about tomorrow and ECT session #9 or #10. I forget what I'm up to. The most depressive thing about ECT is the trip from my ward down to the room where the sessions take place. I'm taken there in a wheelchair like some sort of invalid. I don't usually talk at this time because I grow numb and just look out the windows and cheap paintings on the beige hospital walls as I get pushed down different corridors until we get to the ECT area.

My ruminations continue today about the same issues while they spin around in my brain tornado: job, divorce, money, death, the universe etc, etc, etc. I'm so tired of writing about the same things over and over. Those are steps backwards. It takes a constant effort to fight and change your thought patterns. Like Ellen DeGeneres said in Finding Nemo, "Just keep swimming!"

When I am having a bad day with anxiety, the attacks occur on that schedule I mentioned earlier where it starts, gets bad, hits a certain peak, then lessons, eventually stops for a few minutes and then starts all over again.

The anxieties I have today are mostly centered around having flashbacks of what happened to me at work, and the disciplinary hearings as well. I review them in my mind repeatedly and I start to feel angry and anxious, which is exactly how I felt when the situation was occurring. The reason why I mention this is that because that's what a flashback is: It occurs when you think about a situation in the past and your mind and body react as if it was happening again. I used to think that having a flashback meant that you would hallucinate about the things that happened to you in the past. So, basically for my entire life I have been suffering flashbacks from several events and not knowing that they were flashbacks. I take a little solace in knowing what my thought process is. When you give something an identity and you understand what it is, you can start taking it apart like a car engine. The goal is to be able to rebuild that car engine with improved parts.

 So, yes, today has been a day of thinking about my job and being angry at myself for being a person that doesn't stick up for himself when it is necessary.

I just got my medication for the evening. I have my Seroquel for sleep and my Lipitor for my cholesterol. There's something about the nighttime that makes things quiet and calm. Then, the morning comes and it's like an atomic bomb going off in my body.

Sometimes my ears start with a low ringing and then as the anxiety attack gets worse the ringing gets louder and louder to a point where I go mad.

As I've learned through the years from going to therapy, taking graduate classes in school counselling and most recently talking to people here; anxiety can show up in the body in many forms other than just having negative thoughts. For example, when I was a personal trainer, I had a female client who was in a bad marriage and had a husband who was cheating on her. Her stress level got to a point where she started breaking out with psoriasis on her knees and elbows. She was also breaking out in herpes sores in the corners of her eyes.

Other people cut themselves as a result of anxiety: They need to feel physical pain in order to offset the emotional pain, because physical pain contains a feeling of release. In addition, other people develop terrible back pain and body aches. I believe that the condition known as Fibromyalgia is caused by mental illness.

In addition to my negative thoughts and as I mentioned before, I would scratch my legs until they would bleed. I would continue to scratch open cuts and didn't care if I would bleed. My anxiety was causing my skin to be itching in a psychosomatic way. When I scratched, I felt pleasure. There was also a certain satisfaction of watching blood drip down my legs or if I bled enough on the sheets where Julia would be shocked. I had been accused by Julia of faking my anxiety disorder or trying to milk it in order to get out of things to do with the family. That is entirely 100% not true. I feel a part of me wanted a lot of blood on the sheets to show her that my mental illness was quite real. I used to hide my anxiety attacks from Julia the best I could, so maybe she didn't realize that my illness was as bad as it was. Only she knows, and in my opinion, she can never be open enough to answer the question or shed light on any questions that were left unanswered after we divorced.

Chapter 42: October 09, 2019, Elmhurst hospital, Queens, New York

My sleep was interrupted at one point by Mr. R who banged on my door at about 3:00 a.m. This shook me out of my sleep and triggered an anxiety attack. Sometimes when an anxiety attack happens, I just sit there and I don't even feel scared, I feel annoyed by it. I then go through the paces of feeling sick to my stomach, having no control of my body, I try to control myself from freaking out too badly and ride it out. I have ECT this morning and I look forward to the 20 seconds or so of being wacked out on the anesthesia. It's almost worth going through the therapy.

Today I came back from ECT feeling suicidal. I just sat and dealt with it and convinced myself that I'm not suicidal and that when I do feel like this, it's time to talk to somebody about it. Luckily there is a great staff here of BHA's and nurses who are more than willing to talk you through your problems. They really are special people and until you spend time in a hospital, you'll never know how hard they work and how much bullshit they must put up with from patients and other staff members like doctors and administrators.

I then realize that I've been crying on and off for the past 2 days. Something has changed and I'm not sure what it is, however, it makes me feel that there is no other way out. It's making me feel that I'm never going to get better. I have a terrible headache and I feel like I'm living a nightmare. At this point I feel like a pitcher in a baseball game who has lost his stuff in the late innings and is hoping that the manager will come out to the pitcher's mound and take him out of the game and say, "Okay kid, you did your best, now go hit the showers". In my scenario I don't let the manager smack me on the ass as I leave the pitcher's mound. This must be part of the purging of the mind that ECT causes.

I also received a little surprise today. I was given my favorite pill, Ativan. Somebody on the staff must have noticed that I was having a rough time and must have suggested to the doctors that I should take an Ativan today.

After I took my favorite pill, I went to bed to take a nap. When I woke up, I spoke to my mother and brother on the phone, as well as my sons. I have been calling my sons every day since I've been in the hospital. There is no way in hell that I will let anxiety ever beat me to the point again where I may die. My sons are who I love and must be there for every chance that I get.

Chapter 43: Oct 10, 2019, David Lee Roth's 64th birthday, just saying.

Rumination Warning:

I got out of bed for breakfast today and that was about it. I'm paralyzed and laying in bed all day today doing nothing but ruminating. My suicidal thoughts are out of control. I've come to accept that all these suicidal thoughts might be a side effect of the ECT and that those thoughts just simply need to run their course. Even though I understand, and I am very aware of that, it still doesn't stop me from feeling like shit. It's never going to be totally gone. I had one therapist tell me to remember that life is a journey and not a destination. It made me take a mental picture of a river and what kind of river that I want to float down: Am I going to float down a river with a fast current, dangerous rapids and sharp rocks; or am I going to float down a river with a smooth current that goes slow enough so that I can look around and enjoy life?

After I'm finally discharged, I can never let this happen to me again where I get to the point where I get hospitalized. It would wreck my sons. I love them so much and I miss them. I will never let my anxiety be stronger than my love for my sons ever again.

A good word that would describe today is trapped. I'm trapped with every angle of my life. Trapped with the mind I was born with and trapped in this hospital. More than environment, I believe that my mental illness leans towards being a chemical imbalance. It must be, because it's so severe that it becomes debilitating.

Chapter 44: Oct 11, 2019, Elmhurst Hospital, Queens, New York

The next journal entries in this chapter, which is a long one, cover October 2019 and November 2019. These journal entries contain cycles of my ruminating thoughts. I left them word-for-word because I wanted the readers to get some idea about how the mind races and keeps repeating the same thoughts over and over. I'll be honest it gets a little repetitive and frustrating to read, which is the point. If the reader is getting frustrated, imagine how frustrated I must be with all these thoughts constantly swirling around in my head.

As I look back on these journal entries I start to wonder if I the cycles of my ruminations were worse as a side effect of ECT and that I underwent a chemical change in my brain and maybe that extreme rumination is part of that process. Here are the journal entries:

I just met with doctor C, his challenge for me today is to try to stay in the present moment and not jump to the future because that is what gets me all wound up inside and it is something that I cannot control.

I went to ECT this morning and enjoyed my short time with the anesthesia yet again. When you go days, weeks or months at a time having anxiety and depression, everyday feels like the worst day of your life.

I was just on the phone with my sons and when I spoke to my youngest son who is 9 and he said, "Hi Da Da", in his little voice, tears flowed down my cheeks. How could I do this to them? I feel like I left them. I'm divorced, their mother has a boyfriend who sees them more than I do. What kind of father am I who spends less than 5 minutes on the phone with each of my sons because I'm hospitalized?

Sarah:

Sarah is a new patient who is a braggard. She claims to speak 17 languages, has a brother in the CIA and another brother in the FBI. According to Sarah, she wanted to work for some sort of secret service agency and team up with her brother. I don't know what her official mental illness is, but anybody can tell that she is delusional.

Sarah speaks Spanish because I heard her talking to a Spanish speaking patient. She said she certified in CPR, first aid and how to use a defibrillator. I don't know why she even shared that information because the conversation we were having had nothing to do with first aid. At this point I'm assuming she's delusional because as she continues to tell stories about her life, they get more and more outrageous and unrealistic as she continues to speak.

Sarah is in her late twenties and sort of resembles Katie Couric. Sarah also talks about 9/11 quite a bit and all the people she lost. I'm starting to think that she was at The World Trade center on 9/11 and has PTSD. I am convinced that when you experience trauma, it changes the chemistry of your brain and causes a level of permanent brain damage in the form of any mental illness.

During the current events group we had today, Sarah claimed that her cousin was a field operative in the CIA, she has been in many newspaper articles, lived in Las Vegas, worked as a waitress and turned down the advances of a "very famous" soccer player whose picture was in today's paper. I thought Pele was the only famous soccer player.

Also, while reading the paper, Sarah chose to read all the articles that featured rape and murder out loud. There's a lot going on with Sarah.

RUMINATION WARNING!

My mother came to visit today, and I cried when she got here. She brought me some recent pictures of my sons. We talked about me getting better. There's still that part of me that is dragging me down and trying to convince me to not want to get better.

My ruminations are in their usual cycles today as I mourn the past and worry about the future. What else more can I say that I haven't said or felt a billion times over?

After my mother left from visiting hour, I had a meeting with the social worker, Mr. T. Not the Mr. T that was in Rocky 3, but an Asian Mr. T. Mr. T informed me that I don't have a discharge date yet, which is both scary and disappointing. So, I am now forced to live one day at a time here with no idea of when I'm leaving. My mind then starts to ruminate about how I'm not going to be able to afford to pay all my bills and take care of my children. Obviously, I am now in the middle of a bad anxiety attack. I leave the meeting with Mr. T feeling like that one day I'm going to be homeless.

Monday October 14th, 2019, Elmhurst Hospital Queens, New York

When depression hurts so much that you want to give up on life despite having 3 amazing sons, it's got to mean that I have some sort of chemical imbalance. What else could be the answer?

It's about 8:45 p.m. and the other patients are arguing in the day room because Orlando, another patient likes to tell all the women to suck his dick. Eventually, he pulls out his penis and starts shaking it around and tells everybody to suck his dick. It was better to hear the incident occur from my room than to see it. Truthfully, I could really care less and didn't get a laugh out of hearing a man expose himself to a room filled with people. I've been in a mood where I just want to be left alone and not deal with anybody right now.

Tuesday October 15th, 2019, Elmhurst Hospital Queens, New York

RUMINATION WARNING!

Anxiety is really making my head spin today. I feel that I'm not in control both mentally and physically. For some reason I'm having tremors in my legs. Part of me wants to die and another wants to fight to live at the same time. I must pay attention to that side more. I don't know what I'm going to do when I get out of here in terms of a job or making money. I know that I won't make as much as I did when I taught. How will I pay my bills and pay child support at the same time? I can't believe this is happening to me. I feel worse now than when I got here. Same thoughts repeatedly. What can I do right now to break this cycle? Think fast rabbit! Time to do something different to change my train of thought. I would like to do a NY Daily News crossword puzzle. I'm going to find one!

Friday October 18th, 2019, Elmhurst Hospital, Queens, New York

Today I had my 13th ECT session. Since then, I have been sitting in the day room and staring into space. I worry mostly about money, where I'm going to live, how to raise my kids, seeing my kids, how to wake up every day and not feeling like an anxious wreck and how I'm going to hold down a job without vomiting each day before work.

I once scratched up and dented the passenger door of my car on the corner of a brick column when I was picking some customers up for Uber. When I took my car to be fixed, they said it would be about a week before it would be ready. So, I spent a week sitting at home. I must say spending a week sitting at home and doing nothing is more stressful than being at a job. The reason is that all you can think about is that you should be working, and you feel like a dead beat.

I don't like sitting home alone all day and being stuck with my thoughts. If I did stay at home all day, every day, I know that my mental illness would only get worse.

Right now, I have a choice to make: Do I want to be happy, or do I want to be miserable? It's a decision and choice that is very realistic but hard to make because of self-imposed mental obstacles.

Sometimes I think that having lots of money will cure my mental illness. I then look at celebrities and the extremely wealthy who wind-up committing suicide, and people are left wondering why. They have all the money in the world and the resources to get help. They also have the choice of when they work or when they feel they need a break. Yet, they kill themselves. I can understand losing all your money, family members, and spouse might drive someone to suicide. However, I feel were able to rely on a financial cushion, it would provide the resources to get the help that I needed.

Trying to force or rush to feel better has never worked for me. Recovery is a slow and arduous process that is made up of thousands of baby steps that eventually add up to be hundreds of miles long. As you continue your baby steps, moving forward, you will have the ability to look back on the steps in the past and be able to learn from them.

October 20th, 2019, Elmhurst Hospital, Queens, NY

All day today my anxiety is on high alert.

The reason is the fear of not knowing what the future holds. The doctors say to live in the now and to be in the moment. However, the "now" sucks and so does the moment. Theoretically I know the doctors are right, but for my whole life I've been regretting the past and fearing the future. So, living in the present is very difficult to do.

Who wants to start their life over with nothing at age 50? Almost 19 years of work in the New York City Department of Education down the tubes. 19 years of struggling to get students to participate in my class, and constantly being judged by administrators who can't control the students either. It was no fun working every day and feeling like the administration was looking for any reason to get rid of me.

And now I have thought myself into an anxiety attack. Here comes the cold adrenaline in my sternum, my face goes numb, and my hands and feet tingle. I honestly don't know what I'm going to do or what to do. I'm afraid to go to sleep because I'm just going to lay there and think negatively. I'm overwhelmed with fear, and I would ask for Ativan, but I already took one today and I have ECT in the morning. It's frustrating when you feel that you are improving and then have days where it's like nothing has changed.

October 22nd, 2019, Elmhurst Hospital, Queens, New York

My child support payments are still based on the salary of my job with the New York City Department of Education. Since I have not been working for them, I'm still getting charged by child support as if I am, which now leaves me being in arrears. It's frustrating being in the hospital and trying to navigate bureaucratic red tape while Julia still has time to go to the nail salon and spend money on alcohol and over $2000 on a peloton bike because she makes impulsive decisions and makes impulsive purchases. In addition, at one time, Julia also had a personal trainer. I used to be a personal trainer and I was obviously a gym teacher, so my knowledge of fitness and my availability to exercise with Julia while we were married was never taken advantage of. In addition, the boyfriend she had before me was also a personal trainer. Are you trying to tell me that with all that you've learned from two personal trainers wasn't enough to give you a good foundation about how to exercise? I believe she just wants to tell people she has a trainer.

Tomorrow is my last day of ECT and I'm concerned that maybe it's not helping because I feel I have taken some steps backwards in the last few days because my overthinking has been at a higher level than ever before since I've been institutionalized. Maybe it will take a few more weeks or months for the benefits of ECT to start kicking in. Right now, I could not go home because I would abuse my pills, not to kill myself, but to get relief from this emotional strife. I'm at the point where at least my suicidal thoughts are going away, but I still feel that that I just want to take a bunch of pills and not feel any emotional pain. I also start to think about how there is no discharge date set and that makes me think that I may be hospitalized for longer than I have anticipated. I was also just told that I will be starting lithium again. I hate lithium because it makes you gain weight. I saw it happen to some of my students who had to take lithium for their depression.

One of my students started taking it at the beginning of summer vacation, and then when he came back to school in September, he had gained so much weight that I didn't even recognize him. He looked miserable.

While I don't want to kill myself anymore, the guilt that I have that I did want to kill myself is now coming to the surface. My sons would have been destroyed forever. In addition, I constantly worry about how my stay in a hospital will affect them in the long term. Sometimes I feel like I'm living a self-fulfilling prophecy of living in a nursing home and being on social security and food stamps for the rest of my life.

Meanwhile, we have a male patient who just arrived. His name is Roberto. He is Latino and in his early forties. Roberto told me that his cousin is Tony Orlando (Knock 3 times on the ceiling if you want me). Roberto is also another exhibitionist who likes to whip out his twig and berries and ask if anyone would like to give him a blow job. Sometimes he asks, "Please?", which is polite considering everything else he is doing.

Roberto also has a lot of anger issues towards women, and he argues with them every day on the unit. The latest argument consisted of Roberto asking a female patient why she was licking her lips. Instead of assuming her lips were dry, he assumed she was in the mood to give oral sex. She quickly denied that she wanted to give oral sex at that moment.

This argument then spread onto topics of what famous people they either know or have met in their lives. They try to one up each other and sound like middle school children bragging in the cafeteria.

Then the arguments start to get mean and they question each other about where their kids are, how many baby daddies or baby mama's they have, and they all accuse each other of being bad parents.

One female patient named Alexis just went on a rant about how she is not a corner prostitute but a high-end escort. She says she makes $3400 a week and has an extensive wardrobe. She claims she doesn't look for men and that they just find her. To be with her costs almost $500 a night. She also claims to have once weighed over 300 pounds. Alexis is an attractive African American female, but her body does not look like it used to weigh 300 pounds. She would still have some sagging skin here and there even if she had excess skin removed from surgery. So, I don't think she weighed 300 pounds rather that she probably lost 80 or 90 pounds. In addition, she's nice to me and when we talk, we support each other and can make each other laugh. I'm starting to really appreciate people that are willing to sit with you and listen to all your problems and offer for you a shoulder to cry on. This makes me stronger, so I can sit with somebody and listen to their problems and give them a shoulder to cry on too.

It's not until you start living a solitary life when you learn how important social interaction is and how just one friendly conversation can make you feel like you have a place in this world.

October 23, 2019, Elmhurst Hospital, Queens New York

Today was my last day of ECT. Something was

different about it. I felt a clarity like I never felt before. This was not a good clarity. It was fear. I start to worry about all my financial expenses like my car. I also start worrying about that I will end up in section 8 housing, which aren't in the safest of neighborhoods and that bringing my sons to my apartment would be stressful. I have now created a scenario that is not real where I'm living in an imaginary dangerous neighborhood and that my sons will not be safe when they come over.

Scenarios like that can lead to my obsessing over horrible situations that last for days on end.

The following is an example about how a newspaper story that my friend emailed me that set off a terrible episode of being tortured by horrible thoughts that lasted almost two weeks:

The newspaper article was from Australia, where two 18-Year-old boys were just released from prison. They were arrested and charged with murder when they were both 10 years old: They went to a shopping mall with the intention of kidnapping a child. They kidnapped a three-year-old boy from the mall. They took him to a rural area near some train tracks. They began to beat the boy, cut off his fingers with a scissor, and inserted various items up the boy's rectum including batteries. They beat him some more and he was barely moving. They then placed him on the railroad tracks and waited for the train to come and watch it run over the boy and mutilate his body beyond recognition. Now, I want you to imagine being this boy, his parents or both.

As I was reading the article, I started to cry, I became frantic, fearful and couldn't get the image of what happened to this boy out of my head. It then got worse because at the time when I read this article, my twin sons were almost 3 years old and now I was picturing them in this most heinous situation and that this torture was happening to my sons. I then started to shake and cry more. I couldn't get the story out of my head. I couldn't stop feeling like this happened to my sons. My brain reacted as if this really happened to my sons. Although the part of my brain that knows that it is not really happening exists, it still doesn't stop the other part of my brain that makes it feel real. In addition to knowing that this will probably not happen to my sons, my brain continued to form unwanted questions and statements like; What if it did happen? It could still happen.

As I mentioned above, this news article bothered me for almost two weeks. I told Julia about it and how much it bothered me, and she really didn't know how to react. How is someone supposed to react to that?

 For me, physical affection works to stop the negative train of thought. And I'm not talking about sex; I'm talking about holding hands, hugging and just being able to disappear into someone else's soul for a while just to feel different. The times I was offered solace from Julia, I could feel that physically she wasn't genuine. I could feel that either she didn't understand, which is fine, but I also was aware of her basic lack of empathy in general.

 In my opinion, Julia is the type that will express her empathy and sympathy more for people on the news then she does for people in her personal life. For example, there was a story I believe that took place in 2012 where a bunch of miners in Chile got trapped in a mine. I forget how many days or weeks they were trapped. They eventually got rescued. The rescue of the miners was shown on live TV. I remember Julia standing in front of the TV crying as each minor was taken out of the ground. I had never seen her cry like that before, not even after her father died. I questioned why she had more empathy for these strangers then she did for me? The answer is that having empathy for someone on TV doesn't take a commitment. She could stop being empathetic once the story was over. Being empathetic and kind to your spouse is a lifetime commitment. For a narcissist, that's not convenient. After the news story was over, Julia got to feel good because she expressed some emotion and then feels that she is a good person for crying for these people. That's just my opinion.

I also believe that a narcissist is not capable of truly loving someone or being able to express their feelings like crying for example. Their fear of losing control stops them from sharing their true feelings with the person that they are supposed to be closest with. It's a shame, and it's something that I think about often because during my marriage, I wanted to be the person that she could open up to. There were times that she almost opened up. She would always stop herself from expressing herself further. Pushing her to go further was counter intuitive.

From that train of thought I then start thinking about how life has never been easy for me in terms of my battle with mental illness. It's frustrating to meet every new challenge or change with a frightened attitude. I remember after college I went into a terrible depression. I was not prepared for the real world. Being a music major and hoping your band lands a record deal is a little far-fetched even though we were speaking to insiders in the record industry. If I wasn't going to be a working musician, I had the hopes of working in the music industry in some capacity.

My major in college like I mentioned before was music industry. I took classes in entertainment law (music and literature), marketing, audio engineering, music production and music merchandising. It was difficult to concentrate in classes sometimes because of what was going on with my group in Oneonta and in the surrounding towns. Each day in Oneonta proved to be a new adventure and surprise whether it was being told that we were going to talk to some music industry insiders, girls stalking me, or we had a gig to play. I was always too excited to even go to class because I wanted to get ready for the gig.

The one thing I learned about being a music industry major in college was that if you want to be a performing artist, being a music industry major isn't really that necessary. There are important things that people who want to be performing artists need to know: #1 Never give anybody money. #2 Never give up your copyright. #3 Never give up your publishing. #4 Most importantly, get a lawyer or at least have the connection to one.

If you want to be a studio engineer, audio engineer, work in marketing, be a DJ, manage artists, be an entertainment lawyer etc, then having a music industry degree is necessary.

October 24, 2019, Elmhurst Hospital, Queens New York

I look at all the major life changes I have gone through in the last 10 years, and I realize why I'm burnt out. I feel like I have been punched in the head too many times like a boxer who ends up becoming what they called "punchy". It simply means they have brain damage. You can feel punchy as a result of being hit physically or when so many things happen at once that you cannot emotionally handle it and you burn out.

Every time I have an anxiety attack that's bad, I always say that it's the worst one I've ever had. I get sick of thinking about it and writing about it and have also been able to develop a sense of humor about it because I feel like I'm Fred Sanford faking his heart attacks and saying, "Elizabeth, this is the big one honey! The last thing I'm gonna see on this Earth is your ugly sister Esther's face!"

Sometimes I feel like shaking myself wishing that I could snap out of this cycle of behavior because I think about the same things repeatedly. I have come to the level where I am annoyed at myself and have had enough.

High School:

9th grade was particularly bad with my mental illness. During the 9th grade, my episodes of depression and anxiety went from lasting days to months at a time. There were times during 9th grade where I was so tired of trying to act normal that I would go to the nurse's office and ask if I could lay down because I didn't feel good. When I started coming every day and sleeping for as long as 2 periods, the nurse knew something was wrong and contacted my guidance counselor. From there, I spoke to the school psychologist and explained to him what was going on and informed him that I was in therapy.

My high school was very prestigious and socially difficult. You were judged by the kind of clothing you wore, what part of town you lived in, the amount of money your family had and what kind of car your parents drove.

I looked at school as a social mine field. You had to know where to walk and know where not to walk in order to avoid people that would pick on others. While I was extremely paranoid every day at school because I was worried that I would get picked on. I would spend the whole day worrying and making myself exhausted. It was all for nothing too because I rarely got picked on in high school and blended in. Every day after school, I would rush home I eat about 6 chocolate cupcakes and drink about 32 oz of milk. I would then lay on the couch and fall asleep while watching TV. I would then get up at about 6:00 p.m. eat dinner, do whatever homework that I could do and then watch TV in my room until I fell asleep, or I would listen to Van Halen.

This pattern of being alone everyday would happen over the fall and winter. It would be the spring when I played lacrosse and my anxiety would lessen. I was outside getting exercise; I was around my teammates, and I enjoyed playing. In addition, I hoped that it would toughen me up. Playing goalie in lacrosse means you get hit a lot with the ball when people take shots. Opposing teams love to try to knock down the goalie as well.

I was knocked unconscious 3 times during my time playing lacrosse. The 1st time I got knocked unconscious was at Chaminade Catholic High School For Boys in Mineola, NY. This is the top Catholic school on Long Island. All the students look like Ivan Drago from Rocky 4, while our team looked like a Hebrew school class. I was playing defense at the time and had the ball. As I passed the ball to one of my teammates, I remember one of the Chaminade players hitting me in the sternum leading with his helmet knocking me down and unconscious for about 4 or 5 seconds. The referee called the penalty for spearing.

 The 2nd time I got knocked unconscious while playing lacrosse was when I attended lacrosse camp at the University of Maryland in the summer of 1986. At this point I was playing goalie. I was running down the field with the ball and collided with what I thought was a brick wall. It wasn't a brick wall; it was a kid that was about 6' 2" tall and weighed about 220 pounds and was from Levittown Long Island. When I collided with him all I remember was bouncing off his body. The collision knocked me out for a couple of seconds.

 The 3rd time I got knocked out was during my senior year in high school and we were playing who would turn out to be the state champions and be considered the best high school lacrosse team in the country in 1987. This was Elmont High School. We had a home game against them, and I was playing goalie. One of the Elmont players took a shot at the goal, I made the save but the ball rebounded back into play. I saw that they're biggest player and All-American, was attempting to run and scoop up the rebound to try to shoot again. I decided to run out of the goal and challenge him for the ball. I remember as I ran out of the goal, my coach was yelling "No!". I positioned my body lower so that I could either pick up the ball or try to hit this guy as hard as I could, and to establish myself as a tough goalie. The problem wasn't that I was not tough, rather than the fact that I was outweighed by at least 50 pounds. When I got hit, I got crushed and was knocked out for a few seconds. It wasn't long enough where a timeout had to be called. I just got up feeling dizzy and ran back to the goal.

 I also look back on my time as a lacrosse player and realized how many concussions I must have had while playing. After my car accident in 2013 I had a concussion. The way it felt was the exact same way it felt when I when I had gotten knocked out or the dozens of shots that I blocked with my helmet. It was all well worth it because I loved playing lacrosse at that time.

I also had a strange way of training to be a goalie in lacrosse: I would stand in front of a brick wall, throw the ball against the wall, and instead of catching the ball, I would let the ball hit me. It's funny because many years later Adam Sandler does something similar at a batting cage in his golf movie, Happy Gilmore. While Adam Sandler was only acting, I was doing that shit for real. I remember my coach commenting about on the team bus after a victory in which I played well. My coach said, "You guys played great today! Peter, you were awesome, you're also a maniac too. I heard about how you've been training." He had a big smile on his face. I liked being called a maniac. He was a great coach who also played professional soccer for the NY Cosmos in the 1970's with Pele.

Oct 24th, 2019, Continued

I don't know, I just don't know. I feel like that I've ruined everything and it's all my fault. If you go through life thinking everything is your fault and then someone blames you for something, then you're not surprised. However, the price you pay is living in a constant state of paranoia.

Laying in bed on medications for the rest of my life is something that cannot happen. Right now, this demon is controlling me. Am I afraid to die? Or am I afraid of life? I guess it can be a combination of both. Today feels like I'm stuck under a blanket that weighs a ton.

I also started taking a higher dose of lithium per day. It's up to about 900 milligrams. The lithium is supposed to stop thoughts of suicide, but I hate the weight gain. When I complain to my case worker that I hate the weight gain, she asked, "Would you rather be a little fat and happy, or thin and miserable?". First, the drug doesn't make you happy, it just doesn't make you unhappy. You also become somewhat emotionless like Mr. Spock from Star Trek. Secondly, if I'm thin, then

I'm going to be happy from being in shape. That's better than these bullshit pills; they solve one problem but cause five new ones at the same time.

My case worker is overweight, has a lot of health issues and I'm sure has a past of mental illness, and she is on meds of her own. I refuse to wind up looking like a potato.

The other aspect of Lithium is that blood tests need to be done every couple of weeks in order to test the lithium levels in my system. I have thin veins and most phlebotomists have trouble finding a good vein to poke for blood.

I'm not functioning well, yet not functioning bad either. I'm just existing. Sometimes I feel so numb that my negatives thoughts don't even bother me.

Oct 26, 2019, Saturday, Elmhurst Hospital. Queens, NY

I decided to ask for an Ativan. Why not, right? I have been depending on this pill because it kicks in within 20 minutes. Weed is better, takes less than 10 seconds to kick in and you can't overdose on it like pills or alcohol.

Emotional pain is way worse than physical pain from an injury or a back surgery like mine. After my back surgery, which was successful, I had zero anxiety about the rehabilitation or the physical pain I was in. In fact, I looked forward to the challenge. A physical injury is something that you can identify without confusion and the steps to healing are pretty cut and dry: ice packs, heating pads, stretching and begin exercising again slowly while being cautious. There is no trying to figure out what childhood trauma is the cause for your back being injured in a car accident when you're 44 years old. There's no deep thought about why.

After I came home from the hospital from my surgery, I was told I could start walking with my walker, then use a cane and then rely on myself. In addition, I was told to wait a month before doing exercise.

In less than 2 weeks, I was walking on my own, about a mile at a time, and starting using resistance bands to train the rest of my body. I was assigned a physical therapist who came over once. He saw all my fitness gear and knew of my background as a trainer. I used to train clients who had gone through various types of surgeries and who suffered from illnesses like Parkinson's disease. The physical therapist said to me, "I think I need you more as a physical therapist than you need me". That was one of the nicest compliments I ever received because it made me feel competent.

After dinner tonight, I tried to call my sons, but they weren't home, so I became depressed over that and started my, "I want to die but am afraid to die paradox". I'm slowly learning to accept having suicidal thoughts and just add them to the list of the other thoughts that haunt me. The goal is to compartmentalize the thoughts and try to see them as a signal of something else.

I would like to think that when I took the 15 Ativan, I wasn't trying to kill myself. However, I remember laying down after I took them, and I didn't care about what might happen. This makes me think that I really did want to die. I feel ashamed mostly.

Oct 29, 2019, Elmhurst Hospital, Queens, New York

Today is a fear of death day and other existential questions that have no answer: What is the meaning of life? What happens after you die? What was I before I was born? Before the Big

Bang created the universe, what was there before that? What does forever mean? If the universe is expanding, what is it expanding through? What's exists outside the universe? How many licks does it take to get to the center of a tootsie roll tootsie pop? The owl says 3, but he cheated.

I also worry that in 5 billion years, the sun will turn into a supernova and engulf the Earth. An irrational fear?

As I sit and ponder the universe and why sometimes Pluto is a planet and sometimes it isn't, a patient named Melanie was brought to our unit. I like when there are new patients because it switches my train of thought to what their illness is and in addition, I always learn something beneficial.

Melanie is about 100 lbs. overweight, and her hands shake a lot. I assume it is a side effect from her meds. Her facial expression is nothing less of despair. Melanie has lots of facial hair and she is not taking care of her hygiene. In addition, she doesn't talk because she is so sad. No matter what the cause of your despair is, the commonality is that despair has a certain feeling that we can all relate to.

Today, I'm fighting the urge not to stay in bed all day and the urges to give up on everything and wind up being the person who stays home to watch Maury Povich to find out who the father is.

Last night I had a dream about beating the shit out of my former assistant principal. He is a guy who passes the buck, lied in my observation reports and constantly included things that had nothing to do with my lessons. But I was too scared to stick up for myself for fear that they would make my job worse. It got worse anyway. If I bumped into him in public today, I would have to warn him to walk or run away quick because he would be in danger of getting hit. I'm more interested in humiliating him than anything.

Oct 31, 2019, Elmhurst Hospital, Queens, NY

This is my first Halloween ever without my kids. I love getting into costumes and taking them trick or treating. In my neighborhood Halloween is awesome. Everyone starts trick or treating at about 4pm, there are tons of parents and kids dressed up, people decorate their houses in creative ways, and it feels like it did when I was a kid.

When you miss a holiday or special occasion, it brings you to where you start ruminating. Sometimes I create an imaginary timeline in my head and go over each year of my life and the memories that I have. However, since my divorce in 2013 and everything that has transpired since, it takes up most of my thoughts.

Nov 1, 2019

I have been here since the middle of September. With no discharge date in sight, I start to think about how out of hand this stay in the hospital is getting. I can understand staying a couple of weeks; however, this is now turning into months.

I'm at a point where the nurses can read my mood and will give me an Ativan without me having to ask. It's a little round miracle!

I have started to accept the fact that if I need help from social security, I will take it. It's obvious at this point that my illness is very real. Not that I didn't believe it before, but when you are in the hospital and you have the chance to talk to therapists, behavioral health associates and nurses about your illness, you learn that it is quite real and that having a mental illness doesn't mean you're insane. People who are insane usually don't know it. I'm not insane because I have cognitive thought and can function most of the time even though my mind is in constant turmoil. Just because you are not legally insane doesn't mean that you can't still be afflicted with a mental illness.

The most interesting thing that happened today was that a new patient, who is a 60-year-old female, came into my room and decided to lay down on my roommate's bed while I was resting on mine. She then started snoring like Curly from The Three Stooges and laughing in her sleep. I sometimes think God sends me these comedic situations in order to give me a break from my own mind.

I had no choice but to inform the nurses what was going on in my room. We all shared a good laugh about it. The nurses then came and got her out of my room, had to lock her in seclusion and sedate her. I'm still curious to find out what it's like to get the needle. After this incident ended, my sadness returned as quickly as it disappeared.

My mother also came to visit today. She was feeling guilty about my illness being all her fault. She said she apologized for taking me to the cemetery starting at about age 2, visiting relatives' graves, bringing me to nursing homes to visit great aunts and uncles who were months from dying (and the other patients around them who looked worse!) and not having the common sense of trying to keep me from the behaviors of my father.

Chapter 45: Jan 10, 2020, Elmhurst Hospital, Queens, New York

Yup, it's January and I haven't written a journal in a little over 2 months. The reason is that I keep writing the same things repeatedly. I'm tired of talking about myself. Since November, I was moved to a different floor that houses patients that are scheduled to be discharged soon.

The new ward I'm on is twice the size as the floor below, has a bigger day room with big windows that overlook a park. Every morning from the Day Room, I watch groups of Asian people do Tai Chi and a group of Chinese women who practice a dance where they use beautiful red umbrellas as props. Its peaceful to watch.

Other new views I have is a row of stores including a liquor store, deli, nail salon and a dry cleaner. There's also views of some apartment buildings, the elevated subway tracks and a view of the Manhattan skyline.

I also realize that I have been at Elmhurst since September and that I haven't been outside for over 3 months.

Eden:

Occasionally a patient who is a total character gets admitted to the unit. In this case, it was Eden. Eden is about 32, Caucasian and has short red hair. If Sean Penn's character from Fast Times at Ridgemont High, Jeff Spicoli and Peppermint Patty from The Peanuts had a daughter, it would be Eden: she talked like a surfer and looked a little like the actress, Tea Leoni.

Eden lives in New Orleans and was driving through New York on her way back home from her mother's funeral in Connecticut which she was banned from attending because of her erratic/manic behaviors. Eden told me that she was bi-polar.

When Eden showed up at her mother's funeral, she was turned away. She then waited until nighttime, snuck into the cemetery, dug up her mother's urn (she was cremated and buried) and planned on taking it back to New Orleans.

When she got to New York, she decided to stay for a while and live out of her van. After a few days, she met a homeless man that was about her age, they got engaged and started to plan to have a baby. After about a week of being engaged, Eden and her new fiancé had an argument which led to him calling the police because she was having a manic episode. The police picked her up, put her van in the impound and she was admitted to Elmhurst Hospital along with her mother's ashes, which were put in a storage locker with the rest of her belongings.

Eden's personality is exactly like Peppermint Patty, and I felt like I was her Charlie Brown. If you ever watch The Peanuts, Peppermint Patty is Charlie Brown's biggest cheerleader and emotional support. That was our relationship: She was able to see the old me that my friend Darren describes in the forward of this book.

We would sit together and share our life's stories. I would tell her about my sons, my time in music etc…She would tell me that I was, "Fucking awesome. You have no idea what a great guy you are". Usually, a compliment like that would fall on deaf ears, but not this time. I believed what she was saying about me. Eden had a sincerity there that I rarely see in people. I guess her awareness of being bi-polar, her willingness to be an open book and telling it like it is, are the contributors to her sincerity. Eden was also attractive, and she had mentioned that she found me attractive. So, we became close very quickly. Nothing sexual ever happened because there was no place to sneak off and be alone. Even if you held hands with someone, it was immediately stopped.

Eden and I would sit to next to each other at meals, in groups, walk the hallway together, talk or just sit in the day room to watch the Chinese dancers in the park.

At times, when Eden was manic, she could be found curled up in a ball crying and saying that she wanted to see her mother's ashes. Also, while she was manic, she would skip up and down the hallway while she chewed nicotine gum. Eden hated taking her pills, so when it was medication time, she would push the pills into her nicotine gum so that the nurses believed she swallowed the pills.

I loved Eden's surfer accent; she would call everyone "dude" and her favorite adverb to use was "fucking". For example, she would yell at a nurse, "That's not fucking cool dude!"

After about two weeks, Eden started telling me that she wished that we could run away together. I admit it sounded fun because I started to develop feelings for her. Leave it to me to fall in love with another patient while at a psychiatric hospital. Like Peppermint Patty, she was my biggest cheerleader, ever.

She wanted to travel the country with me in her van. I would never do it because of my sons and because her illness can be quite severe.

The more time I spent with Eden, the happier and more alive I felt. I had mentioned in earlier chapters that my ex, Julia was a parasite who feeds off people's energy without giving anything back. Eden was the opposite. While only sitting close to her, I could feel her giving me all the positive energy that she could. She has the gift of giving love unconditionally and the curse of being born Bi-Polar.

Eden always talked about that when she was discharged, the first thing she was going to do was go to the deli that we could see from the Day Room window and buy a pack of cigarettes. My "relationship" with Eden lasted about 3 weeks and then she got discharged. I remember as she hugged me good-bye, she told me that she was really in love with me. I told her I loved her too. I did.

The last time I saw Eden was right after she was discharged. I watched her from the day room windows as she walked past the Chinese dancers and into the deli. I sat at the window and cried. Sometimes love comes at the wrong times and with the wrong people. I didn't wait at the window to watch her leave the deli. I don't know why.

Words of strength and encouragement don't necessarily have to come from health professionals, friends or family; sometimes it comes from an attractive, bi-polar woman, who is driving around in a van with her mother's stolen ashes!

Chapter 46: Jan 11, 2020

Today my thoughts have been focused on my sons, Julia and relationships.

I miss my sons. On this typical Saturday most people are having fun with their kids. Not me, I've been replaced by Julia's boyfriend. Julia has taken him to Arizona, Florida, Maryland, Boston and a few other places; probably partially on my dime.

Julia has done everything she could do to get every possible cent since divorcing. When I told her I had to declare bankruptcy, she turned around and filed for support modification for more money because I got a raise (maybe that extra money could have helped me when I am with the kids? Ya think?. Meanwhile she makes close to $120k a year. I was making $104k a year and now I make $80k a year. Julia takes joy in causing people emotional pain. She enjoys making her subordinates cry when she observes them at work, she likes when her staff is afraid of her, she thinks she is better than everyone else and is superior. While I knew these things before, my beliefs were confirmed by her ex-boss who I happened to run into at a store.

I had been wanting to talk to this woman for a while because she and Julia started off as good friends. They became such good friends that we would hang out with her boss and her husband. He was fun. After a few years working side by side, Julia's real side came out, their work relationship fell apart along with the friendship.

Julia is power hungry and felt she was the in charge. It eventually got to the point where Julia was removed and reassigned to another location. We had also discussed our marriage and divorce. Ex-boss told me that it wasn't me that was the problem, it was Julia. Her ex-boss also told me it took her 3 years to undo the damage that she did to the staff. It was good to hear that. While I know I have issues, in my opinion, I'm on point about what type of person Julia is.

Another way Julia tried to ruin my finances was by calling her niece who is a CPA and asked how she could, "Screw me with the taxes". The reason I know this was because her niece made it a point to come to one of my gigs and tell me about this information in person. When I told Julia that I knew what she did, she began harassing her niece and sister on the phone so much, that her sister threatened to call the police if she didn't stop calling. The truth was that they liked me more than her and I feel she couldn't handle it. Since that incident, her nieces, nephew and sister do not talk to her anymore.

Another classless thing that I heard from Julia's niece was the following: Julia was engaged to her high school boyfriend. They had an engagement party and received lots of presents. Not long after the engagement party, they broke up. Julia kept all the engagement presents instead of returning them to her friends and family. Apparently, they broke up because his mother was overbearing. I used to believe that. Along with my feelings that Julia is a narcissist, I feel Julia is also a sociopath and will lie about anything so that she looks like the victim. It's not only my opinion, but the opinions of the countless therapists I have talked to over my lifetime, our couple's therapist, who knew Julia well, and some of Julia's relatives and people she used to work with who I bump into a few times a year.

After all that she has put me through why do I miss her? Maybe it's because I know her behavior is the result of trauma, and I can separate her good and evil sides. Unfortunately, her evil side is out on display most of the time and I have a huge aversion towards it.

I sometimes still miss the 5 of us and our family dynamic. I miss feeling that I belong. I miss putting my sons to bed every night, singing Van Halen and Steve Miller songs and telling made up bedtime stories on the fly.

I have had girlfriends since my divorce and only 2 women have met my sons. They both met them once, meaning that there are 2 days in total since my divorce that my sons spent with another woman. I feel wrong bringing another woman around my kids. They didn't ask for it and I shouldn't be forcing them to be around another woman and play "family". That doesn't work for me. I'm also not interested in melding families like The Brady Bunch.

I remember a particular fight with Julia when we lived in Nassau County; she threatened to leave me and take the kids. I think that was her plan all along. That was a constant threat.

Chapter 47: Jan 15, 2020, Elmhurst Hospital, Queens New York

I spoke to the social worker today. I was given news that I was not particularly happy about. The psychiatric team here at Elmhurst feels that I'm not ready to be discharged yet, and want to transfer me to Bronx Psychiatric Center, where they anticipate my stay to be another 2 months.

After I heard two months, I got very upset. This is now officially out of hand. I'm not in control of my own life anymore. Instead of this supposed to be feeling like help, it feels like I'm in jail.

There's way too much spinning around in my head and I'm fucking sick of writing down the same thoughts repeatedly. I'm done.

Chapter 48: Feb 14, 2020, Bronx Psychiatric Center (BPC), Unit 3 North(3N)

I notice that it has been a month since I have written anything. One reason is because I'm tired of writing and in addition, I've started creating abstract drawings with black and colored pencils. I have always been able to draw, and my specialty is of the abstract style.

I was transferred to BPC from Elmhurst Hospital on Feb 3. 2020. I am staying in the main inpatient psychiatric building, which is less than 5 years old. Unit 3 North (3N) where I am staying is divided into 2 halves: On each half are the patients' rooms and bathrooms. Each room is a single. The hallway outside the rooms is very wide with several sections of sofas to sit on.

In the middle of the unit is a large day area with giant windows that overlook the grass yard of the hospital, some baseball fields and a shopping center. This area also has 4 or 5 sections of sofas for people to sit or sleep on. The TV room is separate and only fits about 7 chairs because it's so small.

In addition, the nurse's station, medication window and exit to the elevator are also in the middle of the unit. In addition, the offices for all the therapists for the building are on the 3rd floor too adjacent to our unit.

Like Jacobi Hospital, I have a psychologist that I barely see. Some of the nurses questioned why I'm here because I'm not as mentally ill as the other patients. The doctors informed the nurses that my stay would be about 2 months and that I was transferred here to be close to home and so it would be convenient for me to come here after I'm discharged for their outpatient program.

Some of the patients here will most likely spend the rest of their lives at this hospital. Their levels of schizophrenia, anxiety, psychosis, multiple personality disorders and bi-polar disorders are the worst I have seen so far.

During the day here on 3N, patients are not allowed to be in their rooms after breakfast and must wait until after dinner. The purpose is to keep the patients socialized. However, many the patients sleep on the sofas in the social areas.

The bathrooms/showers are across the hall from our bedrooms and lock from the inside so that patients can have their privacy in the bathroom; that means we can spank our monkeys if we choose too. Only the staff has keys to the bathroom and there is an emergency button to press if a patient has an issue.

Next to the bathrooms is the laundry room which is open for 3 hours in the morning and 3 hours in the evening. We are responsible for doing our laundry and changing our bedding every 3 days. My bedroom window faces the same direction as the dayroom windows. At night in my room, I usually look outside at all the lights and the decorative lampposts that are along the walking path of the hospital property. I don't really get sad anymore. Instead, I just go numb.

When I get bored, I sleep on the sofas too. It makes me feel like I'm homeless. Sometimes in a circle of 4 sofas, there will be 4 patients sleeping. It's depressing to see and be a part of.

Wake up time here is 6:30 am and we get an hour to wash up and take care of our hygiene before they lock our rooms at 7:30. If the purpose for locking our rooms is so that we don't sleep all day; shouldn't there be an effort to keep us from sleeping on the sofas?

We eat our meals in the cafeteria on the first floor. That means at least 3 times a day, we get to leave the unit. In addition, the music room, library, gym, art room, visiting room and chapel are all on the first floor too.

Also on the first floor are the offices for the dentist, eye doctor, foot doctor and general practitioners.

I find that there is a handful of staff members who are rude, lazy and talk down to the patients. I find it uncomfortable to watch. These same staff members will act annoyed if you ask for a favor like a razor and cream to shave. I'm allowed to shave my face and head here on my own without being supervised. Would it not be safer to have patients shave with cordless electric razors?

Anyway, I've been here for 11 days and have had a total of 60 minutes of meeting time with a psychologist: even less with the psychiatrist.

When I met the social worker Dennis, he expressed his curiosity along with the staff of why

I was here. Dennis is the real deal, is a great guy and works hard to make things comfortable for the patients. Dennis said he was not sure what my treatment will be here because I have more cognitive awareness than the other patients. That means I'm aware of my reality and my surroundings. In other words, I wasn't a person who he felt was sick enough to be committed. He saw me as a guy with anxiety that went through a rough time and simply snapped. Dennis said he would do everything he could to expedite my discharge.

At BPC we are given the opportunity to access a computer once or twice a week, we attend a music class and bang on congas to songs that the instructor plays off You Tube. Having the access to any kind of drum or instrument has become a Godsend.

One of the first patients I met here was Temple. Temple is female, is about 6' 1", is African American and looks androgynous. She is a high functioning person with autism and is waiting for a Section 8 apartment to open so that she can be discharged and live on her own. She also has diabetes and is constantly fighting to take weight off. She loves pastries and wants to be a pastry chef when she leaves here. Not only do I believe she can do it, but I also believe she will be great at it. Her autism hasn't affected her intelligence or even the way she speaks. Sometimes she will struggle with some words, but other than that, you would never know she is autistic. I guess her case would be categorized as having Asperger's Syndrome.

I once heard Temple ask a therapist if she could see him to talk. The therapist answered, "I'm not sure, I'm kind of busy today". That would become the standard answer from most of the therapists when asked for even 15 minutes of time.

Today, I experienced my first Unit Community meeting, which is run by 2 patients and Dennis. After a few minutes Dennis had to leave and left us on our own. The meetings are usually about which bathrooms are broken, current events or patients asking that we get more coffee during the day (its decaf so it's not ideal).

Sometimes at the meetings, the schizophrenic patients will tell stories that have nothing to do with the subject matter of the meeting. An older woman named Vida who acts like my grandmother and draws pictures of rabbits and cats, interrupted the meeting by saying that you can only accept God in your life if you accept all creatures into your life as well. She then also said, "I also decided to give up having orgasms in order to be true to God". That's how the meeting ended.

All the psychologists and the psychology interns just emerged from their morning meeting and are headed to the exit of our unit as fast as possible. None of them say hello or make any eye contact with the patients. This is a habit that I have noticed since I got here: Either they are trying to avoid us, or they must see patients on another unit. Right now, there is not a lot of therapy going on.

So far today I have done some drawing, writing, watching TV and even fell asleep on a chair for a while.

We then get called to lineup for lunch. The nurses line us up and do a head count. They then take us to the 1st floor where they give us our meal slips and we lineup like it's a school cafeteria. We are then rushed through our meal. We are given less than 30 minutes to eat sometimes. We are then called to line up to head back to our unit.

I'm fully aware that today is Valentine's Day. I have been putting off writing my feelings about it because of what will get brought up. If I do not write about how I feel, it will fester inside of me like a giant insecure mental cyst.

My heart hurts today because Julia has been with somebody else for a few years now. Its hurtful to know that she is with him and all the aspects that come with a relationship; sex, having fun and playing house with my kids.

I've been pushed aside and started to feel that way when I was blamed for the pregnancy of our youngest son and then she wanted to sell a house that we worked hard on to make it feel like our home etc. Same shit I wrote earlier!

Theoretically, I should not miss her because I feel she needs to be top dog whether it's at home or at work. She micromanaged me during our entire relationship. She would test me by leaving things out on purpose to see if I would put them away.

There's an irony here because part of me does miss her and it's the version of her that she portrayed at the beginning of the relationship. However, that was an act. That person never existed. I still have all the cards she ever got me. I

miss a version of Julia that never existed. I think about what I could have done better. But how can I have done better when I never had a chance to do it my way. I rarely got a chance to try because most of my ideas, thoughts, processes, theories, beliefs and procedures were consistently blocked by
Julia. I either had to argue or deal with the silent treatment if I got something that went my way. I also would like to make the point that some of the things I wanted to do my way would have benefited all of us, not just her.

Along with somebody I believe to be a control freak, I feel Julia was OCD about cleaning and making sure things were put in their proper place, or what she deemed the proper place. Everyone else, meaning me, had to follow suit or else be ridiculed and shamed. It's ironic that Julia Roberts is a supposed narcissist yet played the victim of a physically abusive narcissist in "Sleeping With the Enemy". In the context of our marriage, I was Julia Roberts' character. Hi, I'm Laura!

I wasn't allowed to leave anything on the kitchen counter such as a tub of protein powder. In the bathroom, I wasn't allowed to leave my electric razor charging in the medicine cabinet because it was in her way. I had to charge it in another room. And then of course, sex was used as a reward system if she felt that I did a good job around the house and with the kids. If something was slightly off, no sex. But I was allowed to massage and rub her back and shoulders every night in bed until she fell asleep. I felt she always kept herself one step ahead in order to keep people feeling uneasy.

While I was never physically abused, the constant chastising was hard to take. Julia was only fun when she had a few drinks because the Julia that I first dated would then come out. I guess that's why I would buy her alcohol when she asked.

Vindictive Julia:

3 years after our divorce, she gave me back our honeymoon photos and removed all the ones with her in them.

 Another time, she was throwing out a Valentine's Day bear that one of her ex-boyfriends gave her. Mind you, this happened during the summer. The bear was in the garbage and my youngest son asked for the bear to give to me. Instead of suggesting that they give me something else, she gave my son the ex-boyfriend's bear, and he gave it to me. When he gave it to me, I knew exactly what it was and sent her a nasty text because she knew exactly what she was doing and using our son to do it. Her explanation was, "Technically, it was in the garbage, so it really wasn't from my ex-boyfriend anymore". Those are just some examples of how she likes to hurt me and other people. In my opinion, she enjoys being vindictive. I would say the worst example was the late term abortion threat.

After all that I have mentioned, it's still going to hurt tonight when I'm alone and my soundtrack for the night will be the other patients talking to themselves, banging their heads against the wall or crying.

Chapter 49: BPC, 3 North, Patients and Observations

Walter: Walter looks just like Bryan Cranston's character, Walter White from the greatest show I've ever seen, Breaking Bad, which is why I call him Walter. He is mostly bald with a little bit of red hair. If there were a movie made about this place, Bryan Cranston could play this patient and win an Academy Award.

Walter has a regular speaking voice of someone who would be considered a tenor: basically, he has a high voice which often slips into him sounding like Mickey Mouse. Walter always dresses in a grey sweatshirt, grey sweatpants and sneakers with Velcro straps. We all have Velcro sneakers. Walter sits on the sofa all day and sometimes sleeps as well. When he is awake, he can usually be heard laughing to himself. When anyone says hello to him, he yells "Hello!" back, that's when he really sounds like Mickey Mouse.

I was told by some nurses that Walter has the mentality of a 5-year-old. That becomes apparent when having a conversation with him. You must stick with simple questions in order to keep the conversation going. I like talking to Walter because he is always in a good mood and it's easy to make him laugh. Sometimes I do my impressions of cartoon characters for him.

Walter also likes to be last on line whether we are going to the cafeteria or if we are waiting for meds.

A few days ago, Walter took two sweatshirts from some other patients and threw them in the garbage. I watched him do it. I waited until after he walked away to take the clothes out of the garbage can and return them to the nurses' station. I told them what Walter did it and asked if he would be in trouble. They told me no because it was something that he routinely does. Walter doesn't understand that the sweatshirts are someone's clothes; in his mind, its garbage, and all garbage must be thrown out.

Sometimes Walter gets an evil look on his face like Jack Nicholson does in The Shining when his schizophrenia kicks in and he's sitting comatose at his typewriter. There's also the music in that scene and the way it was filmed that makes that whole movie amazingly creepy.

The times that Walter does get angry is when somebody tells him that he is moving too slow. Walter will then yell, "Fuck You!" repeatedly for at least 10 seconds. When he yells loud, there's a little bit of Axl Rose in there along with Mickey Mouse.

At meals, Walter is always asking for extra food and doesn't take no for an answer and will repeat, "Can I?", over and over until he gets his way. When Walter eats, his hands shake because of his meds, and he manages to not be a sloppy eater. He must be used to the shaking. At the end of each meal, Walter hides in the bathroom because he doesn't want to go back up to 3 North. At least 3 North is a well-lit, bright unit with lots of windows and space. It's very different from Elmhurst and Jacobi: the wards there are painted in dark greens and dark blues which gives off a depressing vibe.

Videa:

Videa is a woman from Jamaica who is overweight, missing teeth and does not bathe. Whenever she is sitting or laying down on the sofa, she has her hand down her pants. Before and after she puts her hand down her pants, she licks her fingers.

I once observed Videa while she read The New York Post. Whenever she was done reading a page, she would take her hand out of her pants, lick her fingers and then turn the page. She's obviously added an extra step in newspaper reading. I no longer read The New York Post.

Videa lies about bathing because she does not feel that she smells. The patients who have poor hygiene usually have dandruff, they wear the same clothes every day and they smell of urine and poop. In addition, when they speak, they all claim to be working for the FBI, CIA or any other spy agency.

Chapter 50: Feb 15, 2020, BPC 3 North

A lot of the patients are in a good mood. For a psychiatric ward, it's about as vibrant as it can get. Walter and Vida are sitting on some sofas. Walter laughs at Vida while she talks about Adam and Eve.

A patient named Michael is sitting next to me and is talking to Videa who has her hand down her pants. I feel like I'm on the subway! Michael discusses the meaning of inner strength and then loses his train of thought and somehow starts talking about the 80's video game, Duck Hunt. When he talks, he gets to a point where his brain shifts on him, and he loses focus. It's unfortunate because he is very intelligent.

Vida then tells all of us that she is excited to have 2 bottles of soda. This means that she took a shower: soda is her reward for bathing. When Vida asked for her sodas, a very nasty nurse said no. Vida began to yell at the female nurse, telling her that she doesn't deserve to be talked to that way. The nurse then said that she had already put the soda order in. She could have said that from the start instead of making a sick woman feel worse. If the nurse was pissed or was busy with something else, it's very easy to say, "As soon as I'm done working on this, I can get your soda. It's a little busy today". Most if not all patients will accept that answer.

Vida then starts to sing songs from the 1950's and 60's and sounds eerily like my grandmother, which gives me some flashbacks.

The building I'm in at BPC is relatively new and looks very nice on the surface, however, when you start getting into to nooks and crannies, you can see where short cuts were taken and inferior materials were used to build the hospital. Some examples include: the locks on the bathroom doors constantly breaking, the water in the shower is hot enough to burn you badly or at least one elevator
will be not in use all the time. There's also cracks in the walls, and you can see where mistakes were made and repaired numerous times.

In addition, in the gymnasium, the exercise bike has no pedals, and all the stations on the Universal machine are broken. I know it sounds petty, but these are things that need to be in place so that the patients can thrive to the best of their ability. Constantly being faced with something broken brings down one's morale.

Like Elmhurst and Jacobi Hospital, the group leaders are nice guys but have the Bob Ross energy and seem to do the minimum that is required. They both always look tired and drag themselves around like sloths.

Mon Feb 17, 2020, BPC 3N

Being that it is President's Day, there are no group meetings. That means that I will not get to use the computers in order to write a new resume. Instead, we went to bingo in the gymnasium and were mixed with the other units here at the hospital. During bingo, there was a fight between a woman and a man. The woman was quite heavy, and the man was quite old.

While the fight did not come to fists being thrown, they were wrestling, and the woman was clearly dominating. The fight was broken up quickly by security guards. The highlight of bingo was that I won a pair of underwear and a bottle of body wash that smelled like Drakkar cologne.

Today is one of those days where I ruminate a lot about the same things that I talked about in the earlier entries. It's the same thoughts and the same old stories repeatedly. It starts off small, then it crescendos and then I crash. My thoughts are mostly about my financial difficulties. For example, my lawyer wants $3500 so she can file a child support modification with family court. I've already given her $10000.

I'm also in a cycle where when as soon as I make improvements on my financial situation, something like a bill from the IRS comes in the mail and says that I owe them $7000. This was because there were 2 sources of income that were not reported when my accountant did my taxes.

I had just consolidated what I owed so that I was living in the black, and now the IRS comes and says they need $7000 from me. I feel like I can't win and can't get ahead. For every step I take forward, something happens which knocks me 2 steps backwards.

Feb 27, 2020, BPC 3N

I just found out that child support services have frozen $20,000 from my bank account for arrears based on my teaching job that I retired from in May of 2019. This still happened even though my attorney filed the appropriate paperwork stating my new sources of income: my pension and SSDI. I'm stuck in bureaucratic red tape. I have no issue paying child support, it's that all these clerical errors are frustrating and stressful. Getting a letter that says that your money is frozen can give you a heart attack. I was paying about $3000 a month in child support in which Julia was not spending properly. Instead of living in an apartment or house where my sons could have at least 2 bedrooms to share, they live in a basement apartment and all 3 sons share 1 bedroom. My youngest used to sleep in the closet, which was bigger than a normal closet, but still a closet, with mommy making about 120k a year plus $3000 a month for child support. Julia sleeps on a fold out sofa and loves to bring that up during her "martyr" act. She has gone on expensive vacations, frequents the nail and hair salon, purchased a Peloton Bike, and had personal trainer at one point. It's the same apartment that I lived with her after we separated for the first time. I wanted to move because I didn't want my son's bedroom to be an oversized closet. It's almost 10 years that they are living there.

It's not hard for me to feel taken advantage of. She's getting everything she wanted, and she bulldozed her way through everyone's lives, including her sons'.

Chapter 51: Feb 29, 2020, BPC 3N

I've been here just under a month. I've been getting to know the patients here a little better. They are all very nice. There aren't any violent people on this unit. About half the patients here are about 60 and over. Some have been here 20 years. Can you imagine?

There's a patient here named Rachel who has a nice singing voice and tells everyone that she loves them. She is about 40 and has been here about 5 years. Most of the time, Rachel is in her own world with the occasional "pop in" to reality especially if she is pissed about something.

I'm starting to feel like a veteran of the psychiatric hospital system for New York City because I'm starting to run into patients from Elmhurst and Jacobi who have been transferred here as well.

Shirley from Jacobi is here; the older women who uses a chair as a walker. Here, she has a walker. I met her in the cafeteria. She is staying on another floor. She told me that she was going to have surgery on her feet which immediately made me lose my appetite. During our reunion, Shirley also informed me that she has stayed here before when the new building was just opening. She also told me that it was her husband and son who had her committed. I'm sure it broke their hearts. Shirley is in her late 60's and will probably spend the rest of her life in a hospital or nursing home.

The other patient that is here from Jacobi is Daniel. He is the man whose legs shake all the time and who shoves his whole hand in his mouth when he takes his pills to make sure they go down his throat.

March 17, 2020, BPC 3N

I haven't written anything in a couple of weeks because yet again, I find myself repeating the same things and have nothing new to say. I've also been keeping busy by drawing my abstract art pieces and I am doing as many crossword puzzles as possible that I can. I've gotten to the point with The New York Daily News where I can finish all their puzzles for each day of the week. Their puzzles aren't particularly difficult, but it's still fun to complete them.

Also, since my last entry, there is a virus called Covid 19 that has started to infect people all around the world. Today on the news, they reported that over 100,000 people have been infected and over 3000 people have died around the world. The first case in New York was in New Rochelle.

Governor Cuomo of New York State said that this virus is like the flu on steroids. All the schools in New York City have been closed and most of the schools in the entire country have been closed. This is like that Dustin Hoffman movie called Outbreak, where a virus took over a town and Dustin Hoffman is the scientist that must save the town. For now, New York City schools will be closed until April 20th. However, both Governor Cuomo and mayor DiBlasio have said that schools could be closed for the rest of the year.

Italy has been hit the worst so far with almost 1000 deaths. The news reported that the virus originated in a lab in China. One theory is that someone contracted the virus in the lab and then it started to spread. There are also rumors that the virus started from a bat that was bought at an open market where people evidently eat bats.

Finally, is the theory that this was done on purpose by the Chinese government.

Everything in New York City is closed and people are being advised to stay home. Even the stock market has taken a huge hit and hasn't seen numbers so low since the great depression. Restaurants can only serve take-out and delivery until 8:00 p.m.

All Broadway shows and movie theatres have been closed. People may not gather more than 50 at a time as well. A new term called "social distancing" is being used all over the place. It means that people should stay at least 6' apart from each other. In addition, all sporting events have either been postponed or cancelled as well as any events where there are large gatherings. This is the exact type of scenario that I would think about when I was a child and obsessing about Armageddon.

Here at BPC, Temple who lives on 3 North with us, was removed from our floor because she had a fever, which is a symptom of Covid 19. It's been 5 days and we haven't heard back of whether she has tested positive. I don't know if we are allowed to know because of HIPPA privacy laws.

One reason that I think that temple has tested positive for Covid 19 is that because our unit has been put on quarantine. We are not allowed to leave the unit. Our meals are now being brought to us and we cannot go to group sessions on the 1st floor.

So far, nobody else is sick or showing symptoms of Covid 19. A part of me feels that it's just a matter of time that one of the older patients who are weaker will eventually get sick. I'm also concerned for my mother who is 86 as well. I am obviously also concerned for my sons. The so- called professionals on TV say that children can fight this virus because they have strong immune systems.

 Given the fact that this is New York City and there are over 10 million people living here; there will probably be an outbreak in the tens of thousands. It only makes sense because you have millions of people living on top of each other in apartment buildings, riding the trains and the buses. From what I see on TV, New York City and other big cities look like ghost towns.

 I'm sitting in the TV Room watching the news and they're saying that New York City may have to do a "shelter in place order". I guess that means everybody is forced to stay home. One of the doctors I see here said the roads are basically empty. The New Jersey governor is shutting down all malls and amusement centers until further notice. Restaurants in New Jersey are allowed to stay open for take-out and delivery.

The news just reported that 4 members of the Brooklyn Nets have Covid 19. They did not report the names of the players. There are also celebrities like Tom Hanks and his wife Rita who have Covid 19. Also, one member of the New York Yankees minor league club and 2 members of the basketball team, The Utah Jazz have Covid19 as well.

A lot of people are going to get sick and die. It's like The Black Plague in The Middle ages that wiped out hundreds and thousands of people in Europe. For some reason I'm not scared of getting it because I don't have any respiratory problems, diabetes or any other physical health conditions that would warrant me getting very sick from Covid.

March 22nd, 2020, BPC 3N

Over the past five days, hundreds of people in

New York City have died. One crazy part is that Elmhurst Hospital, where I was staying before here, has become Ground Zero in New York City for Covid patients. People are dying all over that hospital and on the old floor that I used to stay on. I'm lucky that I got transferred here.

Governor Cuomo has basically declared martial law and that only essential workers like doctors, nurses, police, fire, EMT workers, and MTA workers are allowed to leave their houses to go to work. All other work force people are advised to stay home. People are allowed out to get groceries and their drugs at their local pharmacies. Restaurants are only allowed to serve take-out orders. People are not allowed to congregate in groups of 10 or larger. Small groups must practice social distancing.

So, last night I had a fever of 100 and a little bit of a headache. I thought it was because I was wearing a hoodie and was just tired. Plus, the last time I had a fever was in the 8th grade (no exaggeration, I never get fevers). This morning strangely, I had a fever of 101 and the headache was worse.

This prompted the medical staff to test me and then had me quarantined to my room for the rest of today and tomorrow. Temple's test came back positive, so she has Covid 19. Now this shit is starting to get scary and real.

I'm young enough and strong enough to beat this if I have it. Its torture being stuck in a psychiatric hospital and not being able to see my kids knowing that I might have a virus that could have the potential of killing me. Guess what? This is starting to set off some anxiety. So far, the only medical attention I have gotten was Tylenol. It's working.

March 23rd, 2020, BPC 3N

I don't have a fever today, but I do have a splitting headache. For some people, that's what the virus does; You get a headache or a fever for a couple of days and then it goes away. Hopefully I will be that lucky. Since this has happened, I must stay in my room and eat all meals in my room. It turns out that everyone on the unit must eat in their rooms too. I have no radio or TV in my room, so I stick to trying to get The Daily News and continue with my artwork.

I just opened my door to the hallway to peek outside and see what was going on. Nobody was outside of their rooms. I can hear people singing, talking to themselves and laughing. It sounds like the song, Brain Damage by Pink Floyd.

My good friend Walter White is in rare form tonight. Right now, he's singing "When You Wish Upon a Star", he gets about halfway through the song and then starts laughing in his high-pitched tone.

March 24th, 2020, BPC 3N

I'm trying to keep as busy as I can in my room without thinking about all the things that feed my anxiety and depression disorders. However, the situation feels heightened because of this virus. What if Julia gets it? What if my sons get it? What if my sons get it and one of them dies and I'm in the hospital? What if Julia dies? I always think "what if?" That's my whole life; What if this? What if that? Most "what if's" never come true and you waste days, weeks, months and years of your life worrying about stuff that never happens. There is so much time that I wish that I could get back.

Chapter 52: Thoughts About My Careers

When you are a musician, you are always told to not have all your eggs in one basket. The road manager of the band Metallica gave me that advice while we were having pizza in 1990. He had come to guest lecture in my music marketing class, and I met with him afterwards at dinner with my professor and my friend, Darren to discuss our demo tape. He said, "Peter, if you don't have anything going for you by the age of 25, then have a backup plan. You should still sing and keep trying because there is nothing wrong with your voice or your drumming; your song writing is what has to improve. Also, you're just starting out and these are the first songs you've ever recorded". He was correct. Being a good singer does not necessarily go in tandem with the ability to write good songs. A few examples of great singers who were not songwriters include: Whitney Houston, Mariah Carey and Sebastian Bach of Skid Row.

When I was 25, I took the backup plan advice and I enrolled in graduate school. Two years later, I had a master's degree in physical education. My goal was to teach on Long Island and to coach lacrosse. I had been working as a personal trainer as well, so teaching physical education was the logical next step for me.

During graduate school, ALL my professors told us to not work for The New York City Department of Education. They said to avoid it at all costs. They said we would teach in overcrowded classes, have little resources and get zero support from administrators because most of them are either corrupt, incompetent or on power trips. They were correct on all accounts.

I was once doing a gig at a house party a few years after I started teaching in the city. By coincidence, one of my former professors happened to be one of the guests. She was drunk. When our set was over, we approached each other to say hello. She asked, "So, where are you teaching?" I responded, "At a middle school in the city". She then playfully slapped me on the arm and said, "I told you not to teach in the city! What do you have in the gym; 150 kids and 5 basketballs?". I said, "Yes, that's exactly how it is. It's completely chaotic and then we get blamed if ALL the kids don't participate. One time, we were told we had $5000 for equipment. Two weeks the money went to another program, and we were promised to get some equipment. They sent us a parachute, bean bags, stick ribbons and rubber chickens." My professor then said, and I paraphrase, "What the fuck are you supposed to do with rubber chickens in middle school? All that stuff is for preschool! I told you not to teach in the city. You should have a drink now".

After I finished graduate school, I was a permanent substitute for a middle school on Long Island. It was there that I coached lacrosse and wrestling for two years. I even coached girls' lacrosse when I did my student teaching.

At the end of my 2nd year at the middle school, I attended a job fair in the city that led to me taking my job there. I didn't get hired at the job fair because the principal forgot to show up and I had to come back to the city the next day to be interviewed at the school. At my partner's interview for our school, the principal told him that she knew nothing about gym. In addition, our assistant principal would oversee the gym. This man never taught in a classroom, in a gymnasium or at any school; he was a former boy's and girl's club director. How is it possible that your first job with NYC Schools can be as an assistant principal without any teaching experience? The answer is:

you can if you have your degrees and pass the state licensing exam.

Little did I know that 19 years later, I would be getting pushed out of my job based on a blatant lie. There is something about it that I will never get over. In addition, being thrown into a position where your life is in disarray is very aggravating. And, yes, there are people I would love to beat the shit out of because of this. Being that I don't want to end up in prison, I am pursuing a lawsuit instead.

The building and the gymnasium that I used to work at was physically falling apart. We were barely given equipment yet our observations were done as if they had provided us everything that we needed to teach our classes. If the students who were known to cause trouble felt that they didn't want to participate in my class, I was blamed for it. My partner in the gym wouldn't take any shit from the assistant principal and would tell him "They don't participate upstairs in class either. So, what do you want me to do? 90% of the students are well below their grade levels academically". In addition, if I were a student at my school, I wouldn't want to participate in an overcrowded, filthy gymnasium with no air conditioners or fans. The smell in there was unbearable at times. In addition, my partner's side of the gym was extra hot because it was directly over the boiler room. The wall that divided the gym in half was loose and part of it was in danger of falling off its hinges. The PA system in the gymnasium did not work so we could not hear any school announcements like, if there were an intruder in the school with a gun. The school bell did not ring in the gym and there are no clocks in the gym so that we can see when class was over. On my partner's side of the gym, the school phone had been broken for at least 5 years before they got around to replacing it. The bleachers had been in disrepair for over 10 years and had been left broken with sharp metal corners being exposed. I had emailed the administration about these issues numerous times; however, it wasn't until 2019 that they started to remove the bleachers, using the slowest workers on planet Earth. Each day they took a different part. For example, one day they only took the plastic pieces off the bleachers and left the metallic skeleton of the bleachers remaining. In addition, while the slow removal of the bleachers was taking place, I was still having class in the gymnasium with this dangerous metal structure wide open for the children to mess with.

Because I kept emailing the administration to express my concerns about the gym, it may have given the administration the idea to try to get rid of me because they felt that I was being difficult. I was just trying to cover my own ass because you know full well if a kid ran into the metal structure and got injured, I would have gotten blamed.

March 29th, 2020 BPC 3N

Temple, the woman on my unit that had Covid19 is back with us, and she is OK. She is wearing a mask along with the rest of us. Masks have become the new reality. I stay away from her just in case. Yesterday and today, I feel very tired and slept most of the day. I feel a little weak as well.

I really miss my sons terribly. I hope and pray to get a decent job so that I can afford for us to do things together like going on vacations. I have never been to Europe, and I'd like for the first time going to Europe to be with my sons. Right now, nobody's going to Europe because of Covid. I also think about how Julia hijacked our lives from having a nice house in the suburbs to now both of us living in basement apartments; all because the house wasn't convenient enough for her. I will never forgive her for that. My sons deserved to grow up in that house.

April 1st, 2020, BPC 3N

Today my twins turn 13. Time certainly passes by quickly and I feel guilty that I'm not with them today. This is just one example where mental illness has wrecked the part of my life where I should be celebrating birthdays and holidays with my children. And once again, Julia plays "family" with another man and my kids.

And the irony of this being April fool's day, I found out this morning that I have tested positive for Covid 19. When I got the news, I felt like I was punched in the stomach. In retrospect, when I had the fever, I sort of sensed that I had it. The good news is that I'm breathing fine, my fever is gone along with the terrible headache. I have only been feeling a little bit tired and drained. The doctor told me that that I'm probably at the end stages of having the virus. When the doctor told me that I had it, he had the attitude where he felt that it was no big deal. After all, I never really got sick.

April 3, 2020, BPC 3

A radio that my brother bought me arrived today. I am allowed to have it in my room. Thank goodness because all the silence was deafening.

I didn't sleep much last night because I was listening to the radio and the reports that are going on about Covid and how dozens upon dozens of people in New York City are dying every day.

 This virus likes to attack your lungs so you can't breathe and then you must be put on a ventilator, which is a death sentence. If the ventilator doesn't help, then the patient dies. I just heard that between 2300 and 2900 people have died in New York State.

 The humanitarian effort of doctors, nurses, food service people, police, fire department and EMT's have been very impressive to see; especially during what is probably the most challenging time of their careers. I can't imagine being a part of a medical staff that oversees a morgue right now.

April 4, 2020, BPC 3N

 Today I have a headache and feel very sleepy. The reports on the radio are that between today and tomorrow, the death toll will go up. There are over 1800 cases of cops, fireman, MTA workers and medical workers who have tested positive for Covid 19. I feel that my case of Covid has come to an end.

I decide to switch to the classic rock station on my new radio. God must have been looking down on me because Van Halen was on to save me from some madness today.

As of today, 3350 deaths have occurred in New York State from Covid 19. This is something that nightmares are made of. Furthermore, as of today, there are 1.1 million people in the world who are infected. Over 85,000 people around the world have died. This is just beyond shocking. How did this happen? Was this virus made in a lab and escaped somehow; or was it from a bat sold at a market in Wuhan China where a laboratory happens to exist where they experiment on viruses with the goal of weaponization? I believe World War III has started without one shot or missile being fired. The death tolls equal that of war and the economic fallout that will result be the same as the losing side of a war.

I also found out today that my driver's license is suspended because of the arrears on my child support that is still based on the job that I used to have. I think I've been running around in circles with every possible bureaucratic office in this God forsaken city.

As I sit here thinking about all my psychological problems, my financial problems etc; I hear on the radio that a famous sports photographer just died from Covid. He was only 47 years old and had 2 young kids. I guess everything needs to be put in perspective. In addition, I just found out that Vida caught covid and died a few days ago. She was the older woman who would draw pictures of rabbits, cats and then talk about how she couldn't give herself orgasms anymore in order to look good in the eyes of God. One day I saw a sitting on the sofa talking with everybody, and the next day she was gone.

April 15th ,2020 BPC 3N

Why is it that some people are born driven, and some aren't? There are people born like me, who knows what it takes to get to the next level of success, yet there is a sense of not being able to do it that stops me from completing certain goals. Not only is it a sense of not being able to do it, but there is also the physical sickness that my body experiences with when faced with fear, apprehension and change. This is something that I've discussed with my therapists. I must learn to push through and realize that I am smarter and more competent than I give myself credit for. Most people are more competent and smarter than they give themselves credit for. The problem is when people try to hold other people down with criticism and judgement, it ruins the self-confidence of someone who already comes to the table with low self-esteem.

There are some people, like Julia, who, in my opinion, enjoy breaking people like that. I'm sure everyone has been around at least one narcissist in their lives. There are great videos on You Tube about narcissists that are fantastic. By learning about the personality disorder, you gain a new perspective which aids in your own healing process. Knowledge is power. That's an old phrase that still holds true.

 It can be very frustrating when you know better, and your mental illness gets in your way. I remember being 15 years old in high school and walking down the hallway in the art wing and I couldn't picture my life past the age of 20. All I saw in my mind was a black void. I had no idea what I wanted to do in life. While music was an idea, I didn't pursue it until I got to college.

Like I mentioned before, I went to one of the best high schools in the country and there were plenty of kids to look up to because they were serious students and driven to succeed. If it weren't for some of those students, I would have failed my classes. Watching them reminded me that I needed to do my work, graduate and go to college. I have since thanked those people for being my mentors when they didn't even know it.

The thing I remember most about high school and being in class was that my legs would shake, and I would be constantly sweating from my armpits to where I could feel the sweat trickle down my rib cage. None of my classmates knew I was going through this.

The one negative part about my high school was that there were many social cliques and people could be very snobby. In middle school I felt the pressure to try to be popular and felt extremely insecure. I found that most people except for my close friends didn't really pay attention to me. It wasn't until my 10th and 20th high school reunions where people that I spoke to said they had fond memories of me being funny in class and that I was one of the nicer kids that they knew growing up. I had no idea that most of my classmates felt that way.

Chapter 53: Losing My Interest in Being A Musician

Now that I'm 50, I don't feel the urge to be in a band, play drums or even noodle on a guitar. Maybe it's my depression or maybe I got out of it all that I could. I have played hundreds if not more than 1000 of shows throughout my life, played in great venues, played gigs where my drums sounded like thunder, I got to feel great performing, I met and slept with way too many women and got more attention than I knew what to do with.

One of the last bands I was in was a reggae, soca, disco, reggaeton and classic rock band. I was the drummer/part lead vocals of the band. I joined in 2007. Learning all the styles of music we were playing was both challenging and fun. Our singer/guitarist had a good personality and was driven to get us gigs. In fact, during my time in that band, I never had to make one phone call to book a gig. Being that I used to be the leader of a few bands I was in, I was happy to have somebody else doing the tough work and giving him an extra percentage. "Singer" was the manager, the booking agent and the sound engineer. In addition, he owned the sound system and provided us with any microphones or any other audio equipment that we needed.

We were a busy band and in 2012, we played 77 shows between Memorial Day and Labor Day. I got to feel what it was like to be a full-time musician. I loved it. It was a great summer. I played a ton of gigs, I had fun with my son's, Julia and I were getting along for the most part and we even had a fantastic vacation in Boston. Things were great. I was playing drums, eating great food and smoking some good weed.

In 2011, Singer met a woman named Kathy and they fell in love. I knew he loved her because he would pull me to the side sometimes and tell me in a very shy voice that he really loved her and that he found his best friend. Singer was not the type to break down and open up about his feelings.

Kathy quickly became part of the band's family. She started off by helping us set up for shows and then started to help manage the band. I connected with Kathy because she had fraternal twin sons like I did. Her sons would come to the gigs that we would do at beach clubs. I would show them both how to set up and take apart a drum set. Our keyboardist and bassist took them under their wings as well; showing them the basics on how to play keyboards and bass.

When we were all together, we felt like a team. As band members we got along fine except for the occasional arguments about how certain songs are played. That usually never included me because the other 3 members would be arguing over chords and notes. I didn't have any of that to worry about as a drummer. We worked extremely hard on doing 4-part harmonies. We would spend hours and hours at Singer's house practicing harmonies. We got so good at harmonies that we tried out for America's got talent and made it to the 2nd round of preliminary auditions and got to audition for the producers of the show. While we didn't make it, the producers and the judges before them gave us compliments about our harmonies. 4 middle aged guys aren't making it on America's Got Talent.

In the fall of 2017, the injuries to my lower back from my car accident in 2013 we're getting worse, and I had to quit Singer's band. I then joined a popular top 40 group in Westchester New York. I was eventually fired because I was making too many mistakes on the drums. My body hurt too much to play certain beats and do certain fills. At the end of gigs, my feet would be numb, and my legs would be in tremendous pain. That band never knew I was injured until I told them after my surgery. They thought my mistakes were from not knowing the songs. I didn't tell them I was hurt because they were busy, the money was good, the gigs were fun, and I thought I could push through it.

After I was fired from the top 40 band, I joined an acoustic trio and figured that if I was playing mellow music, my back wouldn't bother me. This did not work either because the type of music you are playing doesn't matter. You still must bring your drums to the gig, setup, play the show, take them apart, load them in your car, bring them home and load them back into your house. It wasn't the playing that was bothering me it was carrying the equipment.

By the summer of 2018, I had a few months of recuperation from my back surgery and was ready to play again. This time I was going to use an electronic drum kit because it folds up easy, it's light, and it also has an infinite number of sounds to add to the show.

I then returned to Singer's band, and we played a show on a Sunday in August of 2018. On the following Tuesday, we were supposed to play outside at a club on Long Island. Our show got canceled because the band that played the night before broke the sound ordinance of the town. The police department suspended the live music license for the club. The band refused to turn down and the residents that lived across the canal complained to the police. In addition, I heard a rumor that the police department and the club owner did not have a good relationship.

I was on my way to the gig when Singer called me to tell me the gig was canceled. He then invited me to dinner with him and Kathy. I declined to go. I decided to stay home. Singer and Kathy went to dinner at a restaurant in Nassau County. During dinner, both Singer and Kathy had drinks. They both liked to drink. When Kathy drank, she liked to smoke cigarettes. Singer was staunchly against cigarettes and any kind of smoking for that matter. The topic of Kathy smoking came up which led to an argument. As they argued, Singer decided to leave and walked out of the restaurant. He was drunk at the time, got into his SUV and started to drive away. He did not realize that Kathy followed him outside and started chasing the SUV through the parking lot. When she caught up to the SUV, she tried to grab the passenger side view mirror and fell. Singer ran her over her unknowingly and she eventually bled to death from internal injuries before the ambulance arrived.

Singer had driven all the way home and then got a call from the restaurant owner telling him that he'd better get back there as quick as possible. When he drove back to the restaurant and saw Kathy on the ground surrounded by EMS workers, he asked what happened. The police told him he ran over Kathy and that she didn't survive.

 I don't remember what Singer's blood alcohol level was, but it was high enough for him to be arrested for DUI and leaving the scene of an accident. The next day, our band was all over the local news. I was even shown playing drums for a second or two. It's more sensationalistic when the people involved are either musicians or artists of some kind. Why bother mentioning the band? It's not like we were famous or even well-known enough on Long Island. If it was an accountant, nobody would have given a shit.

I found out about Kathy's death from our Keyboard player. He sent me a text that said, "Singer killed Kathy". I thought he was texting me a joke and I wanted to beat him to the punchline and texted back, "Well, it was only a matter of time". The keyboardist then texted back that he was serious and sent the links to all the news outlets that were covering the story.

The rest of the band and I went to the wake so we could be there for her sons. We were nervous that her family would reject us and not want us there. On the contrary, we were greeted with hugs by Kathy's entire family and especially her twin boys. Two more kids left without a parent. My heart was breaking for these boys because their father is a drug addict, and he is struggling. He doesn't get to see them a lot. Kathy's sons had been living with her ex-husband's parents. I don't know why, and I never asked why. I couldn't help thinking about; what if they were my kids and they lost me or Julia?

Singer served 8 months in jail for involuntary manslaughter, DUI and leaving the scene of an accident. I don't know when he got out or if he's out already because I've been locked up too. It just dawned on me that I've been hospitalized for about 8 months straight.

After Kathy's death, I decided to take a break from being in bands for a while. My first gig was in 1989 and I had not stopped since then. It was time to clear my head of that life for a while.

April 17th, 2020, BPC 3N Piss Jugs

There are 3 bathrooms across from the bedrooms here on 3 North. They are very close to our rooms. I mention this again because there is a trend amongst most of the men here who I share this side of the unit with who have urine jugs in their rooms. At night, they urinate in their jugs so that they don't have to go to the bathroom. Many times, each day, these gentlemen can be seen emerging from their rooms with their piss jugs filled to the brim and walk to the bathroom to pour the urine out in the toilet. I'm trying to figure out whether they are lazy or have a physical illness. When I see them come out of their rooms with their jugs, I do notice a look of shame on their faces, which makes me believe they have bladder issues and can't make it to the bathroom without having an accident, or maybe their medications cause them to be incontinent. I had the same issue and its one of the reasons that I wanted back surgery. The ruptured disc fragments in my lower back would hit nerves that control my bladder, and I would pee without warning.

 After I had my back surgery, I was stuck using a catheter for the first few days. It was humiliating watching the nurse change my urine bag. After the catheter was pulled out, which is a wonderful experience by the way, I was given a piss jug. I asked if I could just walk to the bathroom since they had me walking a bit anyway. They said no because that would mean I'd have to be supervised every time I had to go to the bathroom, and they couldn't guarantee that someone would be available to be a chaperone every time. To the nurses, it was no big deal because they deal with that and much worse daily. The nurses gave me the jug and showed me where to hang it on my bed so that they could empty it out when it was full. When they would come to my bed to take the piss jug, I felt embarrassed. I then thought I was lucky that I

didn't have to use a bedpan or wear a diaper. As a matter of fact, I don't remember having to take a shit for almost a week after my surgery. I heard that the anesthesia could make you constipated.
April 17th, 2020, Continued BPC 3N

 I just found out that Covid killed another patient here at BPC. He was a patient on another unit. The numbers of deaths per day are crazy; between

700 and 1000 people a-day are dying in the USA. In addition, people are losing their jobs in record numbers, small businesses are closing, and mental illness is on the rise. Unfortunately, there have been some suicides; including a nurse that worked at Elmhurst hospital, where I was staying. I wonder if I knew her.

 I just heard on the radio that 630 people died in New York City in the last 24 hours. I don't think that anybody was prepared for this.

 So, here at 3 North, we are getting used to our new life of being socially distant, wearing facial masks and being quarantined to our rooms.

 I hear from people on the outside and from DJs on the radio that the streets are empty.

Everybody is still being advised to stay home and the schools are closed indefinitely.

I've been listening to lots of talk shows on the radio and a big topic is when professional sports can be started again. One idea that is being floated around is playing games with no fans in the stands. While I love sports, I don't think that they are important enough to go through the trouble of having their seasons while dealing with something that is unpredictable.

When athletes and broadcasters talk about sports, they make it sound like it's the most important thing on the planet and what they do for a living is all that matters. I'll put it in perspective as someone who taught sports and someone who played collegiate sports for a bit: professional athletes get paid millions of dollars to throw and catch a ball. If you miss sports, then play them with your kids. Don't get me wrong, there are athletes like Drew Brees who donated 5 million dollars for hurricane relief. 5 million dollars is an extremely generous donation. To be able to donate 5 million dollars and not have it affect your bottom line must feel damn good.

My point is that if a season of sports needs to be canceled for the safety of everyone involved, then so be it. It's not the end of the world. For other people, the end of the world is happening right before their eyes as their relatives and friends are dropping like flies. Imagine being the person who is losing their business and their relatives at the same time.

April 18th, 2020, BPC 3N

I'm sitting at one of the sofas near the nurse's station. The nurses are having a good time laughing and joking around. It's good to hear people joking around. Sitting 6 feet away from me so that he is socially distanced is a patient named Jayvonne. Jayvonne is about 30 years old and has schizophrenia. He is always either singing, talking or dancing to himself while he watches his reflection in the conference room windows.

Whenever we have a community meeting to discuss issues on the unit, Jayvonne always ends up talking about religion. He usually does start off talking about the topic that is being discussed and then eventually starts "quoting" from the bible. His quotes don't exist in the bible according to the patients who study the bible daily. A female patient once told me, "I don't know what kind of fucking bible he's been reading!"

As this is all happening, the nurses are still laughing and having a good time. There are two nurses that always ask me how I'm feeling and can tell when I need to talk by the look on my face. An amazingly kind nurse said to me, "You are still a young man, you are educated, you have a master's degree, and you are someone that will be able to get a job when you get out. You may not be a teacher, but the fact that you are educated gives you a head start".

After Nurse M's kind words, I started to remember a news story that I saw before I was ever hospitalized: It was about a woman who had just turned 90 years old the same day that she was celebrating her 30th year of working at McDonald's. That means she started working there when she was 60. That is 10 years older than I am right now. So, if I wanted to follow in her footsteps, I'd have to wait 10 more years until I could work at McDonald's. When I watched the story on the news, the first thing that I noticed was that the woman did not look 90 and that her positive attitude was her biggest attribute and what keeps her alive. I just have to develop a similar attitude and have more faith in myself.

Since the quarantine of us having to stay in our rooms is over, the hallway has been busier than ever.

Jimmy, who is 67 years old and told me he was schizophrenic is walking around the hallway and he is telling everyone that he is hearing voices, Videa is asking for everybody's food trays, but nobody understands what she is saying, and a patient named Jerry has just emerged out of his room with his piss jug so that he could wash it out in the bathroom.

The voices that Jimmy hears in his head tell him to hit people. He understands that the voices are there. He has been telling me this for the last half hour. I told him to go see the nurses and that he shouldn't have to suffer.

Jimmy was married when he was younger. He got divorced because he was cheating. The other day he heard I had money problems, so he tried to give me $5. I thought it was very thoughtful. I always share Gatorade and coffee with Jimmy when we get extra. I also gave him my 2 extra rechargeable batteries so that he could listen to his radio. My radio only takes 2 batteries, so I figured I would give Jimmy 2 batteries so that he can listen to music. I also told him that I would charge the batteries for him as well.

April 22, 2020, BPC 3N

The Corona Virus hit my family. My brother's mother-in-law died yesterday at a hospital in Brooklyn. She was in her eighties and had the underlying problems that fuel the virus. She had asthma and a weak heart. She spent about a week on a ventilator. What is sad and unfair is what my brother said, "She had a big loving family and had to die alone because visitors were not even allowed to see her through a window". I've also been hearing stories about the nurses who have been holding the hands of the dying because they are alone.

I worry about my mother because she lives alone, and she is 86. She's in very good shape for her age, which should give her an advantage against this virus, but you never know. The virus is feasting on the elderly and the weak.

My brother's father-in-law isn't in the best shape either; he can barely see, has trouble climbing up and down stairs and has respiratory problems like asthma. I can only assume that my brother and his wife will move her father into their house at some point.

It was also reported today that in New York City, the death count is now averaging about 250 people a day. At one point, it hit 800 deaths in one day. I can't imagine being a hospital worker and being witness to all that death. Where are all the bodies being put?

Soon we will start hearing stories of health care workers suffering from PTSD. How can they not? I wonder if gets to a point for them that the people were slabs of meat to be put in giant Ziploc bags because they developed a numbness to all this.

However, one day the numbness will wear off and their feelings about what they went through will eventually come to the surface. I fear some of them may have suffered so much trauma that they may not be able to live a life that closely resembled their old one.

April 25, 2020, BPC 3N

I heard on the radio today that there are 20 million Americans without jobs. Counting me, that's 20 million and 1.

I decided to have one of those days where I spent most of the day in bed half asleep. I went to bed at 8:00 p.m. last night and woke up at 4:00 a.m. I couldn't fall back to sleep until after I had my morning medications. I've discussed earlier in this journal about the psychological damage that laying in your bed all day causes. It's very tempting to sleep when there is nothing to do. Saying that there is nothing to do is not true. I believe I have said it before, but I need to remind myself that I have many things I can do; I can read, exercise, listen to music, socialize with other patients, write in this journal, work on my art, watch TV or work on crossword puzzles.

Believing that there is nothing to do means that you don't have the motivation to find something to do, like exercise: I started weight training seriously when I was 19 years old. I was taking summer classes at my college and lived in a house that I rented with 7 other roommates. I decided that I wanted to stay there for the summer. I joined the local gym and met the owner named Dave. Dave was a professional body builder and a very nice guy. I was very thin when I joined the gym; I was 6' tall and weighed about 150 pounds.

Dave knew that I was intimidated about being in a gym and being the smallest one there. After about a week, Dave followed me to my car after my workout and said, "Keep up the good work". Those simple words of encouragement made something in me click. I began to start enjoying lifting weights, going to the gym for the comradery with the other members and seeing improvements in my physique. I became so involved in Dave's gym that he would often leave me in charge while he would leave to run errands. I never asked him to pay me or lower my membership fee, because he would give me free protein shakes all the time. He was the perfect person to motivate me to keep training.

Sometimes it's not the message, but the messenger.

I lifted weights and trained hard all through college. After I graduated and I was feeling lost, I decided to become a personal trainer.

One client I was training was a doctor from a hospital in Nassau County, New York.
She was a psychiatrist, and she was working with 5 female teenage outpatients who had anorexia and bulimia. The doctor asked me about training the

girls as they were getting over their eating disorders. I felt it was a good opportunity to try something different and learn about people who had anorexia and bulimia.

The first thing I learned about the girls was that none of them thought that they were fat or obese. It turns out they had anxiety and depression. They couldn't eat. Their stomachs couldn't hold down food because their disorders made them feel nauseous (just like me!) I immediately felt a connection with these kids.

While I taught them to train in a fun and easy way, we would also talk about our feelings. I trained them during the summer of 1995 until they went back to college. It was this experience that led me to want to teach physical education.

April 28, 2020, BPC 3N

Jimmy, my 67-year-old schizophrenic friend, just celebrated his birthday today. Jimmy has been acting out today. As I was sitting on my bed, I heard a commotion, and the nurses were telling Jimmy to go back to his room. He was saying that he didn't want to live anymore. He then came into my room and punched me in the face. While the punch came at me slowly, I was able to lean back enough to where Jimmy's fist only grazed my cheek. I then asked Jimmy why he punched me. He said the voices told him to. I walked with him to the sofas in the hall to sit down. The nurses came over and gave Jimmy some meds. I never told the nurses that he hit me. The last thing he needed was to be strapped to a bed because of "violence". It felt like I got hit with a small pillow. No big deal.

After Jimmy took his meds, he went back to his room. Later in the day he did not come out for snack time which must have meant that his medications really knocked him out.

Jimmy was the first person with schizophrenia that I asked probing questions to about what it is like to hear voices in your head. He would tell me that the voices sound as real as if someone is having a conversation with you in the room, except that there is nobody there. Also, even if you know that there is nobody there and that the voices are not real, it doesn't stop you from being driven crazy. In addition, the volume of the voices in their heads can get so loud that it physically hurts their ears. I guess that's the reason why you see people with mental illness putting their hands over their ears. They are trying to block out the sound from what they think is from the outside world. The untreated do not know the noises are inside their heads.

Chapter 54: Therapy at BPC

A person on the outside world that goes to therapy usually goes once or twice a week for a 45–60 minute session. Others like Howard Stern go about 4 times a week because they feel that their mental illness needs constant monitoring. I've been at the point over the last few months that I need therapy 4 times a day.

Our therapists here at BPC are psychologists who are doing their residency and are assigned to patients for about a month. The sessions with the psychologists are about 3 times a week for about 45 minutes.

My first therapist was Dr. Ellen. She was about 29 years old, Caucasian and had reddish brown hair that was shoulder length. She was a great therapist and would ask questions that would help you either think deeper or start looking at things from more than one point of view before making a decision or a snap judgement. I loved it when she would ask me to analyze things from as many perspectives as I could.

I was able to open up to Dr. Ellen and many times I had to bring tissues just in case of water works. The other great part about Dr. Ellen is that she was responsible for the hospital to start letting us go outside to the yard. In the yard are garden boxes where there are vegetables, berries and sunflowers. Dr. Ellen is a big believer of the healing properties of being outside.

Just when Dr. Ellen and I started to have some insightful sessions, her month with me was over and she would be moving on to another unit to work with other patients. It's a shame because that was the most productive month of therapy I had since Dr. Peart.

I then started with a new resident, Dr. Matt. Dr. Matt and I didn't have therapy sessions. When we first met, he asked if it was alright that our month be spent with me taking psychological tests. In all my years of therapy and now all these months of being committed, nobody ever asked me to take any psychological tests. I found the idea interesting and told him I would do it.

The first round of tests was based on answering questions about your feelings, how you handle certain situations and what triggers your mental illness. The second round of tests were IQ tests which obviously got more difficult as you progress. I'm no Einstein but I'm no Forest Gump either.

The last test was the infamous Rorshach tests, where I looked at ink blots and described what I saw. I was surprised to get that test. I assumed it was an archaic test and wasn't used anymore.

The problem with having a new therapist each month is that you must tell your life's history all over again to another therapist and then try to build a rapport.

In therapy, there needs to be the consistency of one therapist so that trust can be built; this way, you feel comfortable being totally honest and telling them every deranged thought that you've ever had. Can you imagine telling your spouse every deranged thought that you ever had? The divorce rate would be 99.9% if people opened up like that to their spouses. Therapy offers you a safe place to say anything without being judged. When you get to the point to where you are comfortable to say anything you wish, it is most freeing. Feelings and thoughts need to be purged whether it's through telling a therapist, singing, writing in a journal, doing exercise or playing a drum.

April 30, 2019, BPC 3N

I do believe that I have cabin fever. The more I stay here, the more restless I feel. One frustrating aspect is that I keep getting mixed messages from the psychiatry staff about when I will be discharged. My discharge has already been delayed because of Covid 19. The entire hospital is still under quarantine and only the staff is allowed to come and go. Visiting hours have been canceled until further notice.

As the weather improves, so will my mood. Spring, Summer and Fall are when I can control my anxiety by being active outside. I'm starting to feel that I've made enough improvements to be able to be discharged.

The one issue that I struggle with is that I've let certain people get the best of me and I can't get past that. I let myself get pushed around which wound up causing the end of my marriage and my career. Sometimes people are true victims like people who get robbed, raped or murdered. In my case I'm a victim because I allowed myself to be. It's a terrible way to feel when you know that you should fight and take the chance of losing than not fight at all. When you don't fight, you become the victim and it was all your choice. In addition, all those feelings build up inside and it makes you lash out eventually at friends and family. It's like I've mentioned earlier, I have burned the bridges with most of my friends from high school.

 Sometimes people lash out, and it's worse: How many times have you read about the ex-husband, lover or boyfriend killing everyone in the house and then turning the gun on himself. I read about it at least once a week in the newspaper.

 I'm starting to take stock in what would make me happy in life. I know for sure that I want to be around my sons as much as I can. I also hope to own a home again someday that is big enough so that my sons get to experience having their own bedrooms, backyard and driveway to shoot hoops. This was what they had until my twins were almost 3 years old and I feel it's a quality of life that would make them happier. To me, it's unfinished business. That's a part of my old life that I lost, and like I said before I'm going to get it back for my sons somehow.

May 7th, 2020, BPC 3N

The challenge: the challenge for me is to rebuild my life to where I feel I have a healthy level of self-esteem and I can put fear, panic, anxiety and self-doubt to the side in order to lead a productive and happy life. There is a certain amount of acceptance that I must have about the fact that I was born with a mental illness which is not curable. I must learn to take my thoughts, straighten them out and then put them in their proper place.

My challenge has been laid out for me. While I recognize my illness, pushing it to the side has been extremely difficult. It's caused many problems in every aspect of my life from relationships to careers to finances.

After living like this for the better part of 45 years, I always felt that I was a step below other people because I would see them function and adjust to new phases in life without having some sort of existential crisis. Like I mentioned earlier, I used to look at my classmates at school and saw them adjust normally from going to elementary school to junior high school and then to high school.

May 8, 2020, BPC 3N

I saw on the news today that there is a new form of Covid 19 that affects children. One child in New York and one child in New Jersey have died. Of course, I am now worried for my sons and what makes it worse is that I am here and can't be there for them. It's also reported on the news that there are 73 kids that have been hospitalized. I can't imagine what their parents are going through. I don't know what I would do if I lost any of my kids. It is something that I ruminate about sometimes because of the losses that my family has sustained. Witnessing someone grieve over a lost child is a level of despair that words could never describe.

This pandemic has also divided the country. Local and federal governments are bickering over social distancing, people wearing masks and what businesses and occupations are considered essential. Here at 3 North, everyone is still wearing masks when we are not in our rooms. The nurses are covered in jumpsuits, plastic face masks, gloves and anything that covers their heads.

The controversy is between groups who want states to ease up on restrictions and groups who want to keep the states shut down and for people to stay at home. As of today, parts of New York have opened for limited business and most of Florida is open. Florida seems like the best place to be right now. In midwest states where people do not live so close to each other, the cases of Covid are lower.

As of today, about 80,000 Americans have died from Covid 19. Because of that astronomical number, I can understand people's fears and wanting to keep everything shut down. On the other hand, there are 36 million people who are now unemployed. By keeping everything shut down, people will struggle to make ends meet. In addition, there is going to be a rise in drug use, alcohol abuse, domestic violence, crime, mental illness, suicide and pregnancies too.

There have also been many incidents in New York City between the police and citizens regarding the social distancing rules and wearing masks. Videos are online showing police trying to enforce these rules to people who aren't following the temporary mandates that the government has imposed. In many of the videos, you can see the police being harassed and sometimes physically assaulted, which winds up with that person being taken to the ground and cuffed. I think everybody is afraid.

There are also street teams of people who patrol neighborhoods to remind people to practice social distancing and offer people masks if they don't have one. That's a better idea than having the police try to enforce people to stand farther apart and tell them to put on masks. While some businesses are open, places like basketball courts and parks have been closed. Some parks are even closed with locks and chains. I also heard that some of the basketball courts at certain parks had the rims removed from the backboards.

The biggest controversy in New York City right now is with Governor Cuomo forcing senior citizens back to their nursing homes after they had tested positive for Covid because of a law that he said he had to follow that I do not understand. This has resulted in thousands of deaths. These nursing homes have quickly become overrun with Covid 19 cases and hundreds of people are dying every day. Family members are also unable to find out the location of their loved ones and the status of their health. Some people who had lost relatives were unable to find out where their loved ones' remains were. There were also cases where bodies were being piled up in refrigerated trucks because the morgues and funeral homes could no longer handle the volume of bodies coming in. There were also cases of where bodies were being kept in trucks where the refrigeration systems were not working. The smell of the decaying bodies could be smelled if you were in the general vicinity of those trucks.

 I also saw on the news that the Jacob Javits center was being used as a makeshift hospital and a navy medical ship called "The Comfort" was being docked in New York Harbor. The news reported that the navy ship has over 1000 hospital beds and rooms ready to go. There is also a makeshift hospital in Central Park that is made from large tents. Critics of the governor say that he should have sent the senior citizens with Covid 19 to either the navy hospital ship or the Javits Center. Without having access to the internet, I must rely on the news and what I read in the newspapers. I am unable to research anything in order to form an opinion on who is doing things right and who is fucking up.

I believe that President Trump, Governor Cuomo, Mayor DiBlasio or any other politician in charge of a large city or state must be scared right now. Things are probably changing minute by minute, there are thousands of people dying and they are part of the group that must fix it. Lots of pressure right there.

Decisions must be made on whether to completely shut down the biggest city and economic center of the world. If you shut down New York City, you are essentially shutting down the world.

Our leaders must make these decisions while they don't know if a decision could lead to thousands of more people dying or millions of people losing their livelihoods. These are extraordinary and turbulent times like I've never seen before. Democrats blame Republicans and Republicans blame the Democrats.

May 17, 2020, BPC 3N

It is a beautiful morning outside. It's sunny and it is about 60 degrees. I haven't been outside for more than 2 months.

There's nothing like being outside on a nice Spring day and playing with your kids. When I would take my sons to the park, I would have a football catch with one of my twins. The other twin and my youngest would fill up their empty Gatorade bottles with water and make mud pies in the dirt. They would also dig for bugs with sticks. I consider this a wonderful time because not only are we all having fun, but there's also no electronics involved. After goofing around with a football and mud pies, we would go to the Mr. Softee truck and get ice cream. Sometimes my youngest would get ices because he likes when his tongue turns green. I have a great picture of him sticking out his green tongue. He's the cutest!

My youngest son's favorite thing to do at the park is going to the dog run. The dog owners are always friendly and let him play with their dogs, feed them snacks and play fetch with them. The greatest thing to see is when my youngest is petting a puppy and it starts jumping up and licking his face. The giggles and the expressions on my son's face are priceless and will always be in my memory as precious moments.

Chapter 67: Inner Strength

I can't help but wonder where the origin of someone's inner strength comes from. Are we born with it? Does it have to do with the environment that we grew up in? If you are a person that is born with inner strength and born with a will to succeed, then you already have what it takes: If you choose to be a lawyer, doctor, soldier or even an entrepreneur; you will probably succeed because you have inner strength. If you are not born with inner strength, then you may struggle to take advantage of your best qualities, abilities and talents.

With no inner strength, you may flounder through life never getting the job you really wanted, having failed relationships, suffer financial difficulties or you may find yourself alone. People with no inner strength can come from all walks of life; wealthy, poor, having a family or not having one at all.

Anyone can tell you how great and special you are. If you don't believe it internally, your inner strength won't blossom. There is also a certain point that you reach in therapy where you grow tired of talking about yourself and the same issues repeatedly. There's a point in time that you must take all the lessons you learned in therapy and put them to use in real life. There are no magic words and it's up to you to take the difficult and scary first steps in wanting to feel better.

It's important to remind yourself daily of your positive qualities, talents and aspects of your personality that make you a good person. Sometimes it's hard to do that because negative emotions seem to have more power than positive emotions. Negative feelings cause destruction so quickly. This is a mental block that many people must push through. I know all about it because I feel it every day from the moment I wake up until the moment I go to sleep. I'm trying hard to put these feelings in their proper place. Sometimes it works and sometimes it doesn't.

May 26th, 2020: BPC 3N

The exercise bug has finally bit me again. I have started training over the last 10 days. It was tough at the beginning because I haven't trained in almost a year. Luckily, I didn't lose too much strength and I'm not struggling as much as I thought I would.

I have been doing a lot of walking each day for about 3 hours. I walk the hallway of 3 North which is rather long. I would say it's about 1/8 of a mile round trip. I've been walking to the point where I have bleeding blisters on my feet.

Another result of my walking so much was getting an ingrown toenail on my right big toe. I was sent to the first floor to see the podiatrist. The podiatrist told me that he had to cut out the nail and that he would have to do it without numbing my toe because they were out of Novocain.

I sat in the chair while a nurse held my ankle down and the doctor cut into my toe. My entire body started convulsing because the pain that comes out of that small area of your body is excruciating. Luckily, it only lasted about 15 seconds. My toe was gushing blood.

In addition to walking, I have been doing pushups, dips for my triceps, curling chairs for my biceps and doing planks for my abdominals. One challenge that I face is that the medication that I take makes you gain weight. When I was first admitted to Jacobi Hospital in August, I weighed about 165 pounds. I was underweight because my usual healthy weight is 185. To date, I weigh 225.

Since I started training again, my muscles get that old pump that I miss having. When you have a good workout, your muscles feel pumped, and your endorphins are flowing through your body. Not only does it have a lasting effect for the rest of your day, but it has also lasting effects for many days. If you exercise consistently, you will feel your mood improving because you can feel and see a positive change in your body. There's a lot to be said for the adage, "If you look good then you will feel good". I must admit that it feels great when you are with a woman, and she can't keep her hands off you because she is attracted to your body.

This is not bragging but, I have had times when I took off my shirt while being intimate and getting wonderful reactions from women. I never developed an ego from those situations. Those situations simply made me feel that I was wanted and that was more than I could ever ask for. It was more of a relief than anything. I would think, "Thank God I look normal".

Greg:

One of my good friends here is Greg. He is the one that inspired me to start exercising again. Greg decided to start walking about a month ago because he wanted to lose weight. At first, I thought I should be doing that too, but I wasn't ready yet. I then remembered what every therapist told me when trying to make a change, "The first step is the hardest". It was a hard step because I knew I was out of shape, and this would be a challenge.

Greg is originally from Jamaica and has been here for about 10 years. He is soft spoken, and his personality is so friendly that everyone cares for him a great deal. Because of this, the other patients have made him the spokesman of our unit. Greg told me he is learning disabled which caused his mental illnesses to become so bad that he had to be hospitalized.

Out of all the patients here at 3 North, I would have to say I've spent most of my time with Greg and Jimmy. Greg and I spend our time together bonding over watching Family Feud and a crazy reality show called 90 Day Fiancé. Greg also loves Seinfeld, and we watch that as well.

Unfortunately, Greg's mental illness caused him to be violent and he spent some time at Riker's Island Prison. He was then transferred to Bronx Psychiatric Center.

Greg and another patient named Enrique run the underground coffee club. That's where the patients share their instant decaf coffee. None of us have had caffeine in months, and a lot of the patients haven't had caffeine in years. It's not that I want caffeine so much, it's that decaffeinated coffee tastes like shit.

Enrique is from Mexico and is about 60 years old. He loves to draw with his magic markers and shares his artwork with all the patients. There are many days where Enrique and I sit at a table and do our artwork together. At one point, Enrique decided to give me an entire notebook that he filled up with his artwork. He wanted me to have it to remember him after I got discharged.

Another great person I met here was a kid named Santos. He is about 27 years old and is very open about his schizophrenia. One day he opened up to me and told me what his schizophrenia was like. While he knew the voices weren't real, it's still didn't stop him from becoming violent: he attacked his family with a knife. Luckily nobody got seriously hurt but there were injuries to some of his family members. Santos has been here for about 5 years. The one interesting thing about Santos is that he is a good-looking young man that has movie star charisma. Even though he is committed to a psychiatric hospital, it doesn't stop different girls from calling the hospital every day to talk to him. It gets to a point where he doesn't want to take any phone calls because the calls come in so frequently. Santos is a patient that gets day passes from the hospital so that he can go out and meet friends and family and have some time in the real world. I hope for his sake that he is taking advantage of the attention that he is getting from the ladies. Santos is someone that is extremely self-aware of his mental illness, what it caused him to do and the lessons that he has learned from it. I am meeting him at a time in his life where he is improving with his schizophrenia and is making big strides. I hope that one day he gets discharged and we can go to a Yankee game someday with Greg.

I never expected to make such great friends here. These guys are extremely sincere with their words and actions. They realize that we are all in this together and that we need to take care of each other. Greg, Santos, Enrique, Jimmy and even Walter White made me feel comfortable from the first day I got here.

May 28, 2020, BPC 3N

Today my youngest son turns 10. I've already missed my twins' birthday in April. The guilt I feel is beyond measurement. When I spoke to him on the phone, he sounded so cute with his little voice as he was describing his new video game. He also reminded me that my birthday is on June 5th. That was when I really got choked up. For him to remember my birthday was heartwarming.

For me, my youngest son is the reason that I believe in a higher power, God, or whatever created this life and the universe:

When Julia and I decided to have children, Julia was having trouble getting pregnant. At first, she blamed me because I was smoking pot. However, after giving a semen sample, my sperm count was higher than normal. I think it was a blow to Julia's ego to find out that she was the issue and not me. After all, it would be easier for her to blame me than accept her physical condition; especially one that compromises her identity as a woman. I felt, she would be more concerned about what people thought of her more than the deep-rooted disappointment of not being able to get pregnant.

For the pregnancy of our twins, Julia had to take prenatal hormones that had to be injected, prenatal vitamins and we also did a few rounds of artificial insemination.

It turned out that there were 3 fetuses when we went for a sonogram. The 3rd fetus stopped developing after 10 weeks while the other 2 fetuses developed normally. The 3rd fetus eventually reabsorbed into Julia's uterus.

Julia's pregnancy was tough. At the beginning, she had developed ovarian cysts. One day she was in a lot of pain, and we went to the hospital that happened to be less than a block from our house. We were afraid that the cysts would burst and cause a miscarriage. It was the most pain I had ever seen her in. I remember them giving her as much pain medication as they could. I remember being so scared and worried. I thought she was going to die. After Julia fell asleep the first night at the hospital, the doctor told me I should go home and get rest. I said no and wound up sleeping on the hospital room floor next to Julia's bed. I remember not being able to get a chair for some reason, so I just slept on the floor. Do you know how many floors I passed out on in college?

When Julia was released from the hospital, she was immediately put on bed rest for the remainder of her pregnancy. There were a few trips to the obstetrician because her cervix was dilating prematurely.

I remember taking care of Julia during this time period. There were lots of midnight trips to Wendy's to get Julia some junior bacon cheeseburgers. That was her favorite. I would get the chili.

On April 1st, 2007, are twins were born by Cesarean section. In the delivery room, the doctor asked Julia if she wanted her tubes tied while the chance was available. Julia responded, and I paraphrase, "No, we can let God decide if I get pregnant again".

I didn't know that I wanted to be a father until I became one. While Julia was pregnant and we were preparing, I noticed that I wasn't as excited as I thought I should be about having kids. Even when we started buying baby clothes and Julia's stomach got bigger and the babies were kicking, I thought that I would feel more enthusiasm. Instead, I was sort of lukewarm to everything.

That all changed the moment I held my twins in my arms. A warm buzzing feeling came over my body and then I became exuberant about being a father. I realized that I needed to see and hold the babies to make my paternal instincts and love turn on. I believe that women get excited about having babies faster than men do because as soon as they become pregnant, and they know that there is a baby living inside them, their maternal instincts turn on instantly and they physically feel every phase of the pregnancy like when the baby's move or kick. That must produce a feeling that gives your life meaning. It is also the beginning of having unconditional love for your unborn children.

Fast forward to August of 2009. It was a beautiful summer morning and Julia and I had sex. There was something different about it that day. We were both connecting emotionally and physically. It felt like we were both glowing. It was a golden glow. We were both relaxed, were smiling at each other and looking into each other's eyes. That day was the most in love that we ever were. Subconsciously, I must have known that I had just gotten her pregnant. After a couple of days, I didn't give much thought about it. When Julia first told me that she was pregnant again, I Immediately thought of that 3rd fetus that stopped developing after 10 weeks during Julia's

1st pregnancy. Given the fact that Julia had a tough time getting pregnant the 1st time, getting pregnant with no hormones or drugs was not supposed to happen. But it did.

I felt that it was the plan of God or whatever higher power to bring that baby back because there wasn't enough room for 3 babies during Julia's first pregnancy. Like I said, I knew something special was going on that day. Julia got pregnant because of love. To me, this was our love child.

While I was shocked and scared about having another child, I started to prepare mentally and started to become excited about the prospect of maybe having a daughter. It didn't matter to me if we had a boy or a girl if the baby was healthy. But, for a while I was wondering what it would be like to have a baby girl. Either way, it would be great and this time I couldn't wait to see what the baby was going to look like. After all, I was already a father for almost 3 years and for this pregnancy, I grew excited.

And as I explained earlier in my journals, the excitement of this pregnancy was crushed for me when Julia blamed me for the pregnancy which started the chain of events that would lead me to telling her that we should separate. Like I stated many times before, my guess is that before the pregnancy, Julia had probably made up her mind that she would leave me eventually. But that one day, that one magical August morning in 2009 made me believe that our relationship had become stronger.

There were some good times in the relationship especially when we would play Scrabble and have wine. One of my other favorite things that I liked to do with Julia was to order a Turkish pizza called a Lamajun. We would usually get two of them, sit on our living room floor and have a picnic. We also enjoyed watching football and the home renovation shows on HGTV. I even got her into enjoying the heavy metal band Disturbed. I loved seeing her rock out. Julia could also sing but she either wasn't aware of it or was too shy to do it. When she would sing, I could tell that she was on key and had a rather nice voice. I don't know what kind of range she has because I could never convince her to sing out loud and with conviction. I would also encourage her to enter national Scrabble competitions or try out for Jeopardy because I felt she would do well and have fun competing. I believed in her and I felt these suggestions was a way of supporting her. She always said no to those ideas and would never tell me why when I asked.

Unfortunately, there was always some sort of wedge between us. It's hard to explain what it was. I can tell you that the vibe of this wedge made me feel like that it was my fault. Julia was the type of person that if she told you something that she was excited about and you didn't react to the level of excitement that she wanted from you, she would be mad and feel that you didn't care. I had to navigate my way around her feelings in order to keep the peace. She would say the same about me. The truth is that all I needed was a little extra sleep so that I wouldn't get panic attacks due to lack of sleep.

The fall of 2009 was the beginning of my descent that led me to finally being committed to psychiatric hospitals in 2019. It was 10 years of one thing after another that finally made me break like I described in earlier journal entries.

June 14th, 2020: BPC 3N

It's been a few weeks since I have made a journal entry. June 5th was my birthday and I turned 51.

Of course, it felt lonely because I am still hospitalized and can't see my loved ones because the visiting restrictions are still going on because of Covid 19.

I'm getting frustrated about being discharged because they keep changing the date on me. At first, they said I would be out by the 1st week of June. Then they said I would be out by the 2nd week of June. I'm starting to feel like that they are dragging out my stay here so that they can get every dime out of the insurance company.

I have had a few conversations with the head psychiatrist of BPC. I call him Dr. Schmuck because he is full of himself and is not as smart as he thinks he is. In addition, when someone's first impression is arrogance, you know they aren't as great as they think they are. He is no Dr. Peart or Dr. Helen. I will brag about this, Dr. Peart was regarded as one of the top psychiatrists in the tristate area according to New York magazine. I read it in his office waiting room.

During one of my meetings with Dr. Schmuck, the hack and fraud, I found out why they were delaying my discharge. According to him, he felt that before I was completely discharged from the hospital, that I should spend a month in their halfway house on the hospital property called The Haven House.

The Haven House is one of three dormitories that house patients who are almost ready to be fully discharged. The rules of Haven House are that during the day you are allowed to leave the hospital property and spend the day as you please. You are allowed to go home, see your family or do whatever you want. There is a 10pm curfew in which you must be back to check in and sleep in your room.

I got pissed when I was told that they wanted me to go to Haven House. Dr. Schmuck could see it on my face as I told him that this was bullshit and that they have extended my stay here for no reason. I told him that I wouldn't go and that I would appeal his decision.

After my meeting with Dr. Schmuck, a nurse told me to go to Haven House and that after a few days, I could write a letter to the hospital telling them that I felt that I was ready to be discharged and they couldn't stop me. The nurse also told me that Haven House was optional and that they probably signed me up to get a few more weeks of insurance money.

The day after my meeting with Dr. Schmuck, I saw him as I was going to the yard and told him that I changed my mind and that I would go to Haven House. He told me that as soon as a room opened, I would be transferred there. Who knows how many more weeks that will be? It's the middle of June 2020 and I've been institutionalized since August of 2019. This is almost a year of my life spent in psychiatric hospitals.

* This would be my last journal entry from the 3 notebooks that I used at Jacobi Hospital, Elmhurst Hospital and Bronx Psychiatric Center. It doesn't mean that the story is over.

The following chapters describe the rest of my stay at BPC, Haven House, my discharge from the hospital and what I have been doing since then.

Chapter 55: The Haven House and Moving On

It is now June of 2021 and I have been home for almost a year. It took me many months to decide to read my journals and transcribe them to a typed document. It's hard to re-read the parts of the journal because they bring up old feelings. Many times, while transcribing, I would have flashbacks that took me back to certain times. I would experience the same feelings that I did when thinking about different events in my life.

Picking Up From My Last Journal Entry:

I spent the last two weeks of June of 2020 asking the social worker, Dennis, when I would be transferring to Haven House. I grew impatient and started to feel like I was being taken advantage of in some way.

I went through the motions of attending groups that were now available again because certain Covid restrictions were lifted. We started eating in the cafeteria again with the patients from the other units. It was better when we either ate in our rooms or in the activity room on our unit. The cafeteria is extremely depressing. When you are around the insane and you are technically not insane but have issues; you start to feel like you just might belong there.

The last two weeks of June 2020 came and went, and I was still in 3 North. July 1st arrived, and I started to display my anger towards Dr. Schmuck and threatened to file a report with the agency for the mentally ill, who will advocate for you if you feel that your rights are being violated. I was pissed and I let it be known. Did you see what I did in that situation? I stuck up for myself. Not only was I confident in my speech and my demeanor, but it was also the way I carried myself in general; I was intimidating toward them because they had never seen me this way before and they knew that I wasn't putting on an act. During my stay at Bronx Psychiatric Hospital, I made sure I did everything that I had to do to get discharged: I attended all the groups, I always saw my therapists, I never caused trouble, I was friendly with everyone, and I was someone that the staff could ask for help when setting up for group activities.

They took my threats of filing a complaint and a lawsuit seriously as I was transferred from 3 North to The Haven House the next day. Haven House looks like a college dormitory except that instead of drunk college students hanging out outside, there are patients sitting in groups, smoking cigarettes and trying to find ways to get high………just like college students!!!!

Most of the patients are either recovering drug addicts, schizophrenics, psychotics and people with multiple personality disorder. These are the people we ignore on the subway and city streets. To be honest, they looked scary; but you must get over that if you want to blend in and have people to talk to. Everyone there had a story to tell, and I would always take away a nugget of wisdom from each tale.

In order to enter Haven House, you had to be buzzed in by security and check in with security when leaving. On the first floor of Haven House were some staff offices and the cafeteria. The bedrooms, bathrooms and other staff offices took up the rest of the 5 floors. Unlike the nice bathrooms on 3 North, the bathrooms at Haven House were disgusting: the toilets were always left unflushed or clogged up with toilet paper on purpose. Many times, I entered a bathroom to find shit all over the toilet seat and floor. In addition, most of the showers were broken. When I would report that the bathrooms were disgusting, the cleaning staff did the bare minimum by only cleaning up any shit that the patients smeared on the toilet, floor and the wall.

The showers, sinks and lights never got fixed while I was there. I bet they are still broken.

When I got transferred to Haven House, I was given my belongings that included my cell phone. I was also allowed to wear sneakers with shoelaces again. In addition, a woman on the staff who is a head administrator named Teresa, gave me a new pair of Nike running shoes that she had in storage.

Teresa is the administrator who processed my paperwork with when I registered at Haven House. As I was talking to Teresa, I could tell that she liked me: the one thing I learned from being a singer is that I could tell when a woman was attracted to me. Every time she looked at me, she would smile and blush. I thought it was odd. I then began to flirt with her, and it was working. As Teresa and I talked more each day, we realized that we lived only a few blocks from each other. That seemed to pique her interest more in me. One day I said to her, "When I'm discharged and enough time has passed, we should go out for pizza (we always talked about our favorite pizzerias). I could tell that she wanted to say yes, but it would cause a conflict of interest. She was always blushing, smiling and looking at me dead in the eyes to where I could feel that there was a connection. She answered with, "maybe" to the pizza invitation. Since it's been almost a year that I've been discharged, I've been contemplating calling Teresa to ask her out.

I was most excited to get my cell phone back. Do you know what the first thing I did when I got my cell phone back? No, jacking off to porn that I hadn't seen in almost a year was the second thing! The first thing I did was sign up on every employment app like Indeed and I started to apply for jobs. While at 3N I had computer group once a week. I spent that time updating my resume and creating different cover letters that were job specific. I would then email them to myself so that they were ready to go when I applied for jobs.

Haven House had two employment counselors that would give me leads for jobs to apply to online. The first job leads that they gave me were for jobs that I had either already applied to, or they were jobs that had nothing to do with my qualifications. I can work at any music store; sporting goods store and I can still teach; just not for any NYC Public Schools (fuck them anyway and the UFT too!) The social aspect of a job is important as well. Being around people keeps me from feeling too lonely and socialization leads to the feeling that my life has some sort of meaning in this giant dust ball called The Universe.

While applying for jobs, I decided to apply for physical education teacher openings at private and charter schools throughout the city. In addition, I applied for any jobs that seemed interesting like selling solar panels or working for a marijuana dispensary. Applying for jobs on Indeed is very easy. All the information you need about yourself is saved on your account. Most applications for any job take less than 10 minutes to complete.

I had gotten to a point during my stay at Haven House and even after I was discharged where I was constantly applying for jobs. I must have applied for between 70 and 100 jobs.

Anyway, when I first registered at Haven House it was already early evening so any plans for me to go home that day were scrapped. After I registered, I was shown to my room and unpacked my belongings. My room was clean, a good size and the window overlooked the quad area between the halfway house buildings where I could also see all the patients sitting outside. Up until my stay at Haven House, I never had any interactions with people who did so many drugs in their lives to the point where they had permanent brain damage and mental illness because of it. I could only assume that they were doing crystal meth or crack. Their bodies were also destroyed because of their drug use: They were missing teeth, they had trouble with their motor functions, and had trouble speaking. Some of these patients were in worse shape than the most severely ill patients on 3 North. I couldn't understand why they were here and people like Greg and Santos were not here.

The morning after my first night at Haven House, I went home for the first time in 11 months. I decided to walk because it was beautiful outside, and my apartment was only 2 miles away. I knew that as soon as I stepped off the hospital grounds, there would be some deep feelings.

When I walked out of the main gate, I felt a feeling of awe and deep humility. Once you start walking down the sidewalk on your own freewill after almost a year, it feels like you are visiting from another planet. When you see the first real people outside the hospital, you are grateful to see them.

My first stop on my walk home was to Dunkin

Donuts. I love coffee and everything about. I hadn't had a real cup of coffee in almost a year as well. When I entered Dunkin Donuts it was my first reminder of how life used to be. I was never so humbled by the freedom I felt buying my coffee.

My second stop was to a deli so that I could buy my other favorite drink, Muscle Milk. I immediately chugged it and, in my mind, could feel it feeding my muscles. I also realized when I was walking home that the real world wasn't quite the same as it was before I was hospitalized. A lot of stores were closed or out of business and everyone was walking around with face masks. This was my first venture into society since Covid 19 spread to New York City. I suddenly felt like I was in a science fiction movie: I'm a person who just spent 11 months in a psychiatric hospital and now I have been released into a world where there is a global epidemic that is killing people by the thousands daily.

When I arrived at my apartment, I was surprised to see that my landlords were kind enough to paint and installed new lighting fixtures to replace the old fluorescent fixtures that were old and ugly. My apartment looked brand new. If you want to meet the nicest family in the world, just come to my apartment and I will introduce you to my landlords and their children. They are so sweet that it's only natural that they own two bakeries.

As I went through my apartment, I started my new life. As I dusted off my Fender Stratocaster guitar, I sat with it and played for a few minutes. The most amazing thing about that guitar is that it stayed in tune the entire time I was hospitalized. Thank you, Leo Fender!

I had also made plans that day with Julia so that I could see my sons. Of course, when making plans or doing something with Julia, things must be on her terms all the time. The first visits that I had with my sons were at Julia's apartment because she felt more comfortable if she were there when I was with the boys. I don't like going to Julia's apartment because I have to see photographs of her on vacations with my sons and her boyfriend. I don't think anything can hurt as much as looking at a vacation photo with your family and another man. It's like I died and I'm a ghost looking on to what life would be like without me.

One of the worst experiences I had in that regard was when Julia would bring her boyfriend to my son's basketball games. I believe she knew that it drove me crazy, and it hurt me, yet she did it anyway. I even told her boyfriend that he wasn't family and there was no reason for him to be at the game. Julia would claim I was menacing. Menacing would be using intimidation to make someone feel unsafe. I simply spoke my mind, which I had a right to do. At another game, I cut him off as he was walking my youngest to the snack bar. Sorry buddy, that's my son, you're just a pawn for Julia until she gets all that she wants from you.

After one of the games, I had to watch the 5 of them walk away together as they went to Julia's minivan to go home. Watching your children walk away with another man brings you to a whole new low and I understand why people snap and wind up beating up the boyfriend of the ex-wife. It makes it worse when it's thrown in your face on purpose. If you asked anyone who either worked with or used to be friends with Julia, they would tell you that she does these things on purpose. She likes to hurt people. One day, karma will come back big time and bite her in the ass. Maybe if she reads this, she might stop for a moment and try to self-reflect on what she has done to me, her sons, relatives, friends and her subordinates.

 My reunion with my sons was not a highly emotional event. I think it's because I would talk to them on the phone every night while I was in the hospital. It kept our relationship strong. As soon as I saw them, we all hugged and I of course shed some tears and my sons were more interested in showing me their video games and my youngest son's new pet, a chameleon. We immediately picked up from where we left off before I was hospitalized. Julia was her normal cold self and asked me how I was. I could tell she could care less. I'm just a resource of money for her. I feel she uses people for their energy and resources. Once you are drained of all that, you are discarded as soon as you are not a convenience. I truly think that she could care less whether I was alive or dead.

 For the first few months after I was discharged, my only interactions with my sons would be at Julia's apartment for about an hour to two hours. In addition, having to see Julia on this consistent basis brings up mixed feelings. How can you still love somebody that you know for a fact is genuinely not a good person? Most therapists told me that it wasn't love, but an unhealthy attachment masquerading as love.

At a certain point I gave Julia the phone numbers to my psychologist and caseworker and asked her to call them so she can feel comfortable about having my sons visit me at my apartment and resume our lives. Being divorced means that I do not have to see Julia. I feel Julia exudes animosity even when she is being "nice": you can tell that it is contrived. I also feel she does not have the capacity for genuine love and empathy, like I've stated many times. I notice that even my sons are used as props for her self-esteem.

Julia eventually called my psychologist who I gave permission to answer any question or concerns that Julia had about me. She was mostly concerned that I would become violent at some point. My psychologist reassured her that my mental illness was based on fear and not violence. This proved that she knew zero about me. In addition, if I were having a breakdown, I would most likely hide in bed.

While we were married, I explained to Julia the roots of my anxiety disorder and depression many times. She either didn't believe me or never bothered to pay attention. When I would send her links to videos or articles that described my mental illness, she never watched any of them. There were many times in the relationship that I believe I mentioned before where Julia would accuse me of faking my mental illness. Julia never bothered to try to discover the real me and have a healthy connection, even though I was an open book. On the other hand, I had read many articles about women who were sexually abused by family members and how it affects their mental health when they get older. Like I also mentioned earlier, Julia and I agreed to help each other with our shortcomings when we first got together.

After speaking to my psychologist, Julia agreed to start having the boys visit me at my apartment and now I did not have to see her and only communicated with her through text messaging. Talking to her live on the phone also brings up old feelings and I get flashbacks. Just her voice alone causes me to feel sick to my stomach.

Before we had kids and Julia was pregnant, Julia had a book about how to take care of babies and wanted me to read it. I never read it. Either I was not ready to face the responsibility of parenthood coming up or I didn't like how Julia presented that

I read the book. It was more like an order than an asking. Remember, sometimes it's not the message that sucks, it's the messenger. She was disappointed. We wound up taking a new parent class at one of the famous baby clothing stores. I started watching videos at home on You Tube and after the twins were born, there were classes and videos for new parents at the hospital. We went to all the classes. The best class was giving our babies a bath together for the first time. The twin I bathed was born with hair, so I got to comb his hair for the first time. I also learned how to and when to feed, swaddle, dress and change diapers. I may not have learned about taking care of babies the way Julia would have liked, but I still learned in my style and did become good at all the aspects of taking care of a baby. Did I make mistakes? Hell yeah! One scary mistake was that I didn't notice that my youngest son once had a small piece of cardboard tucked up in his mouth by his cheek. The cardboard was about a half an inch big and was from the lid to a box of nose drops. I never saw him put it in his mouth. I was mortified when I found out from Julia. You can only imagine the verbal lashing I took that day.

It was hard raising twins being first time parents. We were tired all the time; Julia did do the majority of 2am diaper changes mostly because I had to take Klonopin for sleep and it was sometimes difficult to wake me up. This would make her angry. I would tell her to then try harder to wake me up. I didn't have a problem getting up to change or feed them in the middle of the night. If she couldn't wake me up on her first try, she would get angry and give up. Even our marriage counselor told Julia that she felt Julia liked being angry with me so that she could complain about her husband like what her friends did. After all, in my opinion, anger and antagonism are what fuels Julia.

For some reason I'm reminded of a funny story about me and Julia: it was our first Valentine's Day together and Julia had bought me black silk pajamas and a black silk robe. We enjoyed having wine and cheese together and were preparing everything at the kitchen counter. As I bent down to throw something out in the garbage, I accidentally farted. I was mortified because it was the first time that either of us farted in front of each other. I said, "Oh my God, I had no warning or feeling that I had to fart!" And I stood there with an embarrassed look on my face. Julia then said, "Do you know that since we have started dating, I haven't been able to make a poop while around you because I was embarrassed? Some nights when you left my apartment, I was relieved that I could take a poop ". I said, "The floodgates are now open". As a couple we got to the point where we would be pooping or peeing in front of each other while one of us was washing our face or brushing our teeth at the bathroom sink. To me that was a form of bonding because you're doing your most private things in front of your wife and feeling zero embarrassment about it. I miss those sorts of aspects about my marriage and it's unfortunate that we divorced. I consider it a profoundly monumental failure that I'm not sure that I will ever completely get over. I don't think anyone really does. Those who do say they were probably never in love with their spouses to begin with. A part of me will always pine for the past. It's something that I know at this point in my life to put in its proper place.

Discharging Myself From the Hospital:

After about 3 weeks at Haven House, I was not only frustrated with the ineffective help I was receiving for employment; my room was broken into and some of my belongings were stolen like my new sneakers, my radio and my socks. Why would someone steal socks? The thief was my neighbor across the hall who steals from every person that he can.

I got my sneakers and socks back, but he must have traded my radio for cigarettes, drugs or money. Since the patients can leave the hospital grounds, it is easy for them to hook up with old friends and get high. None of them ever invited me! Those bastards!!!

 This incident was the last straw that made me decide to write the letter that I wanted to be discharged. I immediately wrote the letter and gave it to Teresa. She asked me if I was sure that I felt healthy enough to leave because this would be my final discharge from the hospital. I told her yes and filled out the paperwork, packed all my stuff and headed out as fast as I could. In fact, I had gone home the day before and drove my car to the hospital with the idea that I would be checking myself out. Teresa was kind enough to give me a few nice duffle bags to pack my belongings. She looked disappointed that I was leaving, thus confirming my belief that she was interested in me. Since it has been almost a year,

I'm considering calling her. I should call. After all, I have nothing to lose. If she says yes and we go out, I won't have to explain anything about my past. She knows everything about me already. To have someone accept you despite your checkered past is a blessing and a testament to the fact that there are empaths in the world.

On July 22nd, 2020, I officially became a free man after being hospitalized for 11 straight months and the 2 months combined before that. I'm not so good at math, but I believe that adds up to 13 months.

Chapter 56: Adjusting to Life

After being hospitalized for 11 months, there is a period of adjustment that you go through when you get home and back to your old life. You see people that you haven't seen in almost a year, and they ask you where you have been. When this happens, I'm open and honest and tell them the short version of what happened. Then there are some close friends that I didn't call while I was away who were worried about what happened to me because I disappeared.

During one of my first days at home, I sat and thought about what I had been through and that while the hospital was designed to help me, I did experience things that made me feel like I was truly insane. That is something that I must get over as well. It's been almost a year that I have been discharged and I still feel the experience of the hospital. I have a caseworker that told me to slow down with trying to find a job so quickly because she wanted me to take some time to adjust to being home. In July of 2020, I had a pension, I was collecting social security disability and I was on food stamps (I still am). When a person collects disability benefits, you are allowed to earn $1200 a month at a job. That's basically part time for $15 an hour.

I decided that a relatively stress-free job would be delivering food for Door Dash, Grub Hub and Uber Eats. I was not interested in driving people around anymore, so I decided to deliver food instead. The only stressful part of the job was when I had deliveries in high crime neighborhoods.

I drove food delivery for a few weeks and decided that I wanted to work around people. Delivering food is a solitary job where you are trapped alone in the car with your thoughts. I began to feel depressed, and I stopped delivering.

The next job I had at the end of August of 2020 was with Federal Express in Yonkers, New York. I got a job scanning and loading packages onto delivery trucks. I enjoy manual labor because I turn it into a workout. My shift was from 3am to 7am, 5 days a week. I would go to bed at 8pm and wake up at about 1:30am and get ready for work. My plan was to climb the corporate ladder at FedEx and eventually work there full time. For the first few weeks, I enjoyed loading the trucks. It was simple and I was getting great exercise. However, being 51 years old with metal rods in my back comes with its risks. First, I started having tremendous knee pain. I attributed this to when I was a lacrosse goalie and would get hit in both knees on a consistent basis from lacrosse balls traveling at about 80 mph. My old injuries were catching up to me and I wasn't recovering from each shift in time for my next shift. It was during one shift that I felt pain in the area of my back where the surgery was. As I was in pain, I looked around and realized that I was the oldest person there loading trucks. Everyone else was in their twenties. It was then I realized that I probably should quit before something happened to my knees or the hardware in my back. A day or so later, I woke up at 1:30 am to get ready to go to work. My entire body was so sore from lifting boxes, that I couldn't move. I texted my supervisor and explained my physical condition, my surgery and explained that I'm too old to be loading trucks at that high intensity for 4 hours straight. My mind loved it, but my body did not. I wound up quitting Federal Express in Sept of 2020. Had I taken a job like that at age 25, I would have thrived.

After quitting Federal Express, I put even more effort into applying for physical education jobs. At the same time, I started to look through all the artwork that I created while I was hospitalized. I then came up with the idea that these designs would look great on leggings, handbags, shoes and other fashion accessories.

An old friend of mine turned me on to a company called Contrado, in England. The company provides products for you to put your designs on and sell through their website. Here's how it works: Contrado has over 400 products to choose from. All the products are white. You then choose and item to add a design, like leggings. You then upload an image of your artwork and use Contrado's design software to experiment with your design until you create something that you think would look good on leggings or anything else you decide to create. You then post your designs in your store on Contrado's site. Customers can then order your products. The products are manufactured by Contrado, and they take care of packing and shipping. In return, I get 20% of the sales. It's worth it because all I have to do is design and post. I didn't have to worry about purchasing inventory and being stuck with what I didn't sell.

During September and October of 2020, I went through a phase of creativity that was new for me: I was designing leggings, handbags, shoes, bedding, bathroom items, mouse pads, laptop cases, bathing suits, hats and shirts. I created over 300 items which are currently for sale. The web site is www.contrado.com/stores/peter-vox-designs just in case you're interested in seeing my designs.

I try to get internet traffic by constantly posting photos of my products on all social media platforms. I even buy social media promotion when I have the money. I make it a point to post at least once a day. I've sold a few pairs of leggings, some covid masks and some coffee mugs so far. In addition, I also email the CEOs of apparel companies, or anyone involved in product development. I introduce myself, tell my story and share images of my products. The trick is to be different, and I haven't seen much artwork that looks anything like my style. I even email the owner of SPANX, the top leggings company in the world, on a weekly basis. She happens to be married to a guy that I went to high school with. He owns an NBA team. I email him as well. Either the emails aren't being read on purpose or because they must get hundreds of emails a day and don't have the time to answer everyone. So, I keep emailing with the hope that one day, they decide to open some emails and read mine. I would love to get a licensing deal with an established company, but I know it is very difficult to do. So, for now, it's self-promotion. I'm also considering renting space at fashion trade shows to display my designs and make sales that way. Either way, creating these products has been a lot of fun. I have enough items for now to choose from. I just have to keep pushing and find ways to get attention for my designs.

In late September of 2020, I accepted a job as a school monitor at a private school on the upper east side of Manhattan. My job there was to escort students from class to class, making sure that they maintained social distancing and wore their Covid masks. During their classes, I would sit at a desk outside the classroom door for hallway duty. I used that time to design my products on Contrado. In addition to escorting the students to class, I would also stay with them at lunch, which was being served outside in a giant tent where each class had their own roped off section with classroom desks set up 6 feet apart. Once November and December rolled around, it started getting cold in that tent and the kids were freezing.

I enjoyed the job partly because it was in Manhattan, and I wanted to be someplace different and see new people. In addition, I was taking the bus and subway to work. I didn't mind because even on a bus or a subway, I wanted to see new people.

As I continued to work as a school monitor, I continued to apply for jobs. I had a few Zoom interviews and a school for autism in Manhattan offered me a full-time physical education position. The salary was to be 67k per year. I was excited because between my pension and this new job, I would be making more than I was at the time that I retired. I was offered the job in February of 2021, and I started to complete the online training courses that were required before I could start teaching. In addition, I had to clear their background check.

After I completed the training, it seemed that it was taking a long time for my background check to clear. The reason why it took so long was because I now have a record of being accused of corporal punishment in New York City Schools. This school for autism was partially funded by NYC Schools. When the false allegations came up, I had to have a phone conference with a human resources representative to discuss what happened. It was humiliating to say the least. After the phone conference, I emailed the woman who hired me and told her what happened and that I would not be pursuing the position. Because my record although not true, I didn't get the job.

So now, it's virtually impossible for me to get a new teaching job because my record is not clean. I had mentioned in earlier journal entries that I have filed a lawsuit against NYC Schools and am just waiting for my case to come up. It very well may take a few years.

One idea that I considered for a new career was being a home inspector. I wrestled with it for a while as I kept searching for work. I was also thinking about getting my CDL license to drive trucks, but I'm currently on 6 medications for my illness and would never pass their drug test.

So, by the beginning of March of 2021, I had no job and started to focus on applying to retail businesses that where I could sell what I knew best which would be drums and sporting goods. I applied to Sam Ash, Guitar Center and Dick's Sporting Goods.

I had an interview with Sam Ash and then an interview with Dick's Sporting Goods. I was hired by Dick's on the spot. It took Sam Ash a month to inform me that I didn't get the job. No wonder people hate working for Sam Ash or Sam's Ass, as some musicians like to call it.

So, from the end of March of 2021 thru August of 2021 I worked part time at Dick's selling equipment. My experience as a Physical Education Teacher, personal trainer and athlete made the job easy for me because I'm well versed in 90% of the products they sell. The job was also fun because I got to meet new people every day.

When I was teaching, you saw the same people every day. Each September there would be a handful of new teachers, so for 19 years, I saw basically the same people every day.

At Dick's, there were people from all walks of life. I goofed around with the customers, and we had a good time picking out what they need. Lots of times people shared their stories about their time playing sports when they were kids. I even met a customer who played baseball for the Pittsburgh Pirates for about 5 years.

It's been over a year since I've been home, and I still feel like I haven't fully adjusted to being out of the hospital.

I have worries and concerns about what I tell new people that I meet and who I get close with. Telling them what I've been through can sometimes be tough even though I want to be honest with people.

Another concern is that if I meet a woman and a relationship starts to build, I'm going to have to tell her what I've been through. It's a lot of baggage. When I read dating site profiles, the essays women write sound more like a ransom list of what they demand in a man. Having no baggage seems to be the biggest prerequisite. As I read more profiles and see how obnoxious some profile essays are, I start to think that being alone might be healthier for me. Over the last decade or so, people in general have become so selfish and self-absorbed. They love themselves too much to have room to give love to anyone else. In the meantime, they have no problem draining you of your love.

Some people like to blame social media. I don't. I blame the people who use social media as an ego boost. If your life revolves around how many comments, "likes" and emojis you get; it means you are living for the quick dopamine fix from compliments by strangers and you will become unable to sustain a relationship in the real world. How can one person compete with 300 likes and 100 comments about how hot you are? Some people don't realize that this is all fantasy that causes unhealthy delusions of self-importance.

One woman who accepted me and that I mentioned earlier was Natasha. I saw her for the first time since my discharge in October of 2020. I would be remiss not to admit that I wanted to see her so that I could have sex. At this point, it had been over a year since I had even held a woman's hand. I also thought that maybe if I spent some time with her, I would develop feelings. Instead, during the few weeks I spent with her, a lot of red flags were raised; she would make comments on how she wished I acted a certain way, she immediately wanted a serious relationship, she was OCD and was controlling. I felt like I was in a similar situation that I was with Julia. Before Thanksgiving of 2020, I ghosted Natasha. I know it wasn't right, but I was stressed and wasn't up to having a breakup conversation. I admit it was cowardly and mean.

Chapter 57: Life Over the Past 10 Months

Since being home, my main concern has been focusing on my sons and making sure that their mental health is ok. being alone. The fact that they live on top of each other and don't have their own bedrooms is one reason for my sons' getting on each other's nerves. Even though Julia makes more than enough money to rent a place with three bedrooms, to my knowledge, hasn't made any plans to move yet. None of my sons have a place to disappear to in order to experience some peace and quiet. In addition, Julia got a promotion, a raise and got transferred to a new location for her job that is less than 1/10 of a mile from her apartment. So, she got everything she wanted at the expense of the children not living in a space big enough for all of them. Now that she lives so close to work, I don't see her moving anytime soon. What I am seeing is a person hoarding all the money that she can. My sons are getting older and the window for them to enjoy a home with their own bedrooms while they are still young enough is just about closed.

I do credit Julia for pushing the boys to do well even though I feel her narcissistic personality pushed them to do well so that she could look like she is a great mother. Julia is a very efficient mother and my sons have benefited in the fact that they are good students and opportunities will present themselves to my sons if they keep up the good work. Part of me is worried that they will burn out due to her overbearing personality and will start to resent her. I'm starting to see hints of it.

One day at work, I met a college freshman who was wearing the sweatshirt of my sons' future high school. He told me it was the best 4 years of his life. Not many kids say that about high school. In addition, the dean of the school is a former student who loves it there. Also, the brother of a woman that I dated went to the school, he loved it and still has a relationship with the school. So, I'm cautiously optimistic that my sons will adjust to high school without too much fear and uncertainty. I have to show them that they will be going to a school that thrives on nurturing the individual talents of their students and hopefully points them towards a path that they are interested in following. I consistently share career ideas with my sons. I also make sure to tell them that my suggestions are just that, suggestions. They obviously do not have to choose a career that I suggest. I feel Julia, on the other hand

will probably give them a hard time if they choose a profession that isn't acceptable to her. I just want them to be happy.

My Mother's Health:

Another thing that occurred over the past 10 months has been the beginning of the deterioration of my mother's decision making and physicality. In February of 2021, she fell into her bathtub while trying to move a rack that she keeps in the bathtub that you can hang clothes on to dry. She says she doesn't know how she fell and wound up stuck in the bathtub for 4 hours. Her story made no sense and led me to believe she was leaving out details.

My brother had called me to tell me he had been trying to reach her, but she was not answering her phone. When I called and got no answer, I then decided to go to her apartment. When I got there, I couldn't get in because she had locked her top lock and neither me nor the building staff had the key to that lock. I only had the bottom lock key. I knocked on the door and there was no answer. I yelled, but no answer. I could hear that her TV was on very loud, and I could also hear the wind howling because her window was open. At this point, I thought she was dead. I then called 911 and my brother called my mother's landlord to bring the key to the top lock of her door. The police, EMTs and the landlord all showed up at the same time. The police went in first and found her stuck in the tub. Her phone was on top of the toilet tank, and she couldn't reach it to call for help.

For many months, my brother and I were trying to convince my mother to get a Life Alert System and she kept refusing. However, when one of the police officers suggested she get one, it became a great idea.

It turns out that the real reason my mother fell in the bathtub was because she was only wearing one sandal instead of two. The reason was because she had a cut on her big toe and the sandal was uncomfortable. So instead of just not wearing anything on both feet and being properly balanced, she decided to walk around her apartment with one sandal on that has at least a one-inch heel. She's 86 and her balance is not good anymore and now she was teetering back and forth while walking to the bathroom, reaching into the tub while not balanced and fell in. She had some bruising on her back but otherwise she was ok. It took weeks for me to find out the real reason she fell because she was avoiding telling the truth. I had been telling her that her sandals were not sturdy and there was no reason to be wearing them in her apartment. For some reason, my mother always turns a simple procedure into a project. And she still insists on wearing the sandals. She'll deny wearing them while they are on her feet.

It's like she saves her neurotic behavior for my brother and I. For example, if I am looking for something to eat, she will always offer me cold cuts. I stopped eating cold cuts 25 years ago and I answer," No mom, I don't eat cold cuts anymore", and then she would respond with, "I know ", I then ask, "Well if you know, why do you keep asking me every time I decide on what to eat?", she then says, "I don't know, humor me". I get pissed and say," Humoring you is asking me the same questions that you know to answers to over and over because you think frustrating me is funny?" I then said, "Don't you think that being hospitalized was enough for me to deal with? And now you want to push the buttons that you know drive me crazy?" It's as if she has learned nothing. This isn't due to age, it's something else. I don't know what to call the behavior where someone keeps asking you the same questions your entire life while knowing the answers. What is that? Is it schizophrenia? Is it a simple case of wanting to bust my balls? Whatever it is, it makes me want to stay away but she needs my help.

Even though the doctor said her memory was fine, I see it slipping a bit. It's either that or her neurosis is so bad that she forgets what she is doing. One day, she picked up her cell phone and asked me if I knew what a cell phone was. She denies the conversation, but it's true. The other obstacle when talking to my mother is that she doesn't stop talking to let you say what you need to say. She will ask a question and when you start to answer, she immediately starts to interrupt. This has been going on for her entire life. I remember hearing my dad yelling at her to let him talk if she's going to ask him a question. Their fights were frustrating to listen to because I didn't know who was crazier.

After her fall in the bathtub, I slept at her apartment for about 2 weeks until my brother was able to arrange home health care.

I must admit that as I got older, I started to resent my parents more and more because of their lack of common sense. If you have a mental illness and have been to therapy for most of your life; how do you not recognize that your child needs more help than what you're doing?

 Since my father died, I never really grieved. I think I was too angry with him for years of exposing me to his illness with zero effort put towards trying to not let it affect his kids. He used nothing he learned in therapy in real life and didn't see how a parent's behavior affects their children, like his mother. A part of me felt a sense of freedom after his death because I knew I would never have to witness his neurotic behavior ever again. These are harsh statements and feelings that I have about my dad. I'm just being honest about the thoughts that cross my mind. Like I said earlier, those feelings need to be analyzed. Other people may have these same thoughts and may find solace in reading about someone who shares similar thoughts. Thoughts are just thoughts: they do not make you a bad person. Your response and actions to those thoughts are what really determine what happens to you and how your character develops over time.

Chapter 58: My Social Life

Since coming home, I have not been interested in going out socially yet. Even with Covid restrictions being taken away, I don't have the motivation to go out with friends or even date. My schedule has been the same since I got home in July of 2020: I only go out to see my sons, run errands, do laundry and go to work. Other than that, I'm home alone. I go through periods of painful loneliness, and I try to combat it by working out, playing drums, singing, designing my clothing line and playing guitar. But, every night, I'm alone. It especially hurts when I drop my sons of at Julia's after a day together and I know that her boyfriend is there. As I drive away and the sting of loneliness kicks in. Still, I would rather be alone than with someone who I do not get along with.

In Jan of 2021, I started vaping cannabis oil again. It works better than any of the pills that I take and there aren't any side effects like weight gain and having a beer belly. To me, that is unacceptable. If I'm in shape and training on a consistent basis, I do just fine.

Since recreational marijuana has become legal in New York, I see no reason why I can't wean off these pills and have marijuana as my medication regime. Like I've claimed before, marijuana immediately takes away my anxiety and gives me the freedom to live in the present and participate in life.

I'm not dating anyone and have seen my friends a total of three times since I've been home. Maybe it's because I've been going out almost every weekend since 1987 and I'm probably fried, which is ok. When I don't feel lonely, I enjoy the quiet. I'll start going out again when the decision comes without any internal debate.

I'm on a few dating sites and if I start texting someone, I start to wonder if I'm really interested in a relationship or if I'm there for the possibility of sex. There are also times where I make plans to meet someone and then cancel. Am I not ready to date, or is it that I'd rather meet someone by chance with love at first sight? Love at first sight is one of the most exciting feelings a person can experience. The reality is, it's LUST at first sight, not love. Lust at first sight crashes and burns quickly.

With all the overthinking about relationships and messing around on dating sites, I have resigned myself to the possibility that I may never find love again and right now, that is ok. I may not be interested in finding love again and won't waste the time of a woman who wants more.

Instead of focusing my energy on a contrived search for love, I have started to do all the old things that bring me joy; drumming, singing, playing guitar and training. Recently, I answered an ad to sing for a band that plays the same music that I love. The band members are my age and just want to have fun and maybe play out twice a month. I accepted their invitation to audition, and we are waiting until the rehearsal studio can reopen when their Covid restrictions are lifted. I'm excited to sing, make new friends and have some fun. Even if we just rehearse and don't play gigs will be fine with me.

I must fix myself first before worrying about a relationship. I would like to meet someone fun but my priorities are my sons, using what I've learned in the hospital, embark on a new path, rebuild my financial safety net for my sons and rediscover the old Peter.

As my story here starts to come to a close; I must remind you that it doesn't end like a movie with Julia and I reconciling and the 5 of us living together again as a family. I'm not the guy that gets the girl. Not getting this particular girl is probably a good thing in the long run.

This chapter of my life ends with me now as a free man who has been given a chance to continue to be a loving father. I have been given the tools thanks to a few therapists, nurses and me on how to continue living with mental illness and find happiness wherever I can. I know what I must do. The decision is mine. The decision is also yours if you are going through similar issues. In the end, only you can fix you if you want it bad enough.

There is more healing that must occur for me to truly move on from everything that occurred in my life; like my earliest memories of being brought to cemeteries, my divorce, my career and finally being committed to psychiatric hospitals.

It's up to me know what to do with my life. The one thing that I know is that I won't try to commit suicide again, wind up in a hospital and being away from my sons.

In August of 2021 I registered to get my certification to become a home inspector. The training starts in October 2021. I'm excited at the prospect of making a better living than I previously did and starting a new career. By the time you read this, I should be a licensed home inspector.

My plan on getting back my life, starting a new career, rebuilding my finances and eventually buying a house for my sons is underway.

I will finish my attempt in creating meaningful literature with some useful pieces of knowledge that I learned during the events of the past year and my entire life:

If you feel that the only answer to your problems is suicide, use your suicidal thoughts as a signal that you have simply run out of ideas on your own and it's time to collaborate with others who can help you. In this day and age, it's not hard to get help. If you don't know where to turn, call 911, tell them what's going on and they will get the ball rolling for you.

Roger Waters of Pink Floyd once said, "If you're a bad musician, surround yourself with better ones to help you get your project done". Get it?

Improvements in life don't happen overnight. They come in baby steps with the occasional times where you make tremendous progress. There are also days where you regress too, but you must remember that those days get few and far between when you use what you have learned.

There's no shame in getting help. I'd rather ask for help than being dead and leaving my sons without a father.

I hope my experiences and views about mental illness help people gain a new perspective of what living with mental illness is like and everything that comes with it. In addition, I'm hopeful that I provided useful and interesting insights into what living in a psychiatric hospital was like as well.

 There are no cures, only improvements that depend on the effort that you put forth. With enough psychological breakthroughs, it's possible to get to a point where you can manage your illness and live a happy life.

I never did get that needle!

Is this the end? Nope, it's just the beginning.

National Suicide Prevention Hotline

1-800-273-8255

www.ingramcontent.com/pod-product-compliance
Lightning Source LLC
Chambersburg PA
CBHW060511230426
43665CB00013B/1481